Resurrecting Erotic Transgression

Gender, Theology and Spirituality

Series Editors: Lisa Isherwood and Marcella Althaus-Reid

The Gender, Theology and Spirituality series explores the notion that theology and spirituality are gendered activities. It offers the opportunity for analysis of that situation as well as provides space for alternative readings. In addition, it questions the notion of gender itself and in so doing pushes the theological boundaries to more materialist and radical readings. The series opens the theological and spiritual floodgates through an honest engagement with embodied knowing and critical praxis.

The Gender, Theology and Spirituality series brings together international scholars from a range of theological areas who offer cutting edge insights and open up exciting and challenging possibilities and futures in theology.

Forthcoming in the series:

Patriarchs, Prophets and Other Villains
Edited by: Lisa Isherwood

Our Cultic Foremothers: Sacred Sexuality and Sexual Hospitality in the Biblical and Related Exegetic Texts
Thalia Gur Klein

Queering Wisdom
June Boyce-Tillman

Women and Reiki: Energetic/Holistic Healing in Practice
Judith Macpherson

For What Sin Was She Slain? A Muslim Feminist Theology
Zayn R. Kassam

Through Eros to Agape: The Radical Embodiment of Faith
Timothy R. Koch

Baby, You Are My Religion: Theory, Praxis and Possible Theology of Mid-20th Century Urban Butch Femme Community
Marie Cartier

Radical Otherness: A Socio/theological Investigation
Dave Harris and Lisa Isherwood

Resurrecting
Erotic Transgression
Subjecting Ambiguity in Theology

Anita Monro

LONDON   OAKVILLE

Published by
Equinox Publishing Ltd., Unit 6, The Village, 101 Amies St., London SW11 2JW, UK
DBBC, 28 Main Street, Oakville, CT 06779, USA

www.equinoxpub.com

First published 2006

Cover artwork: Megan Clay

British Library Cataloguing-in-Publication Data

A catalogue record for this book is available from the British Library.

ISBN-10   1 84553 103 5 (hardback)
          1 84553 104 3 (paperback)

ISBN-13   978 1 84553 103 4 (hardback)
          978 1 84553 104 1 (paperback)

Library of Congress Cataloging-in-Publication Data

Monro, Anita.
Resurrecting erotic transgression: subjecting ambiguity in theology/
Anita Monro.
     p. cm. -- (Gender, theology, and spirituality)
Includes bibliographical references and index.
ISBN 1-84553-103-5 (hb) -- ISBN 1-84553-104-3 (pbk.)
1. Feminist theology. 2. Feminism--Religious aspects--Christianity.
3. Kristeva, Julia,. 1941- 4. Other (Philosophy) 5. Objectivity.
6. Ambiguity. I. Title. II. Series.
BT83.55.M655 2006
230.082--dc22
                    2005034644

Typeset by S.J.I. Services, New Delhi
Printed and bound in Great Britain by Lightning Source UK Ltd, Milton Keynes

CONTENTS

ACKNOWLEDGEMENTS

This project, first begun as a doctoral thesis, has had a long gestation. There are many midwives to be acknowledged.

I offer my sincere thanks for support and encouragement to Dr Francie Oppel and Dr Elaine Wainwright R.S.M., my doctoral thesis supervisors; the Brisbane College of Theology (BCT) which forms the School of Theology of Griffith University, Brisbane, Australia; the Alcorn Fellowship Trust of the Queensland Synod of The Uniting Church in Australia (UCA); Coolamon College, the National Network for Distance Theological Education of the national Assembly of the UCA; United Theological College, the recognized ministry training college of the UCA in the Synod of New South Wales and part of the School of Theology of Charles Sturt University.

During the course of this project, I had the opportunity to present elements of my thinking in the following forums: BCT Postgraduates' and Feminist Postgraduates' Colloquia; the National Assembly Sexuality Task Group of the UCA; the 1994 Australian Concurrent National Conferences in Theology and the Study of Religions in Adelaide; the 3rd National Gathering on Women in the UCA in Brisbane in 1996; and the 1996 UCA Queensland Synod Review Task Group Colloquium. Some of these presentations resulted in publications in the journals *Colloquium* and *Trinity Occasional Papers*. I thank Lisa Isherwood and Equinox Publishing for this current publication opportunity and Valerie Hall and Norma Beavers for their editorial work.

Many other individuals have provided support, encouragement, and conversation along the way. I particularly thank Val and Barry Monro, Elizabeth Nolan, Christine Digby, Carol Bennett, Ros Martin, Wendy Brunckhorst, Ella Mangan, Val Graydon, Jayne Clapton, Colleen Geyer, Colin Gurteen, Lyndall and Paul Moore, Adele Neal, Lorna Collingridge, Keree Casey, Lauren McGrow, and Sarah

Mitchell. Other members of the BCT Feminist Postgraduates' Colloquium; the Planning Group for Women Clothed With The Sun, the 3rd National Gathering on Women in the UCA; the planning committee for the inaugural conference of Women Scholars of Religion & Theology (1998); The Professional Association for Ordained Women (Inc. in Queensland); the Home Hill, Maryborough and Stanthorpe Parishes of the UCA; and the faculty of United Theological College have also shared the journey.

Most of all, I thank my husband and chief supporter, Russell Morris, who believes in me even when I don't believe in myself.

Introduction

SUBJECTING AMBIGUITY: OUTLINE AND IMPETUS

Plurality, diversity and difference are catchwords of the early twenty-first century and its emphasis on the global in communications, economics and ecological concerns. At the same time, such global movements also engage in hegemonic tendencies: the representation of one kind of solution, dominant economy and subjectivity or identity for all global constituents. Within these broad parameters, smaller institutions and movements are clearly faced with a diverse membership, a variety of pressing issues and a lack of resources.

The Uniting Church in Australia, of which I am an ordained minister, is one small institution which, since its inception in 1977 from three Protestant strands, has proclaimed the catchcry of 'unity in diversity'. Yet faced with issues on which there are clear and often polarized divisions among its membership in relation to matters such as the authority of the scriptures, the ordination of people with a homosexual orientation and the rights of indigenous people, the threat of schism looms continually.

The Uniting Church, as institution, is but one very small component of the global phenomenon of the Christian church. Its divisions are replicated elsewhere, and many of these divisions no longer follow denominational lines but are cross-denominational. How does a church, or indeed the whole Christian church, negotiate an age where diversity is increasingly emphasized and definitive institutional monolithic responses seem no longer relevant? How does Christian theology both maintain its identity and manage diversity within that identity? If not the survival of the church as institution, then the survival of the church as Christian movement, the called forth/together people of God, remains a significant question for me.

Feminism, one of the emergent influences in Christian theology threatening the neat categorization of orthodoxy and orthopraxis, is itself diverse and complex. Drawing from Marxist, liberal and an assortment of other ideological foundations, feminism too must cope with the reality that there are no definitive feminisms. Challenges to dominant Western feminisms by Asian, African, Latin American and indigenous women emphasize the differences inherent in the 'women's movement'. Men responding to feminism also raise questions about the allowances made for their own explorations of gender constructions and differences. Issues of sexual identity and orientation as well as the role of institutions such as the church in contributing to patriarchy produce a myriad of responses among feminists as well. Yet for me, one of the key visions of feminism or the 'women's movement' is the solidarity of women. How is solidarity able to be practised by such a diverse and eclectic movement? How can solidarity with women who do not regard themselves as within that stream be achieved? How do feminist women offer the same respect to other people, including men, which we demand for ourselves? These may not be relevant questions for all feminist women but they are for me, particularly in the context of the diversity of the Christian church.

Finally, the diversity of human existence itself, and not just its diversity but also its ambiguity, defies neat categorizations of any kind: us and them, self and other, good and bad. Yet the categorization of people along such lines persists. As I was working on this project in its thesis form, the Australian media was wallowing in the aftermath of the tragic killing of 35 people by one individual in the small tourist community of Port Arthur, Tasmania, on Sunday 28 April 1996. The demonization of that person, suggested by some to be suffering from an untreated mental illness, was well-established. There was little questioning of the process of vilification. Even representatives of mental illness associations were found to declare the person as 'not one of us'. Such a person, who caused such a horrific event, can only belong to the 'other', never to us. Nearly a decade later, there are innumerable examples of the demonization of the other to be cited in responses to 'terrorist attacks', justifications for military action, political apologetics for policies on asylum-seekers, and the re-emergence of the abortion debate (to name but a few).

This type of vilification, through separation along dualistic lines, persists in less media-grabbing situations: in the church as fundamentalists and liberals call each other names, and in feminism as people are defined in or out of the movement. Is it possible to discuss the ambiguity of human existence without demonizing some people and excessively valorizing others, by recognizing the ambiguity of life, the power to create and to destroy which exists in all of us? Is it possible to overcome the necessity of separating us from them and self from other? These are important ethical questions for me. The addressing of ambiguity is a matter of personal integrity: a question of dealing with other people and positions with the same recognition that I demand for me, and the willingness to demand that recognition for my own ambivalent existence.

What, then, do these concerns for diversity, ambiguity and integrity in the face of multiplicity mean for me as a feminist Christian? What kind of theological method is available to me to deal with the resources of my faith in a manner consistent with such concerns? I answer that question by proposing a feminist theological methodology based in poststructuralist theory. This methodology claims the possibility of bringing into discourse, and therefore into recognition, the ambiguity of human subjectivity: both dia-anthropically and syn-anthropically—across humanity and within the human person.[1] The word 'discourse' does not only refer to spoken or written texts, but also to the fabric of human communities, societies and cultures, although texts retain a primacy of place because of their immediacy as observable phenomena and the constraints of the theological context.

Methodological Overview

Poststructuralism, and its associated term, postmodernism, nominally cover a complex, nebulous and largely eclectic range of sources, activities, theoretical positions, critical analyses and practical applications, creating of them a body of work through the activity of the naming itself. The natures of poststructuralism and postmodernism are controversial. Even more so is their presence in the realm of theology. In that context, my project belongs to a variety of poststructuralist postmodernism which defies David Ray Griffin's dualistic categories of '*deconstructive* or *eliminative*' and '*constructive* or *revisionary*' postmodernism (Griffin 1989: x); moves through Mark C. Taylor's vision of an 'utterly transgressive' 'a/theology' (1984: 6); and seeks the creative, reclaiming, reconstructive, prismatic dance of the 'metaphorical postmodern' identified by Carl Raschke (1992: 102).

---

1. The terms, dia-anthropically and syn-anthropically, are plays on the linguistic distinctions, diachronic and synchronic, made by Ferdinand de Saussure, originator of linguistic structuralism, a precursor of poststructuralist theory.

This double movement is also particularly related to both the feminist and the Christian concerns embodied in this project. Working with the definitions and self-definitions of various poststructuralist and feminist theologians from a variety of sources, I call the type of postmodern poststructuralist play in which this project is involved: 'erotic transgressive resurrection'.

Julia Kristeva

This methodology is grounded primarily in the work of Julia Kristeva (b. 1941). Kristeva is generally, although controversially, described as a 'French feminist'.[2] She is more acceptably, although equally as anomalously, tagged as a poststructuralist theorist, since some commentators would question the appropriateness of the juxtaposition of the words 'theory' and 'poststructuralist'.[3] Kristeva's particular poststructuralist position is informed by Lacanian psychoanalysis from the viewpoint of a practitioner, as well as by literary theory, and her own brand of semiotics, 'semanalysis'. Her work bears the mark of an interest in matters religious and theological. It is specifically her notion of the peculiar power of poetic language, described as revolutionary, and the particular role of the 'otherness' of language and subjectivity in both creating and subverting meaning and identity which I appropriate here. In recognition of this concentration, I call my proposed hermeneutical method for interpreting language, discourse and identity 'poetic reading'. This naming signals the focus on Kristeva's socio-linguistic concerns

---

2.   While Kristeva writes in French and works in Paris, her country of birth is Bulgaria. Having received her early education from French nuns, she moved to Paris in 1966 to continue her literary theory studies. She has remained there since that time (Roudiez in Kristeva 1980: 1-2). Her early work is influenced by Russian and Eastern European scholarship. The identification of Kristeva as 'feminist' is also problematic for three reasons: her repudiation of that epithet in a French context; her standing as a theoretician separate from any feminist associations; and her ambivalent status among other feminist scholars. The epithet 'French feminist' is retained here because of its widespread use in an English-speaking context in relation to Kristeva.

3.   Linda Alcoff, for example, with some sympathy to elements of poststructuralist thought, suggests that the position of Julia Kristeva is 'wholly negative': 'deconstructing everything and refusing to construct anything' (1988: 418). While Alcoff does not restrict the word 'theory' from use with the word 'poststructuralist', she expresses some of the sentiments which undergird the tendency for others to do so.

maintained in this work, and the deliberate omission of exploration into the bodily or psychosomatic[4] implications of her work at this stage.

In this appropriation of Kristevan theory, theology is viewed as essentially hermeneutical or interpretative. This view is taken because of theology's reliance on key primary sources as its basic tools, i.e. Scripture and the often creedal or formulaic, accepted traditions of Christian orthodoxy; and on the necessity of reinterpreting these primary sources for each new context in which theological communities find themselves. The theological methodology described claims the heritage of Christianity and, specifically, of Western Protestantism. It is also indebted to the late-twentieth century production of significant bodies of theological work arising from feminist perspectives. Such feminist theological ventures discuss a variety of issues related to the treatment and characterization of women and the feminine in Christianity. These considerations often cross traditional Christian boundaries such as church or denominational adherence.

Poetic Reading

The project of poetic reading is described as having a hermeneutical goal of *jouissance*, a transgressive (boundary-crossing and category-breaching) method with a series of specific strategies, and a methodological imperative of confronting the abject in language and culture. 'Jouissance' and 'the abject' are Kristevan terms. Both terms rely on the assumption of the existence of an 'otherness' in language and subjectivity. Foundationally, the methodology outlined is concerned with exploring that otherness through the ambivalences or ambiguities manifest, because of it, in the discourses of the Christian community—written, spoken or otherwise enunciated. These discourses include the primary theological sources of scripture and tradition as well as the tapestry of Christian community. In a Protestant context, scripture takes priority. That priority is mirrored in this book in the focus on the reading of scripture in the context of Christian community and attention to hermeneutical method in the reading of scripture prior to the exploration of the use of that method

---

4. This term is used in its formal sense of the intersection between bodiliness and mental operations in human experience.

in theological discourse. I argue that a feminist theological methodology based in poststructuralist theory provides the means for 'subjecting ambiguity', i.e. for bringing into discourse, and therefore into theology and Christian community, a recognition of the multiplicity of human language and identity. This recognition is founded in a process of sustained attention to the 'otherness' or alterity of language and subjectivity.

Argument Outline

Poststructuralism is a simple nomination for a complex and eclectic set of practices and theorizations. Chapter 1 provides a broad overview of the theoretical directions generally indicated by the term. This overview is followed by an examination of the major theological objections to the use of poststructuralist theory, together with arguments addressing these critiques. A brief survey of the use of poststructuralist theory in theology is included. Particular attention is paid to the prominence of feminist theologians amongst poststructuralist theologians, and to those theologians who have explicitly used elements of the work of Julia Kristeva. Kristeva as theologian is also briefly considered in this context. The chapter concludes with a series of comments setting the project of poetic reading in the context of other poststructuralist theological projects by highlighting significant points where my approach differs from other poststructuralist feminist theological works.

　　Chapter 2 offers two examples of the application of a methodology of poetic reading: one textual and the other experiential. These two applications are related, emphasizing the practical as well as hermeneutical possibilities of a poststructuralist feminist theological methodology. The 3rd National Gathering on Women in The Uniting Church in Australia was held in Brisbane from 25–28 January 1996. As a member of the Coordinating Group (Executive Committee), I had responsibility for the oversight and development of the programme for this event. The development of the programme was a response to the hopes of the members of the larger Planning Group, and the evaluations of the two previous conferences. The programme sought to respond to the ambiguity of women's lives by offering a context where each woman's story would be treated with equal care, and where recognition would be given to the variations in women's life and faith experiences through a multi-layered strategy. The theme of the gathering, 'Women Clothed with the Sun', was drawn from the story of the woman clothed with the sun in Rev. 12: 1–6, 13–17. The text required attention to its own ambiguity as the basis for a programme which sought to recognize the diversity of women and their experiences in the Uniting Church. Such attention is given in chapter 5 where the story of the woman clothed with the sun becomes the first specific example for demonstrating the methodological direction required of a hermeneutical method that seeks *jouissance*. Chapter 2 demonstrates that the methodology for 'subjecting ambiguity' involves not only the poetic reading of texts such as Scripture, but also the poetic reading of social discourses such as community interaction.

Chapter 3 outlines some clear principles of structuralist theory underlining poststructuralist agendas. In particular, this chapter highlights the assumption of an inherent duality extant in human language and culture, together with the understanding of the crucial role of language, in its broadest sense (as systems of communicative symbols), in determining human experiences, or at least the perception of them. This chapter makes use of the pioneering linguistic work of Ferdinand de Saussure (1857–1913) and to the later assimilation of his structuralist methodology into the realm of other social sciences, particularly anthropology, by Claude Lévi-Strauss (b. 1908). Saussure envisaged a linguistic split between signifier and signified, that which stands for and that which is presumed to be represented in the composite whole of the sign as a basic building block of communication. This split was identified as being replicated in other socio-linguistic arrangements by Claude Lévi-Strauss. For example, the organization of whole societies was observed by Lévi-Strauss to occur around series of binary divisions. The primary link between language and social organization established by structuralism is an important base for the explorations of poststructuralism which both affirms the usefulness of inherent organizational duality as a theoretical base for understanding social arrangements and considers the areas of language and society where that duality is transgressed, concealed or, for all intents and purposes, obliterated. The assumed determining connection between language and culture is also an essential legacy of structuralism for poststructuralism. This legacy allows connections to be made between linguistic structuralism, cultural phenomena and versions of Freudian psychoanalysis focusing on the 'talking cure', for example Lacanian psychoanalysis.

Chapter 4 characterizes the movement from structuralism to poststructuralism through an investigation of the work of psychoanalyst Jacques Lacan (1901–1981) and literary theorist Jacques Derrida (b. 1930) as exemplary moments in that shift. Lacan's unique incorporation of structural linguistics into his interpretation of Freudian theory can be regarded as a key step in the transition process. His focus on the concept of an inherently split human subjectivity is direct heir to the structuralist concern with primary dualities. The psychoanalytic emphasis on sexuality ensures that the dualities— Male/Female and Masculine/Feminine—become centrally and even problematically placed in the poststructuralist enterprise. Derrida, preferring to focus on the linguistic implications of the groundwork laid by Lacan, seeks the gaps between the dualities of language which reveal the 'otherness' that is outside such constraints. This otherness or 'alterity' is characterized as feminine in the constructions of language. Such a characterization follows the model of the psychoanalytic triangle (Mother-Father-Child) and the diminution of the maternal figure in the struggle between Father and Child.[5] The possibility of something beyond the inherent dualities of language and subjectivity is the key motif/motive for the investigation of poststructuralist theory in chapter 4. This lays the groundwork for an exploration of Julia Kristeva's concept of *jouissance* as a discursive means of accessing alterity. Poststructuralism both recognizes the patterns of duality inherent in language and subjectivity as observed by structuralism and looks beyond that patterning via reference to a notion of otherness or alterity. This notion of otherness raises questions about the nature of human identity, challenging the idea of a unitary, conscious human subjectivity.

In the context of the work of poststructuralist scholar Julia Kristeva, the concept of *jouissance* provides a notion of a viable threshold to this posited otherness or alterity. *Jouissance*, for Kristeva, is the outcome of discourse: a discursive product. Using the background work offered in chapters 3 and 4 as the foundation for understanding

---

5. 'Mother', 'Father', 'Child', while related to 'real' people, must primarily be regarded as archetypal. That is, direct correlation between the archetypes and familial relations should not automatically be assumed. The archetypes should be regarded as attempting to highlight something that is not simply a matter of family relationships, but rather a socio-cultural phenomenon.

the significance of poststructuralist theory for a theological framework, in chapter 5, I offer my own interpretation of the possibilities contained within a poststructuralist theoretical framework for a theological methodology. This interpretation revolves around the argument that *jouissance*, as well as being the outcome of poetic language (discourse that manifests ambiguity), may also be the outcome (and therefore goal) of poetic reading—a hermeneutical approach that identifies ambiguity in discourse. The concept of *jouissance*, not simply as an exercise in the production of discourse but also as a hermeneutical goal, is the topic of chapter 5. Through an exploration of the discourses of abjection and apocalypse as characterized by Kristeva and an examination of various approaches to interpreting the biblical Revelation to John, chapter 5 presents the possibility that the interpretation of a text may be *jouissant* whether its production is or not. That is, the ambiguities and ambivalences of the text may be identified in interpretation, thereby defying even the most apparently strict binary divisions contained within the text itself. A *jouissant* interpretation of a text such as Revelation, a discourse often identified as dualistic, presents the possibility of both identifying the inherent dualities of the text and of identifying the otherness on which such a text is dependent, rendering a reading which is capable of enjoying the complexity of the text and momentarily bypassing or subverting the dualities presented therein.

Chapter 6 continues to explore the possibilities of this poststructuralist theological method based in the work of Julia Kristeva by outlining the specific strategies or method by which the hermeneutical aim of *jouissance* might be achieved. The methodology of poetic reading is described as essentially transgressive. That is, it crosses traditionally identified boundaries in both text and method. It involves a three stage process: articulation of the dualities present in the focal discourse; subversion of these dualities through a variety of strategies; and the re-presentation of the focal discourse emphasizing its multiple or ambiguous nature. Such a method is developed from a combination of the deconstructive strategies of Jacques Derrida, together with the notion of the dual oscillating nature of all discourse as developed by Julia Kristeva. The method of poetic reading seeks the revolutionary potential of poetic expression, the linguistic manifestation of *jouissance* for Julia Kristeva. In this manner, there is an attempt to re-present overtly in discourse the ambiguity or alterity which is assumed to exist outside of, under and covertly within it. The use of the outlined method is demonstrated in the interpretation of the story of the Canaanite woman (Mt. 15: 21–28) based on the textual work of Elaine Wainwright.

A comment should be made here on the re-introduction of the notion of re-presentation. Poststructuralism, as the inheritor of structuralist precepts, does not envisage the representation in language of any identifiable concrete entity. Rather, it is in language that such entities are created. The attempt to re-present alterity in language is thus not a representation of a concrete entity, but an attempt to create something outside the previously determined dualistic boundaries of language and subjectivity. The nature of the methodology and the assumptions on which it is based ensure that such a project is never complete in itself, but in the process of constantly reinventing discourses.

Chapter 7 argues that one of the clear implications of the transgressive method of 'poetic reading' is the continual facing, and indeed confrontation with images of the abject in language and culture, since such images represent the alterity which is beyond both of these. In a Christian feminist theological context, a transgressive hermeneutical method will entail a confrontation with otherness or alterity as it is characterized in a Christian theological context. One archetypal manifestation of this otherness for Christianity has been the image of the wanton, unruly and evil woman, the 'whore'. This archetype, also an archetype of transgression itself, can be correlated with the (m)other image of alterity inherent in Kristeva's work. The archetype of the 'whore' together with its counterpart the 'virgin' has had profound effects on the characterization of women in Christian communities. Chapter 7 argues that not only must this duality be subverted for the imaging of women in Christianity, but, in contemporary attempts to reinvest the image of God with feminine motifs, the 'whore' must be incorporated too. Since *jouissance* remains a continuing aim in this confrontation, the outcome of the encounter is never definitive. A confrontation with otherness implies the immediate re-characterization of that otherness and the necessity of continuing the transgressive strategy.

The conclusion considers briefly the implications for a continuing poststructuralist feminist systematic theological project of transgressive method and its intended *jouissant* outcome. It suggests that four factors are continuing marks of the methodology proposed:

1. A continuing exploration of dissonance without reconciliation or synthesis.
2. The revolutionary focus of the project as its transgressive programme remains movably identified with the unwanted, repressed otherness of language and subjectivity.
3. A lack of definitiveness in its product and a constant openness to transformation as a corollary of this lack.
4. A continuing political programme of transgression.

Despite the confrontational nature of the terminology used to describe this poststructuralist strategy, its simultaneous sense of closure and non-closure remains faithful to the Christian tradition. *Jouissance* becomes the promised culmination at once awarded and deferred. In a final account of the argument, I affirm the place of the methodology described herein within the tradition of Christian theology and recognize the disputation that may occur because of this affirmation.

My Approach

Through the process of the argument, the poststructuralist feminist theological methodology proposed here is grounded in both appropriate and articulated underlying theoretical assumptions, and the demonstrated and practical application of its hermeneutical approach, textually, theologically and communally. The methodology of the process itself is essentially explorative and integrative. That is, a particular theoretical strand has been chosen, that of poststructuralism, and within it, a particular theorist, Julia Kristeva. Through a heuristic strategy of identifying the key assumptions and projections of the theoretical position and applying these assumptions and projections to discourses in a theological context, the possible outcomes of that theoretical position are explored for a theological context.

The illustrations of chapters 2 and 5 to 7 are thus essential components of the argument, and not simply examples of a more abstract discussion. In this way, practical and theoretical concerns are integrated into the exploration of the possibilities of a poststructuralist theoretical position for a feminist theological context, both through the explorative, integrative methodology used and the discourses—textual, theological and communal—chosen as illustrations.

Context remains an important contribution to this process. In addressing the primary and personal impetuses of this exploration here, I have signalled the key role that I believe that context plays. The integrative nature of this work relies on my own multiple concerns of reclaiming the biblical text, offering sound pastoral practice, maintaining a feminist ethical position, and the necessity of all of these being grounded firmly in consistent theory and good theologizing. If the latter concern for consistency, and indeed my earlier question of integrity seem oddly placed beside poststructuralism, then for myself the juxtaposition is not so difficult, because, as I will argue, poststructuralism is perhaps best understood primarily as the rigorous and consistent application of the structuralist agenda to its logical and splintered conclusions. This rigor is precisely the reason that poststructuralism offers the possibility of bringing into recognition the ambiguous nature of language and subjectivity itself, thereby giving a suitable theoretical base for addressing the three concerns I raised earlier: diversity, ambiguity, and integrity in the face of multiplicity.

Chapter 1

RESURRECTING EROTIC TRANSGRESSION: POSTSTRUCTURALISM AND THEOLOGY

A Poststructuralist Theological Project

In describing my project as an 'erotic transgressive resurrection', I use the term 'erotic' because this project begins with a premise of unfulfilled desire, primarily for meaning. The project explores possibilities for the liminal, momentary and deferred satisfaction of desire for meaning in *jouissance*. It also takes seriously the relational and power aspects of human meaning systems at the level of socio-linguistic relations. I describe this project as 'transgressive' because it seeks to cross established boundaries, particularly those of Western dualities; is confrontational in certain of its exploratory strategies; and defies conventional constraints against the examination of loss and death in its willingness to face the loss and death of meaning. I use the term 'resurrection' because the whole project is based on the assumption of a constant process of meaning construction, deconstruction, destruction,[1] and reconstruction, and the validity of reinvigorating Christian symbolism with relevant contemporary meaning.

This project does not assume that the presumed destruction of meaning, because of the processes of deconstruction, is the end of either the poststructuralist enterprise or of theology. Rather, in the words of the opening paragraph of 'The Funeral Service' of The Uniting Church in Australia, this project 'affirm[s] the Christian

---

1. 'Destruction' is used in addition to the word 'deconstruction' in order to highlight the distinctive role of deconstruction which is not, in the first place, destruction. Deconstruction is, in effect, a detailed examination of meaning construction. One of the possible results of this process, although by no means the only one, is the destruction of meaning (or at least certain meanings) for the examiner.

conviction that while death is the end...it marks a new beginning...'
(The Uniting Church in Australia Assembly Liturgy Commission
1988: 456), i.e. while deconstruction exposes the constructed nature
of meaning thereby rendering current meanings and systems
unsatisfactory, and therefore 'dead', new meanings are constantly
being created in order to satiate the human desire for them. These
new meanings are, in turn, exposed to the rigours of deconstruction,
and the cycle continues in the constant twofold motion of death and
resurrection—an oscillation which is never content with either of the
polarities, but instead demands a situation which is both beyond and
within the artificial structures created by them. Accordingly, this
chapter places this project in the context of other contemporary
poststructuralist theological projects and, in particular, those of
Christian feminist scholars.

Erotic Transgressive Resurrection

The words '*eros*' and 'erotic', although part of the feminist agenda
for a number of years, have only become more prominent in the
feminist theological arena in comparatively recent times. This late
emergence has been perhaps partly due to the often strict division
enforced in certain Christian theologies between *eros* (and sexuality)
and *agape*, 'true' Christian love. This division is being challenged by
feminist theological reinvestments of *eros* with positive connotations.
Rita Nakashima Brock, for example, proposes a 'Christology of erotic
power' in her book, *Journeys by Heart* (1988). Brock describes 'erotic
power' as 'the power of our primal interrelatedness' (1988: 26).

Brock's explanation of *eros* is very positive, but somewhat too
idealistic for my tastes. There is no acknowledgment of other than
positive elements within it. Yet, the specific linking of *eros* with power,
to my mind, demands a recognition of the latent ambiguity—terror
as well as celebration—which lies in such an association. The
characterization of erotic power as the power of our primal
interrelatedness, 'the fundamental power of existence-as-a-relational-
process' (1988: 41), holds the possibility of that recognition. This
possibility is not explored by Brock except in the context of relational
power being 'denied and crushed' (1988: 36). There the emphasis is
on the repression of relational power, not on the terrifying aspects of
its exercise. The recognition of the ambiguity of erotic power is a
possibility able to be envisaged in a Kristevan theoretical base.

Jouissance is the concept from which this project launches itself. Connotatively tied to notions of sexual pleasure and thereby to the sexual aspects of the psychoanalytic triangle, in the context of this thesis it is primarily defined as a product of discourse. *Jouissance* as an outcome of discourse is appropriated as a hermeneutical product in Chapter 5. In this appropriation, *jouissance* is defined as the specific enjoyment of subjective ambiguity—but not as an enjoyment which is only joyful or celebratory. Rather, *jouissance* is interpreted as the ambivalent celebration of ambiguity: the recognition of both the pain and the joy of the meaning-making process—the point where 'Gravity becomes frivolity that retains its memory of suffering and continues its search for truth in the joy of perpetually making a new beginning' (Kristeva 1987a: 51–52). As such, *jouissance* is an outcome of desire for meaning, but not an outcome that requires the illusion of meaning as reality. Rather, *jouissance* 'joys in the truth of the self-division' of meaning and subjectivity.

Elizabeth Grosz suggests that the concept of desire can be associated with two distinct philosophical traditions: one where 'desire is conceived as a fundamental lack in being, an incompletion or absence' (Grosz 1989: xv) and the other where desire is a 'positive force of production' (1989: xvi). Grosz associates the former with Plato, Hegel and French psychoanalyst Jacques Lacan (1989: xv); and the latter with Spinoza, Friedrich Nietzsche, Michel Foucault and Gilles Deleuze. In the context of this project, if desire represents an incompleteness then it is an incompleteness that cannot be regarded as abnormal and therefore as either necessarily or possibly able to be fixed. Rather, desire is regarded as a symptom of the ambiguity of human consciousness: the identification of an absence which is neither absent nor identifiable. Consequently, desire does represent a 'positive force for production' in its very recognition of 'lack'.

This dual characterization of desire is probably in part attributable to the use of Kristevan theory in this project. While Kristevan theory is influenced by the psychoanalytic concepts of Lacan, the peculiar combination of literary and linguistic analysis melded with post-Lacanian psychoanalytic formulations produces a system which recognizes lack as a construct, understands the resulting condition of desire as an illusion, and enjoys the halting, confused and varied attempts of humans to fill a space which does not require satiation (and indeed cannot be satiated). In the Kristevan schema, desire produces love and love, following the security discovered in relationships of transference, produces meaning. Love also may be illusory in these terms, but illusion has 'therapeutic and epistemological value'. For Kristeva, it is the role of the analyst to restore the fullness of this value to illusion, thereby bringing about healing and recovery (Kristeva 1987a: 21). This healing or recovery assumes a loss or death which is retained anamnestically as part of the *jouissance* which is a celebration of ambiguous subjectivity. That recovery is based on illusion created by desire and has both positive and negative consequences.

A Kristevan theoretical model assumes a constant interplay of two elements which are never absorbed by a third, although neither are those elements static in their manifestations. In this respect, the 'erotic' linguistic play of this project assumes a constant interplay based in a desire which is never fully consummated by any form of synthesis. Desire remains even at the height of *eros*. Subjectivity is always ambiguous. The significance of the dual characterization of desire coincides with the two-fold poststructuralist movement that this project continually advocates: deconstruction and reconstruction. Grosz notes that feminists have used the notion of desire as lack to explain the position of women in patriarchy, and the concept of desire as a positive force of production to directly explore the possibilities of 'power and resistance' (Grosz 1989: xvi). This project suggests that both elements—critique and production—are useful feminist operations, and that desire offers the possibility of both.

In a theological context, Charles E. Winquist (1995) explores the notion of desire in relation to the desire for theological meaning: 'I have equated desire for a thinking which does not disappoint with a desire to think theologically' (Winquist 1995: ix). Winquist sees in this formula 'a secular mandate for theology'. He also sees a theological mandate for the use of poststructuralist theory (1995: x). His account of the relationship of desire and theology places theology itself in the realm of *eros* or relational power: a position which I am happy to endorse in all its ambiguity.

Transgression

Transgression indicates a passage across something and also a straying or, in Mark C. Taylor's terms, an 'erring' (Taylor 1984: 11–12). This project, as a theological enterprise, primarily transgresses theology as its 'master' discourse. That transgression comes through a willingness both to critique and to produce. In critique, this project exposes the underlying principles of construction, most notably the role of dualities, of the master discourse. Such critique is prepared to endure the loss of meaning, in order to search for new meanings. In production, this project dares to present alternative constructions which challenge the hegemony of the master discourse. Such production relies on the previous loss, and is constantly aware of its own ephemeral position. Both critique and production stray into each other as well as transgressing the boundaries of the master. Yet they are also separate moments. As transgressors, they are also confronters and liable to be labelled as such. Their transgression envisages the possibility of something which is described as 'impossible' within the master discourse, and yet something which is integral to it: resurrection. Resurrection requires a transgression of its own—through death.

Resurrection

I have deliberately used the word 'resurrection' because of its theological overtones. This project is very definitely theological, despite its transgression of theological discourse. It is also resurrectionary from a number of points of view. It is resurrectionary of theology in both a feminist and a poststructuralist context; it is resurrectionary of meaning in a poststructuralist context; and it is resurrectionary in the sense that it presupposes a passage through death or loss.

There is no resurrection without death. Every reconstructive attempt requires a prior deconstruction of that which existed previously. This project pursues a constant, rotational, double movement of meaning transformation—death and resurrection, death and resurrection—a continual 'seeking [of] the renewal or rebirth of theology by way of a passage through the end or death of the primal ground of the Western theoretical and theological tradition' (Taylor 1982: xi) and whatever paradigms purport to emerge in its place. Christian theology has always had within it the potential to allow the coexistence of oppositional terms, and thereby to flout the hierarchical boundaries of dualities because of the death/resurrection motif. Yet, as Taylor suggests, this potential has not always been evident (1982: 9). This project assumes the mutual and equal positionality of both binary oppositions, asserting the relevance of both, the arbitrariness of both, the indivisibility of both, and the inability of avoiding either. In this respect, it is grounded firmly in a Christian tradition which has always struggled with the ambiguity of its central symbol, the person of Christ—'in two natures, without confusion, without change, without division, without separation' (the definition of Chalcedon 451 CE; Bettenson 1963: 73)—even if historically that tradition has failed on many occasions to enter into the *jouissance* that is discovered in the recognition of the otherness (alterity) that is beyond, within and uncontained by the dualities of Western meaning systems.

Just as this attention to the double movement of death and resurrection is profoundly Christian, it is also profoundly feminist for feminism is essentially born in the critique of the dominant patriarchal system: the deconstruction of a system which is revealed as unsatisfactory, particularly for women. Feminism, however, has never been content to precipitate the demise (already and not yet fulfilled) of patriarchy. Always, there has been the search for a new way of operating: a way which might supersede patriarchy in both time and achievement. The 'perfect' feminist system has, of course, not been found yet, and perhaps will not and cannot be. Nevertheless, the search continues: a search which is at one time deconstructive and reconstructive, highly adaptable to and probably a contributing precipitator of the poststructuralist agenda. Indeed, as I have suggested above, it is feminism which demands the deconstructive component of any postmodern theological enterprise, in addition to any reconstructive attempts made in the face of perceived crises in the Christian faith.

Post-Structuralism

Poststructuralism is essentially *post*-structuralist. This statement implies that poststructuralism basically begins or, more appropriately, launches itself from certain structuralist premises:

1. Human meaning systems are arbitrarily constructed according to certain structures, albeit deeply unconsciously embedded ones.
2. These structures are essentially binary or dualistic.
3. The construction process of meaning systems governs the nature of the constructed meanings within them, i.e. the unconscious binary structures produce dualistic systems of meaning.

4. There is no real referential relationship between language (and other symbols) and the 'objects' which they purport to represent.

In *The Thinking Muse: Feminism and Modern French Philosophy*, Jeffner Allen and Iris Marion Young characterize the legacy of structuralism as 'the Saussurian proposal that meaning resides not in a relationship between an utterance and that to which it refers, but in the relationship of signs to one another' (Allen & Young 1989: 5). In this relationship, a world of dualities is understood to be constructed arbitrarily. The dualities, the process of the construction and, following all this, language, symbols and meaning are laid open to intense scrutiny, scepticism and, in the final analysis, rejection as conveyors of any absolute 'truth'.

Poststructuralism, in following the principles of structuralism to their inevitable conclusion, raises issues about the validity of meanings and systems given their apparently arbitrarily and automatically structured construction. In this focus on the constructed nature of meaning, the structures undergirding systems and meaning are revealed to be neither inevitable nor absolute. Rather, structures are shown to be highly determinative of meaning and systemic content, yet arbitrary, fallible and flawed. The validity of meanings and systems is thus called into question, and alternatives outside of such structural constraints are sought. The invalidation of constructed meanings has major implications for epistemology. Allen & Young comment that 'Every form of subject-object epistemology, including the phenomenological distinction between the constituting subject and the experience it constitutes, comes into question by this move of structural linguistics' (1989: 5).

The difficulty of envisaging anything outside of that which constrains our meaning and thought leads poststructuralism to use complex, creative and transgressive tactics which deliberately undermine the sense of safety and security which people find in the assumption that we say what we mean, mean what we say, and actually refer to 'real' things in language. Poststructuralism challenges that assumption by exposing the possibility that we say what we have learned to say, mean what we can only mean within the constraints of our systems of language and communication, and refer only to the categories we have constructed for ourselves in those systems, not to any concrete or existential reality. In this respect, it provides a major challenge to Western epistemologies in general, and theology, with its peculiar metaphysical pretensions, in particular.

Feminist ethicist, Edith Wyschogrod, in describing 'postmodernism' rather than 'poststructuralism', uses a phrase which is equally apt for the latter as it is for the former: the 'subversion of philosophical language' (Wyschogrod 1990: xiii). Poststructuralism, as an aspect of the postmodern theoretical agenda, undermines the security of all epistemological efforts. In doing so, it relativizes various knowledges and, some would say, enters the slippery slope to nihilism.

Certainly, poststructuralism disempowers dominant epistemological paradigms. This disempowerment is, for me, the source of the promise of poststructuralism in a feminist theological enterprise. For, as poststructuralism relativizes dominant paradigms, it conversely and unexpectedly validates alternative epistemological models. This validation is not the replacement of one dominant paradigm with another but rather the recognition that another (and *perhaps* every other) paradigm offers a contribution to the human search for illusive 'truth', i.e. meaning; or, more accurately, no meaning construction can be regarded automatically and uncritically as providing an accurate account of what is 'real'. Thus, for epistemologies which find themselves sidelined by modernism, e.g. theology, and those which have failed to gain a legitimate and firm foothold in long-established power structures, e.g. feminism, poststructuralism offers the validation of their place among a pantheon of epistemologies. This place is not secure, but it is no longer any less secure than any other paradigm. Indeed, in circumstances where these epistemologies are transgressors, they may be more welcome in a poststructuralist milieu than are those paradigms which seek to perpetuate dominant stances. This welcoming of transgression is an oscillating process as various paradigms gain varying degrees of acceptance at different times and in different places, thereby demanding closer analysis and scrutiny of their constructed nature. Poststructuralism both warns that no paradigm should be taken too seriously, and welcomes alternatives that transgress dominant motifs. In this respect, it aptly fits the postmodern agenda.

Post-Modernism

Chronologically, poststructuralism refers 'to currents of philosophy that have prevailed in France [and become increasingly influential elsewhere] since the early 1970s' (Allen & Young 1989: 5). Sequentially, poststructuralism proceeds from structuralism. For theologian and deconstructionist, Mark C. Taylor, this firmly places poststructuralism on the postmodern theoretical agenda.

Using G.W.F. Hegel (1770–1831) as his fulcrum, Taylor determines poststructuralism to form part of the 'extended critique of Hegel's systematic philosophy'. Since 'Hegelianism is the culmination of modern philosophy', a full-blown 'structuralism' developed from Hegel's 'protostructuralist' theory, poststructuralism is postmodern. That is, it belongs to a theoretical agenda that supersedes and disrupts modernity, as well as arises from it. The significance of Taylor's characterization of poststructuralism is in its association of the modern agenda with Hegel and 'latter-day Hegelianism' (Taylor 1990: 19). If poststructuralism is postmodern, then it must be regarded as challenging specific and foundational elements of the modern philosophical method from a theoretical base which essentially arises from that method. Postmodernism must, as its name implies, transgress, transcend or supersede the 'modern' agenda as well as 'completing' it in the sense of bringing it to its inevitable conclusion, both theoretically and terminally. If Taylor is correct, then both the complementary and disruptive characteristics of postmodernism for the modern agenda may be discerned by attending to specific legacies of modernity.

In the context of this work, and its focus on ambiguous subjectivity, the modern agenda is best characterized by the use of three motifs:

1. The assumption of an autonomous self-conscious subject.
2. The necessity of a dialectical process for progress.
3. The dominance of the scientific method (including its ideals) in epistemology.

All three motifs carry Hegelian overtones. This description of the modern agenda and its completion and/or disruption by postmodernity is not exhaustive. Rather, it is a description of key motifs which characterize modernity and postmodernity and are relevant to this project.

The Subject

Epistemologies of the modern era rely heavily on the notion of the thinking, knowing subject. Taylor offers a widely accepted truism when he asserts that the 'modern period in philosophy is generally acknowledged to have begun with Descartes's [René Descartes 1596–

1650] decisive turn to the subject' (Taylor 1984: 21). This thinking, knowing subject is regarded as the actor in the realm of epistemologies. Similarly, Grosz observes that, for Hegel, 'the precondition for historical development or dialectical change is provided by the postulate of a self-conscious, as self-identical being' (Grosz 1989: 3), a subjectivity which is self-aware. Modernism assumes that the subject is identifiable, knowable and knowing, and self-conscious. As such, this subject is presumed to have the capacity to learn, to experiment and to amass greater and greater knowledge and understanding of itself and the world which it experiences. In this concept of the subject, autonomy is valued and pursued since autonomy is also what validates the subject's knowledge as much as the subject itself. In *The Phenomenology of Mind*, originally published in 1807, Hegel talks of a 'pressing forward' to a 'true form of existence' where consciousness would grasp 'its own essence' and attain 'absolute knowledge'. This process of grasping absolute knowledge is contingent on the laying aside of 'what is foreign' to the subject (Hegel 1931: 145).

In fairness to Hegel, there is ambivalence in the position just identified. The account of the movement towards absolute knowledge may also be read as incorporation into consciousness of the appearance or 'semblance of being hampered with what is foreign' (Hegel 1931: 145) to consciousness. That is, it is possible to draw from the Hegelian account of consciousness, a recognition of something that belongs to subjectivity, but is unrecognized by it, so that this appearance of difference is incorporated into an understanding of subjectivity that encompasses difference. The Hegelian ideal is still an 'absolute knowledge' based in a complete consciousness but, in this second reading, the seeds of the poststructuralist agenda are clearly evident. The possibility of subjectivity being more complex than an autonomous self-consciousness is raised, if not pursued. Such a double reading of Hegel accounts for Taylor's description of Hegel as 'protostructuralist' and Hegelianism as a full-blown 'structuralism' (Taylor 1990: 19). The motifs of modernity may belong more clearly to a particular reading of Hegel than to Hegel himself. Nevertheless, consciousness and knowledge through consciousness remains a significant component of both the philosophy of Hegel and the modern philosophical agenda.

The Hegelian Dialectic

For Hegel, the movement or development towards absolute knowledge is predicated on a dialectical process which presumes the existence of at least two autonomous self-conscious subjects, and an antagonism between them. Grosz writes that, in Hegel's schema, it is only when what is presumed to be *other* to the subject is discovered to be *another* subject that progress or 'history (as dialectical overcoming)' occurs. That is, paradigm shifts demand the contradictory and 'dialectical antagonism' of two self-conscious subjects (Grosz 1989: 3). In the contradiction between the two knowledges, a synthesis or third alternative (and presumably closer to absolute) knowledge is sought for 'reason *cannot* rest with what is self-contradictory' (Stace 1955: 93).

Again, within this schema, there is ambivalence. The original consciousness or knowledge is the 'thesis'; the arising contradiction, the 'antithesis'; *but* the antithesis is found *within* the thesis: 'the fixed and stable existence carries the process of its own dissolution within itself' (Hegel 1931: 115). Here again are the seeds of the poststructuralist agenda in this 'protostructuralist' philosophy. The dialectical process is something 'which consciousness executes on itself' (Hegel 1931: 142). That is, for all intents and purposes, the dialectical subject is essentially divided. This account of a divided subject in Hegel is anachronistic though. In Hegel's schema, the manifestation of an 'other' is regarded as a result of imperfect knowledge, a phenomenon to be overcome by successive dialectical confrontations and syntheses resulting in the perfect thesis. Nevertheless, the 'other' is also a 'radical *negativity*' and the resulting conflict encountered by the thesis with the antithesis is a confrontation with 'another self-consciousness fundamentally similar to itself, distinguished from everything other than itself by [that] radical *negativity*' (Grosz 1989: 3). That this 'other' is internal to the originally postulated self-conscious subject is the beginning of the postmodern 'loss' of the autonomous, unitary and self-conscious subject.

In the poststructuralist schema, the 'other' becomes that on which the subject is dependent for existence. It cannot be overcome; nor can the resulting conflict which is internal to the subject be synthesized; nor is this 'other' presumed to be necessarily self-conscious or consciously perceived by the self-conscious subject. Poststructuralism presumes that an 'other' exists within and, indeed, under the subject itself. That is, the subject, although presuming self-consciousness, is confronted, knowingly or otherwise, by an 'other' entity whose consciousness is somewhat indeterminate (and perhaps non-existent)—a part of the self which the self does not know, but upon which the self is predicated. This recognition introduces an *ambiguity* into subjectivity. The subject can no longer be regarded as self-conscious. Consciousness itself is questioned as a state of 'being' and even as an epistemological position. Furthermore, this 'transgression' of modernity is traceable to modernism itself. Grosz attributes some of the poststructuralist developments specifically to a mid-1930s reading of Hegel by French phenomenologist and Marxist, Alexandre Kojève: 'the fate of the subject is necessarily bound up with the existence of the other...the essential condition of self-conscious' (Grosz 1989: 6).

The Scientific Method

The scientific model is indebted to the Hegelian dialectic: the notion that movement in knowledge, epistemology and ideology can be charted in terms of a dialectical and conflictual opposition between a thesis and an antithesis, resulting in an ensuing synthesis which consequently becomes the thesis in a repetition of the pattern. Important elements of this model include the binary and oppositional nature of the thesis and antithesis, the resolution of this opposition by a third term which supersedes the prior two, the progression envisaged and the continuing reliance on the dual form. The goal of an 'absolute' knowledge is also significant, as is the notion of self-conscious subjectivity and autonomy. In this schema, the antithesis is found through considered reflection; the synthesis, in conflict. The goal of the dialectical process is the point where no antithesis can be found and, therefore, no synthesis need be sought. The end point is the moment when 'knowledge is no longer compelled to go beyond itself, where it finds its own self, and the notion corresponds to the object and the object to the notion' (Hegel 1931: 137–38)—perfect referentiality.

The breakdown of the concept of the subject as self-aware and knowledgeable disrupts the scientific method which relies on the ability to 'trust' the subject's observations—on autonomy in the subject's observations. Similarly, the severing of the referential relationship between concept and 'reality' (sign and object) disrupts the possibility of a perfect referentiality. Poststructuralism, as the result of the very search for knowledge which modernity envisages, takes the modern scientific agenda to its inevitable conclusion when it theorizes that the subject is constructed as much as any of the other objects of study. In this respect, nothing can in anyway be considered autonomous and no position can be regarded as external to that which is being studied. In a sense, Hegel's quest for an absolute self-consciousness is swamped by the very process by which he envisaged attaining it—the incorporation of the 'semblance of being hampered with what is foreign' (Hegel 1931: 145) into an epistemology of subjectivity. Thus, as Taylor observes, 'Carried to its conclusion, the pursuit of self-possession actually dispossesses the searching subject' (Taylor 1984: 30). Not only is the subject dispossessed but any notion of epistemology on which the identified subject based its search, research and conclusions is also displaced. The removal of these certainties of method and exploration undermines the security of knowledge and 'truth'. Because of this, poststructuralism has faced accusations of nihilism.

Nihilism?

If nihilism is the loss of meaning, then it is part of the poststructuralist journey, although not its culmination. If nihilism is the loss of the desire for meaning, then it negates the very basis of poststructuralist theory. For poststructuralism is the result of the desire for meaning taken to its inevitable conclusions through the vehicle of modernity. In this respect, there is a loss of meaning involved, and a questioning of all structures and explanations of reality. In contrast, there is no loss of the desire for meaning so that even poststructuralism can be described as another system of meaning attempting to somehow meet 'truth' although no longer in modernist terms. Consequently, nihilism is more correctly attributable as the outcome of modernism rather than postmodernism. Edith Wyschogrod remarks, 'nihilism is not *post*modern in any straightforward chronological sense' (1990: xiii). Conversely, nihilism cannot be regarded as being outside the realm of the experience of the postmodern. Rather, as Taylor suggests, it is a part of the process of the development of the postmodern which, when taken seriously, may be a 'mark of strength' not a 'sign of weakness' (Taylor 1984: 33).

Taylor makes a distinction between 'the partial nihilism of the modern humanistic atheist' and 'the crucifixion of selfhood' which is the thoroughgoing nihilism of the postmodern: 'For the writer who suffers the crucifixion of selfhood, nihilism is the mark of the cross. On Golgotha, not only God dies; the self also disappears' (Taylor 1984: 33). This latter nihilism is a loss of the illusion of autonomous subjectivity and, with it, the mirage of knowledge. It is not, however, a loss of hope and even promises an entry into another sphere of 'consciousness' by direct confrontation and indeed assimilation of the death of meaning, language, subjectivity and God. The word 'consciousness' is highly problematic here because the postmodern agenda in fact questions the validity of any subject's self-consciousness. Nevertheless, the term serves to highlight the deep connection between the goals of modernity and the outcomes of poststructuralism. Its use also serves to highlight an aspect of the loss of self for poststructuralism that is not 'simply nihilistic'. For Taylor, the 'disappearance of the subject' is also the mark of 'the emergence of the trace': a Derridean account of the signs of the 'otherness' that pervade subjectivity. 'The trace concretely embodies the ceaseless interplay of desire and delight' (Taylor 1984: 15). Thus, the nihilism of the poststructuralist paradigm is not a death which is terminal. Rather, it is a death which envisages, although does not hasten, a resurrection, but not of subjectivity in its pre-demise form.

Poststructuralism and Theology

The accusation of nihilism is also one which raises questions about the validity of poststructuralism as a theoretical base for theology. In my opinion, poststructuralism is, at least potentially, theological in several of its motifs: mystery; otherness; death and loss; and resurrection. My particular interest, however, is in its construction of subjectivity as ambiguous. This construction, in my opinion, presents the possibility of addressing the concerns of diversity, ambiguity and integrity which are outlined in the 'Introduction'. This construction conforms to the specifically Christian motif of the ambiguous subjectivity of the person of Christ. The goal of this project is to construct a methodological framework that will take into account ambiguous subjectivity, thereby transgressing the dualistic tendencies of Christian faith, theology and practice, and upholding the central motifs of Christianity which defy such dualisms. In this respect, the indivisible Christian motifs of death and resurrection are perhaps most poignant in the following examination of ways in which poststructuralist theory has already become a part of theological investigations, and the manner in which my own project fits into that context.

Constructive or Deconstructive?

Self-defined constructive postmodern theologian David Ray Griffin distinguishes between 'constructive or revisionary' postmodernism and 'deconstructive or eliminative' postmodernism. For Griffin, constructive or revisionary postmodernism seeks the construction of a new worldview: a synthesis of 'scientific, ethical, aesthetic, and religious institutions' built on the triumphs of modernity. In contrast, deconstructive or eliminative postmodernism is regarded as stripping away the possibility of worldviews altogether, and, with that possibility, any hope of meaning, truth, purpose, God and self—an 'ultramodernism' carrying through the premises of modernity to their logical conclusions (Griffin 1989: x). The movements of post-structuralism belong in the latter category.

Terrence Tilley perpetuates Griffin's distinction in *Postmodern Theologies: The Challenge of Religious Diversity*. For Tilley, constructive postmodernism, 'the postmodernism of completion', extends and completes the modern project, purifying not destroying the 'religious world' (Tilley 1995: vii). In contrast, deconstructive postmodernism, the postmodernism of 'dissolution', employs 'distilled and concentrated modern acids on religious and theological constructs' (Tilley 1995: vii–viii). The irony of this characterization is that both constructive and deconstructive postmodernisms are regarded as the heirs of modernity.

The distinction employed by David Ray Griffin and Terrence Tilley is not a helpful one. First, it has been used to downplay the efforts of feminist theologians to lay bare the nature of the patriarchal order and to deconstruct the prevailing hierarchies. Second, it maintains the extant Western dualities and their hierarchical positioning in theological thought. Third, it fails to recognize the deconstructive component that is always part of reconstruction, and the recon-structive move that is always part of deconstruction.

Anti-Feminist

From a feminist perspective, the distinction made by Griffin and Tilley between 'deconstructive' and 'reconstructive' postmodern theologies is highly suspect, not the least because it has been used to sideline the work of feminist theologians from the identified 'mainstream' or 'legitimate' theological enterprises yet again. For example, the only woman (Edith Wyschogrod) used as a significant example by Tilley in the sections of *Postmodern Theologies* (1995) which address constructive and deconstructive theologies is placed in the deconstructive category. This category is ultimately rejected as a positive theological solution by Tilley in the context of his focal issue of dealing with the dilemma of religious diversity (1995: 167). To be fair to Tilley, he does end up with a feminist theologian in his favoured category in his final chapter, when he conflates the 'constructive' theologies with the 'theologies of communal praxis'. In this movement, Sharon Welch, identified as a theologian of communal praxis, is placed in Tilley's preferred category. The significance of Welch's contribution is moderated, however, by a reference to her work as being 'less distinctively "christomorphic"' (Tilley 1995: 166).

More obviously, in a paper entitled 'A Survey of Contemporary Theologies that Move Us in the Direction of the 21st Century' and presented at a colloquium sponsored by the University of Queensland chaplains in April 1993, Scott Cowdell, an Australian Anglican scholar, used Griffin's distinction between constructive and deconstructive postmodern theologies to banish feminist theology in general to the suspect deconstructive category. This assessment was made without any significant reference to varying methodological strategies. Rather, because of the critical foundation of feminist strategies, the efforts of feminist theologians were regarded as 'deconstructive', a word which is often equated with the notion of 'destruction', whether or not their methodological strategies conformed to the poststructuralist agenda.

The analysis of patriarchy found at the heart of feminist critiques is, in one sense, profoundly deconstructive, and in another sense cannot be equated with deconstruction as such since a variety of strategies are involved. Nevertheless, the critical (and sometimes deconstructive) process is an integral component of feminist analysis.

The critical moment is important for feminist analyses. It is also a significant element of good scholarly work. Terrence Tilley partially acknowledges the importance of the critical movement in contemporary theology when he recognizes that the process of dissolving constructions leaves 'an empty space for the Light' (Tilley 1995: viii). The process of deconstruction, however, for Tilley, is the exposure of a 'Nothing' which relativizes all positions without establishing a unifying commonality or any criteria for establishing distinctions in value. At this point, Tilley also rejects such approaches as being 'postmodern'. They are only 'ultramodern' (Tilley 1995: 162–64): a point which I have already suggested is at least partially correct. Nevertheless, equally correct is the observation that Tilley fails to recognize the continuing role given to human constructions by deconstruction.

Although at times it may seem so, poststructuralism does not envisage a vacuum at the site of meaning loss. The process of meaning-making is more complex and continuous. Indeed, poststructuralism participates in that process itself. In the mere activity of deconstruction, the deconstructor has already created another layer of meaning demanding the sort of attention which has just been given to the object of the deconstruction. The void, if indeed it is ever exposed, is already filled either by other constructions requiring deconstruction even at the moment that the vacuum is discovered, or by the 'traces' of the 'other'.

Poststructuralism cannot be discarded simply because of its critical element even if that critical element is prepared to enter the realm of the unknown, i.e. of loss, even more fully than other critical approaches. Interestingly, Italo-Australian feminist philosopher Rosi Braidotti suggests that 'mainstream' and feminist readings of 'the crisis of modernity' differ because 'for the former the "crisis" stands for loss and decline, for feminists it marks the opening-out of unexplored possibilities' (Braidotti 1991: 276). Perhaps, it is also the case that, for at least some feminists, deconstruction is not a threat because the very nature of feminism has always ensured that the critique and untangling of patriarchal ideology has been a central feature of its basic endeavour.

Maintains Dualities

David Ray Griffin's approach to describing postmodern theologies is also deficient because it maintains the dualistic structure of Western thought which postmodernism directly confronts and attempts to move beyond. This maintenance is not so much discovered in the binary division of his taxonomy (although that division is significant in itself), but rather in the hierarchical positioning of the resulting opposition: reconstruction is good; deconstruction, bad. Feminism, confronted by the socio-political realities of dualisms, and poststructuralism, wary of the constructed nature of these dualisms, must view such a hierarchical taxonomy with great suspicion.

Feminist Christian ethicist, Beverly Wildung Harrison, for example, notes the relationship implicitly assumed between a whole range of dualities within human meaning constructions (Harrison 1985: 135–39). In this context, it is hardly unexpected that a distinction between constructive and deconstructive postmodern theologies would end up being conflated with the male/female binary opposition in a judgment which ensures that one term is the lesser in the duality. Indeed, feminist moral philosopher Elisabeth Porter situates the female/male opposition 'at the heart' of the myriad of dualisms so constructed (Porter 1991: 51 n. 2). In a patriarchal order, where the constructed dualities envisage the lesser nature of the 'feminine' term, the distinction made between constructive and deconstructive postmodernisms, and the use of this distinction to continue the marginalization of feminist critiques cannot be ignored. If Griffin is really to bring about his postmodern world which transcends 'individualism, anthropocentrism, patriarchy, mechanization, economism, consumerism, nationalism, and militarism' (Griffin 1989: xi), then the order(s) which maintain those regimes *must* be deconstructed, i.e. their constructed nature must be exposed, including the dualities through which they operate.

Ignores Ambiguities

The maintenance of dualities means that Griffin ignores ambiguity: precisely the motif in poststructuralism which is perhaps the most promising for theology. The ambiguity which Griffin fails to take into account is primarily the interrelationship of construction and deconstruction. This failure is reflected in the accounts of both sides of the duality he creates: deconstructive and constructive postmodernism. In the deconstructive category, Griffin sees only the eliminative and 'anti-worldview' aspects (Griffin 1989: x); in the reconstructive category, only the preservative and revisionary aspects

(1989: xi). Yet clearly, through deconstruction, something is created, and through revision, something lost. The rejection of either aspect—creative or eliminative—is a further false dichotomy which denies the ambiguous nature of any task.

Mark C. Taylor

Mark C. Taylor, undoubtedly a candidate for Griffin's deconstructive category, envisages a poststructuralist a/theology which does indeed encompass deconstruction to the point where he himself has been accused of nihilism: an accusation which he is pleased to confirm, explore and connotatively correct as shown above. Taylor's project, an 'erring a/theology', is described as 'utterly transgressive' of concepts and categories. For Taylor, the 'erring a/theologian is driven to consider and reconsider errant notions' such as 'transgression, subversion, mastery...death, desire...' (1984: 6). This consideration and reconsideration is 'neither *properly* theological nor nontheological, theistic nor atheistic, religious nor secular, believing nor nonbelieving' (1984: 12) as the '"hermeneutic" of the death of God' is explored (1984: 6). Certainly, there is an undeniable emphasis in Taylor's work on death, loss and deconstruction. Yet also clearly, within this a/theology which is so eager to explore the significant motifs of loss and death, there is a reclamative, creative, reconstructive component. Taylor, for example, admits to a 'deconstructive reformulation' of 'God as writing, self as trace, history as erring, and book as text' (1984: 13). Inherent in this a/theology is indeed both a deconstructive and a reconstructive move—although perhaps the reconstruction is not nearly so creative or reconstructive as others might prefer.

Carl Raschke

Carl Raschke (1992: 101–102) draws a distinction between 'analytical' postmodernism and 'metaphorical' postmodernism from the work of contemporary arts theorist David Levin. While, at first glance, this distinction seems to be a mere repetition of Griffin's dichotomy, on closer inspection, it becomes evident that the category of 'metaphorical' postmodernism, at least, is an attempt to encompass both deconstructive and reconstructive moments. While 'analytical' postmodernism is regarded as 'the formalist reappropriation of the anti-metaphysical propensities within modernist culture and thought', 'metaphoric' postmodernism is defined as 'the transcendence of nihilism', the movement beyond 'the emptiness of all frames and representations, including the dys-representative entropy of the deconstructive campaign' (Raschke 1992: 103). What is significant here is the characterization of metaphoric postmodernism as transcending or moving beyond the deconstruction of meaning. Metaphoric postmodernism assumes a deconstructive stage in contrast to the constructive, revisionary postmodernism of Griffin which seems to avoid any notion of dissolution or dismantling.

The difficulty I have with Raschke's classification of metaphoric postmodernism is in his over-eagerness to farewell the deconstructive moment. Raschke is impatient to be rid of the reductionism of deconstruction, and to replace it with a 'fundamental ontology of the body' (1992: 102). The problem with discarding the deconstructive moment is the surrendering of any tools to assist in the prevention of the solidification of the new system in the process. Even in reconstruction, there is a necessity for deconstructive moments. For me, the point of feminist critique and revisioning, critique and revisioning is precisely that there is never just one deconstructive moment. Rather, every system, new, old or resurrected, demands continuous vigilance against the solidity that threatens to reinstigate oppression and repression. Similarly, the message of post-structuralism of the Kristevan variety is that, as meaning-making beings, humans are constantly involved in an oscillating process of deconstruction and reconstruction, of attempts at solidity and revolution. Both forces are constant elements of linguistic formation, deformation and reformation. Because of this eagerness to move beyond deconstruction, Raschke assigns the work of Taylor to the 'analytical' category, accusing him of failing to 'embrace the "metaphoric postmodern"' and arriving at an 'insurmountable impasse' (1992: 102).

Deconstructive and Reconstructive

I wish to struggle with the best elements of the analysis of postmodern theologies that Taylor and Raschke have to provide. On the one hand, I wish to claim from Taylor the fearless entry into the deconstructive moment of loss and death; on the other, I want to claim the creative, reclamative, reconstructive, prismatic dance of the 'metaphorical postmodern' of Raschke; and with both hands, I want to uphold the ambiguity which each recognizes within both moments. This appropriation of deconstruction, reconstruction and ambiguity accords with the ambiguity of the Christian message itself which cannot envisage a death without a resurrection, or a resurrection without a death in the central motif of the Christian faith.

Within this ambiguity, the deconstructive moment can never be ignored or relegated as an historical moment; and the reconstructive activity never venerated as the only continuing work. Rather, just as there is a constant liminal aspect to Christian faith and life, so there needs to be a constant liminal aspect to this project which must never take itself too seriously to prevent it from keeping vigil at the tomb of its own death while expecting further resurrectionary transformations in theology. For this reason, in characterizing the nature of my own poststructuralist theological project, I choose neither to borrow Raschke's notion of metaphoric postmodernism nor to appropriate Taylor's account of a/theology. Rather, I offer my own category, 'erotic transgressive resurrection', in the context of the persistent feminist motif of deconstruction and reconstruction as the dual theoretical move required in the face of patriarchy.

Feminism, Poststructuralism and Theology

In 1993, the publication of *Transfigurations: Theology and the French Feminists* (Kim, St. Ville & Simonaitis) marked the significance that French feminist theory, as a subset of or an overlapping set with poststructuralist theory, was beginning to have in the arena of English language feminist theology. This volume included essays from feminist philosophers such as Elizabeth Grosz and feminist theologians such as Rebecca S. Chopp and Sharon D. Welch. The first footnote in the text indicates that Chopp's work was considered to show the most influence from the French theorists (Kim *et al.* 1993: 1). The French theorists most in vogue were Luce Irigaray, Julia Kristeva and Hélène Cixous (1993: 5). Of this triumvirate, Chopp argues that the work of Julia Kristeva offers 'some productive strategies' for critiquing the depth of patriarchy, and some 'modes of possibility' and 'new ways of understanding' for transforming theology (1993: 48). Chopp's major work, *The Power to Speak: Feminism, Language, God* (1989), explicitly seeks to challenge 'reigning discourses' (1989: 3), arguing that a feminist perspective can envisage 'emancipatory transformation' in the context of 'narcissistic individualism,

representational language, and the politics of self-preservation'
(Chopp 1989: 9).

Kathleen M. Sands considers the problem of theodicy in *Escape from Paradise: Evil and Tragedy in Feminist Theology* (Sands 1994). Her theoretical sources are varied, including Mark C. Taylor, Michel Foucault and Margaret Miles, who uses the work of the French feminists in her *Carnal Knowing: Female Nakedness and Religious Meaning in the Christian West* (Miles 1989). There is no explicit debt to Kristeva in Sands. There is, however, a very definitive motif of ambiguity. Sands argues that a 'tragic consciousness' is an appropriate 'heuristic foundation' for a feminist theodicy. Within this notion of 'tragic consciousness' are elements of both sadness and hope.

Interestingly enough, my own project began with the question of theodicy and the dilemma of the ambiguous nature of people and events: people who commit horrific acts remain loved members of families; celebratory events that create identity as well as excluding. For Sands, a 'tragic consciousness' is the means for coping with such ambiguities, just as *jouissance* becomes the way into a methodology for addressing my own concerns. Sands explicitly emphasizes both critique and production. Her feminist theology both 'disturbs the tomb in which patriarchal theology buried evil' (Sands 1994: 166) and is involved in a 'messy multiform continuance' of hope where we are invited to 'mourn and laugh and dance until our flesh remembers how the world goes on' (1994: 169).

Explicitly using the work of Julia Kristeva, along with that of Michel Foucault and Maurice Merleau-Ponty, Diane Prosser MacDonald seeks a theology of 'transgressive corporeality' (MacDonald 1995: xii): 'not a new way of systematizing the movement of the sacred among us, but rather a transgression of those orders of thought and being that effectively resist the call of the sacred' (MacDonald 1995: xiii). In the concept of transgression, MacDonald is interested in ideas of madness and wildness. The emphasis on 'corporeality' indicates an interest in bodiliness and sensuality. MacDonald develops a concept of theology as the somatology of 'wild love' (1995: 129). She is eager to explore both the deconstructive and reconstructive elements of this suggested theological paradigm. For MacDonald, the deconstructive moment exposes the 'remainders that resist the violence and counterviolence of structures of binary oppositions'. The remainders are also the 'originary site' for 'a new theological imagination' (MacDonald 1995: 142).

Paula Cooey is concerned also with the body and religious imagination. In *Religious Imagination and the Body: A Feminist Analysis* (Cooey 1994), she argues that 'religious traditions' provide the site for the 'transfiguration of human pain and pleasure in ways that continually recreate and destroy human subjectivity, the world within which it emerges, and the transcendent realities with which the subject seeks relation' (Cooey 1994: 9). The body, being the site of a power struggle because of this meaning-making process centred on the explanation of pain and pleasure, is also the site of the imaginative construction of feminist theologies (Cooey 1994: 128–29): theologies that challenge the epistemological judgments of the body made on the grounds of gender (Cooey 1994: 9). MacDonald and Cooey represent an element of poststructuralist theory which remains unexplored in this thesis: bodiliness. Yet, Cooey's focus on encrypting the body with meaning is not unrelated to the exploration of images of women in Chapter 7, and the use of the image of God as whore in that same chapter. Cooey's work suggests an area of further exploration in such imaginative reconstructions.

Sharon Welch, one of Terrence Tilley's 'theologians of communal praxis'/'constructive theologians', is very much concerned with an ethic of transformation in a communal context (Welch 1990: 166). In this context, she is painfully aware of both 'the forces that bind us' and 'the forces that free us' (Welch 1990: 10). In this respect, she remembers the pain of resistance to injustice and also its joy. The concept of *jouissance* is introduced in the discussion on the joy of resistance (Welch 1990: 170–71). She is also aware of the ambiguous nature of all resistance attempts: 'All of these movements are holy; all of them are flawed'. The locus of this ambiguity, however, seems to be in a struggle between 'exploitive forces' and 'oppression', and 'the power of divine love and healing at work' (Welch 1990: 180). Ambiguity, for me, lies in the existence of polarizing influences in the one entity. I prefer an account of 'the power of divine love' that recognizes the ambiguity of power. Nevertheless, Welch is optimistic about resistance, and that is certainly an aspect of this project also, with its emphasis on the revolutionary potential of poetic reading.

Mary McClintock Fulkerson's work, *Changing the Subject: Women's Discourses and Feminist Theology* (1994) is an exemplary work in feminist pastoral theology using poststructuralist theory. Fulkerson develops a model for dealing with the 'generic pretensions of feminist theology's subject' undergirding the assumption of the 'universality' of 'women's experience' (Fulkerson 1994: 3). Her intention is not to 'lose the subject "woman", but to *change the subject*' allowing 'the complex production of multiple identities' to become 'basic to our thinking' (Fulkerson 1994: 7). Fulkerson uses poststructuralist theory to explore 'a new definition of difference' which allows that multiplicity to be incorporated into a specifically feminist theology. Elements of the 'theological warrant for respecting difference' which emerge from this exploration include a focus on narrative telling, hearing and enabling the 'stories of the other to teach us' and a recognition of the creation of identity in relationship with others (1994: 12). Fulkerson's recognition of the multiplicity and ambiguity of subjectivity comes closest to my own. Her project has a number of resonances with the practices explored in Chapter 2 and their emphasis on hearing *and* respecting women's diverse stories.

Conclusion

In the course of the chapter, I have categorized my project as one of 'erotic transgressive resurrection' with a double movement through death, dissolution and loss of meaning to reconstruction and renewal. This double movement is an oscillating process. Deconstruction and reconstruction are constant partners in an 'erotic' interplay which presupposes the drive of desire for meaning, the role of interrelationship in constructing meanings, and both the value and danger of meaning constructions. In this account of the place of this project, I have maintained an emphasis on its underlying concerns: the multiplicity, ambiguity and diversity of subjectivity and subjective integrity within that context.

Chapter 2

WOMEN CLOTHED WITH THE SUN: RE-PRESENTING IDENTITIES
WHICH ARE NOT ONE(S)

Community and Identity

Communal identity has been a major focus of contemporary feminist theological enterprises since their inception. In 1960, when Valerie Saiving asked the question as to whether traditional Christian concepts of sin and redemption were appropriate for women, women's theological and corporate identity in Christianity was problematized (Saiving in Christ & Plaskow 1979: 25–42). Elisabeth Schüssler Fiorenza attempted a reconstruction of women's involvement in early Christianity and proposed an *ekklēsia of women* or *ekklēsia gynaikōn* (Fiorenza 1983: 343–51, Fiorenza 1992: 125–32). Rosemary Radford Ruether appropriated this concept for *Women-Church: Theology and Practice of Feminist Liturgical Communities* (1985). Letty Russell (1987) proposed the 'household of faith' as an appropriate concept for a liberation community.

Community has been an important element of Christianity from the 'table fellowship' of Jesus (see Dutney 1993: 64–78) through the shared meals and belongings of the early Christian groups to the development of the institutional church. Both feminist theological goals of community and ecclesiastical definitions of community have struggled with assumptions about the singular unitary identities either of 'women' and/or 'Christians'. Increasingly, such assumptions have become untenable. So, what kind of community can one envisage in a context which does recognize ambiguity, multiplicity and diversity?

At the beginning of 1994, a group of women within the Queensland Synod of The Uniting Church in Australia considered this question. The product of their efforts was the 3rd National Gathering on Women in The Uniting Church in Australia held in Brisbane, Queensland from 25–28 January 1996 (henceforth 'the Gathering'). While the theoretical appropriations of this chapter for that enterprise were not fully formed during that period, they are a direct result of my own involvement with that group and, in their intuitive infancy, they did inform my involvement in the process of developing the Gathering. My official role in that process was as Programme Convenor, a position that involved the development and oversight of the overall programme structure.

Mary McClintock Fulkerson makes a distinction between mere inclusion strategies and liberative community practices which actually have the theoretical depth to allow analysis of one's own meaning-making as well as that of others (Fulkerson 1994: 18). I believe that the method of poetic reading offers that depth because of its emphasis on otherness, and not simply on an outside otherness but an interior one: 'the stranger within ourselves' (Kristeva 1991). In seeking the gaps, silences and disruptions within discourse, poetic reading acknowledges the complexity of discourse, and consequently, the multiplicity of subjectivity.

While what I present in this chapter might equally be applied to the subjectivity 'Christian' (and indeed must be in the face of the challenges of diversity, ambiguity and multiplicity for Christianity), it is the subjectivity 'women' or more accurately 'woman' that is the focus of this discussion. I argue that the method of poetic reading offers an appropriate theoretical base for developing a concept of community that does encompass diversity, ambiguity and multiplicity. In line with the underlying linguistic assumptions of poststructuralism, I suggest that the development of such a concept allows for the possibility of collective events which transcend the anxiety about communal identity provoked by the postmodern crisis of institutions. Such transcendence is possible because the developed conceptual environment acknowledges and accepts the existence of groups of disparate people for common, if not commonly understood, purposes for varying lengths of time and in a variety of different formats. Such acceptance recognizes the diversity, ambiguity and multiplicity of the collected company rather than attempting to produce a singularity of identity among participants, and conformity to a set conceptual framework.

This strategy is in itself paradoxical because it relies on a theoretical base to which it cannot bind participants. That is, one of the implications of the method of poetic reading for the development of community is the inappropriateness of coercive attempts at external control, even on its own account. It is also paradoxical because, even as the method renounces coercion, it participates in it as do all attempts at codifying structures in language and systems.

So, by beginning with the impossibility of defining a singular subjectivity in relation to the concept of 'woman', I will explore how the method of poetic reading can be used to problematize any neat subjectivity. Following from this recollection, I will indicate how certain strategies adopted in relation to the Gathering coincide with strategies of the method of poetic reading. In introducing discussion about the role and location of the reader in the method of poetic reading, I will suggest that the poetic reader can be internalized in one's self as other. I will show how this internalization within a community context can contribute to the development of an expectation for community that is not singular or unitary, but embraces difference. The problems and failures of such a strategy are also addressed.

The Identity 'Woman'

'Woman' as an identity is problematic just as any identity is problematic in the context of poststructuralist theory. But it is also problematic because, in a phallologocentric[1] order, it has been cast as the identity which is not one. In an interview with the Psychoanalysis and Politics group from the French Women's Liberation Movement (Psych & Po 1996), Julia Kristeva asserts that ' "woman" is something that cannot be represented or verbalized; "woman" remains outside the realm of classifications and ideologies' although the concept has had a useful role in the unpacking of a political agenda for women (Psych & Po 1996: 98).

This lack of identity has had a number of consequences:

1. The abjectification or negative characterization of 'woman' and therefore women.
2. The associated tendency to ascribe a negative unitary identity to women without allowing for difference, a corollary of the process of abjectification.
3. The dismissal of women's voices because they have not been the voice of all women, a result of the need to see women only as a group which does not have a subjectivity in its own right.

1. An order characterized by the patriarchal construction of 'reality' in language.

4. The valorization of women's voices which uphold the patriarchal order, a recognition of identity only in the terms of the prevailing regime within the symbolic order.
5. Expectations of non-conflictual communities for women, another result of the non-identification of women as individual subjects.

In seeking to redress such non-identity, feminism has valorized the subjectivity of 'woman', attempted to establish an identity of 'woman' and, in the process, albeit unwittingly, repressed the voices of women who would not submit to this new ordering of subjectivity, however it was characterized. For feminism also is a discourse of the symbolic order, and must be aware of the dangers of that order for women and the effects of feminism as part of it.

In an interview about her conception(s) of women in 1975 (Boucquey in Guberman 1996: 103–12), Julia Kristeva notes the dual dangers for women in this context: the identification with the power structures of identity; and the attempted, but impossible, rejection of the power dynamics of signification. Women who adopt both positions look for non-contradiction in their social environments (1996: 105–109). In critique of Kristeva, Andrea Nye notes that the distorting power of the 'categories of patriarchal language' embroil the woman speaker in an apparently unresolvable dilemma: to speak is to risk distortion; not to articulate a position is to remain in the subjective wilderness (Nye 1987: 665). This is precisely the dilemma that arises for the subjectivity of women in a Kristevan theoretical environment: a dilemma that demands some kind of recognition and/ or acceptance of ambiguity and multiplicity in relation to women's identities in order that women can have some integrity in their subjective locations, both individually and as communities.

There are a number of feminist attempts to reconstruct subjectivities for women that are not based in unitary, singular identity but difference and multiplicity.[2] In a theological context, such attempts have been prompted especially by the critiques of non-Anglo women who do not see themselves represented in first world white feminist discourse.[3] Fulkerson notes the increasing problematization of 'the generic pretensions of feminist theology's subject, a subject that

2. For example, Rosi Braidotti speaks of a developing nomadic feminist subjectivity (1994).
3. For such a critique in a theological and Australian context, see Pattel-Gray 1995.

invokes universality, implicitly if not explicitly, by virtue of its appeal to "women's experience"' where the 'specificity of the race, class, and sexual particularity of this experience has come under scrutiny' (Fulkerson 1994: 3). She provides an example of an attempt at reconstructing subjectivities for women which attempts to take into account multiplicity and difference. Her intention is 'not to lose the subject "woman", but to *change*' it so that 'the complex production of multiple identities becomes basic to our thinking' (Fulkerson 1994: 7). This project is also concerned with the recognition of alternate expressions of subjectivity which seek to account for diversity, ambiguity and multiplicity. By a threefold method and various strategies, poetic reading offers the possibility of just such a recognition: by identifying dualities, subverting them, and re-presenting alternate readings which highlight alterity and evoke *jouissance*.

Poetic Reading and Community

But how can the method of poetic reading, as essentially a hermeneutical method, interact with what is basically a matter of human community? First, in the context of poststructuralist theory, human community, like any other identity, is constructed according to established patterns. The relevance of a hermeneutical method becomes readily evident when this perspective is recognized, for community becomes a text which is able to be 'read'.

Communal identities are constructed in similar ways to that of individual identities: I/we identify myself/ourselves as not being the 'other'. A community attempts to hold its own unitary, singular identity as much as any individual. The apparent panic when this identity seems no longer relevant, unitary or singular is clear evidence of this attempt. Witness the inability of many current institutions, for example churches, to cope with the diversity within their midst. Because of the parallel construction of communal identity along similar lines to that of the construction of individual identities, a hermeneutical strategy directed at reading a communal identity as ambiguous offers the prospect of 'subjecting ambiguity' in a communal context.

Poetic reading is characterized by its attention to otherness: that otherness both within and beyond the constructed sociolinguistic realm of human meaning systems. Such otherness is re-presented in language by the abject: conceptual elements that do not conform to neat dualities and remind us that it is 'otherness' that undergirds our own identities. Kristeva suggests that by 'questioning the identity of "the foreigner" or "the woman"', characterizations of otherness outside identity, 'metaphysical notions' of identity can be dissolved 'in a series of representations, conflicts, and strategies' as 'otherness' is revealed to be within identity. Such questioning produces a '"nonidentificatory" approach to problems' (Guberman 1996: 260) where the 'unity of man [sic] reduced to his consciousness' is rejected (1996: 259), and the possibility of a subjectivity other than a unitary singular one is embraced. The method of poetic reading when set in a communal context offers a theoretical base for such an identity-dissolving 'series of representations, conflicts, and strategies'.

Identities of Women

In the very early stages of the planning process of the Gathering, it became clear that, even in the limited group of women who had met together in various convocations over an initial period, there was a diversity of interests, identities and expectations for the project. The women involved had different levels of ability and availability, different types of skills and different levels of commitment to the process. Some members identified themselves as feminist and others did not. A variety of feminist perspectives were present among those who identified themselves as such. There were clear generational differences among the women. A diversity of responses to the previous conferences on women in the Uniting Church existed among those who had attended them. In addition, the geo-political context of the host Synod (Queensland) meant that particular aspects of the diversity of women's identities were highlighted. For example, the varying concerns of rural, regional and urban women were recognized.[4] In contrast, while some of us were aware of women associated with the project who identified themselves privately as having lesbian or bisexual orientations, other women involved could

4.   Queensland is a large state which covers about one-fifth of the continent of Australia which is roughly the size of mainland USA. Queensland has a significant urban population concentrated in its south-east corner where the capital Brisbane is situated. Strong regional centres occur along the coast and inland. A large number of small towns/rural communities and vast areas that are sparsely populated complete the geographic picture. Because infrastructure is centralized in Brisbane, distance and access to resources are major concerns, hence the significance of regional centres.

not even conceive that such might be the case.[5] More positively, the executive of the indigenous Uniting Aboriginal and Islander Christian Congress[6] is situated in Queensland, emphasizing the differing concerns of Aboriginal and Torres Strait Islander women to other church women. Ethnic congregations and members of the Uniting Church other than Anglo and indigenous groups were not well-integrated into the life of the Queensland Synod at that time: an observation which raised further matters of difference.

This brief outline in no way exhausts the diversity which confronted the Planning Group as the planning process unfolded, nor the tensions involved in that confrontation. However, it does illustrate the general recognition of diversity which was present in varying degrees among the group, and the corresponding desire to produce a gathering of women that could encompass such diversity. The early minutes of the Planning Group show the desire for a conference on women for women[7] that did not assume a singular, unitary identity for women.[8] For example, the list of objectives for the 'Gathering', a name deliberately chosen because it indicated to the Planning Group 'a chance for sharing in a less sophisticated, non-intimidating way', shows that key aims for such an event were 'mutuality and sharing'; 'open to and responsive to all "cultures" within Australia'; 'a place where women define the space' recognizing the diversity of the individuals present (21 April 1994).[9]

5. At the time, it was not safe for people with gay, lesbian or bisexual orientations to identify themselves openly in the life of the Queensland Synod of The Uniting Church in Australia due to officially adopted positions of that Synod which reject their contribution to the life of the church and the strong presence of an anti-homosexual lobby known as the 'Evangelical Members of the Uniting Church' (EMU).

6. The Uniting Aboriginal and Islander Christian Congress is also referred to as 'the Congress' within the Uniting Church.

7. Men are able to attend Uniting Church conferences on women, but their participation has been limited to 10 per cent of the total number of registrations. Requests for attendance at the Gathering by men did not exceed this set limit.

8. Note that despite the emphasis on diversity in the planning of the conference, there were also clear limits established for the group, i.e. women in the Uniting Church. While Uniting Church men, and women of other Christian denominations ultimately attended the Gathering, the focus was always identified as 'women in the Uniting Church'.

9. The source of this original concern among the Planning Group for the inclusion of 'others' was probably strongly influenced by a number of factors including (i) the socialization of the women as women and in conservative Christian environments with an emphasis on responding to the needs of others (see, for example, Gilligan 1982); (ii) the politically conservative environment of the Synod of Queensland where

Problematizing 'Otherness'

The identification of 'otherness' is integral to the identification of self. Already in the recognition of some of the diversity amongst the Planning Group and among women in Queensland, the identity of the 'other' was problematized. For who is the 'other' when she is sitting beside you and identified as part of you in a collective situation? Who is the other for a group which has already been acknowledged to be disparate, especially when the desire amongst the group is for 'others' to feel comfortable within the group? Who is the 'other' when 'I' am 'other' to my neighbour? Who is the 'other' when she is consciously and unconsciously within? The profound duality of self and other is clearly disrupted in an environment that valorizes 'otherness'. The question that confronted the Gathering Planning Group concerned the way in which such an environment could be developed and sustained through a whole event of several days.

The Gathering attempted to create such an environment where 'otherness' was indeed problematized through a series of strategies related to the method of poetic reading:

1. The valorization of a subjectivity for women which emphasized diversity and ambiguity.
2. The diffusion of sources of input from women's perspectives that attempted to avoid the valorization and/or denigration of any one source.
3. The re-visiting of the same symbols in order to evoke different responses to those symbols.
4. The explicit description of symbols in ambiguous terms.
5. An emphasis upon speaking from and listening to various perspectives in community.
6. A valuing of the unconscious processes of women's meaning-making.
7. The placing of each individual woman as her own reader of herself, the community and the overall event.

feminist women have always had to struggle to show that they did not exclude while seeking their own inclusion; (iii) social justice concerns carried by the women especially in relation to indigenous and rural women; (iv) the work roles of many of the women in 'caring services' e.g. parental roles, work with people with disabilities, psychology; and (v) the presence among the Planning Group of a number of women engaged in academic study in areas of theology, ethics, social science and clinical practice on projects related to questions of 'otherness'.

This series of strategies performs two functions (or at least attempts that performance):

1. The development of a community using the principles behind the method of poetic reading to establish a collectivity that did not shun multiplicity and ambiguity; and
2. The guiding of that community in the poetic reading of a specified text, in this case, the story of the woman clothed with the sun.

The second stage of the method of poetic reading, as outlined in Chapter 6, has a number of strategies:

1. The privileging of the lesser term of a duality, which may result in a reversal of the hierarchical ordering of the dualities.
2. The treatment of the lesser term as the precondition for the dominant one, not vice versa.
3. The introduction of a third term outside and precedent to the dualities identified.
4. The highlighting of spaces or gaps in the discourse which undermine dominant and unitary interpretations and their assumed dualities.
5. The playing with the slippages of terms both contained within the discourse itself, and infused from the contexts in which the discourse is placed.
6. The paying of attention to the intertextuality of the discourse, the intersection between the focal discourse and other texts.
7. The placing alongside each other of differing interpretations of the discourse under consideration, offering different readings of the textual dualities.

These strategies correspond with each of those identified in the previous paragraph as strategies undergirding the Gathering programme.

The Gathering Theme

The theme of the Gathering was structured around five key images from the passage in Revelation concerning the 'woman clothed with the sun' (Rev. 12: 1–6, 13–17). Sub-themes articulated around these five images provided the thematic directions for the conference programme:

1. The Celebration of the Woman Clothed with the Sun (Rev. 12: 1) — *Celebrating Women's Diverse Gifts and Experiences.*
2. The Birthing Experience (Rev. 12: 2, 4b, 5a) — *Recognizing the Pain and Joy of Women's Creativity.*

3. The Loss of a Child and the Threat of the Dragon (Rev. 12: 3, 4a, 5b, 13, 15, 17) — *Remembering the Struggle and Grief of Women's Lives.*
4. The Desert Experience (Rev. 12: 6, 14b) — *Recognizing the Emptiness and the Nourishment of the Dry Times.*
5. The Gift of Eagle's Wings and the Rescue by the Earth (Rev. 12: 14a, 16) — *Exploring New Ways of Being and Doing.*

Valorizing Diversity and Ambiguity

The focal and titular image from the Revelation passage for the Gathering was the woman herself; hence the major theme, 'Women Clothed with the Sun'. This major theme was articulated in the sub-themes as 'The Celebration of a Woman Clothed with the Sun—Celebrating Women's Diverse Gifts and Experiences'. The association of a plural 'women' with the singular 'woman' began the thematic attempt to valorize diversity and ambiguity within the gathered community and their interpretations of the biblical text. This strategy has connections with several strategies in the second stage of the method of poetic reading. By valorizing diversity and plurality over unity and singularity, the identity 'women' was privileged (first strategy in the second stage of the method of poetic reading) or treated as a precondition (second strategy) for understanding the term 'woman' in the context of the Gathering. In a sense, the use of the term 'women' was also an introduction of a third term (third strategy) outside of the duality 'woman/not-woman': a variation of the identity duality 'us/not-us' that can dominate any community struggling to achieve recognition. The 'programme notes' sent out to participants prior to the Gathering began with the following paragraph:

> This event is an opportunity for women across the diversity of the Uniting Church to share our stories with each other. Listen to and speak with one another. Discover and reaffirm the validity of your own stories and those of others. Celebrate our mutual place in the complex creativity of God.

In valorizing diversity, the Planning Group sought to create an event where difference was accepted rather than feared, where 'woman' was never just a singular, unitary identity.

The association of a plural term with a singular one also introduced a note of ambiguity: an identity which was not one. This note was further enhanced by the recognition of the ambiguity of the interpretation of the focal text and specifically the character of the woman clothed with the sun; and by the ambiguous associations given some of the five key images in the articulation of their sub-themes. This pattern coincided with several strategies in the second stage of the method of poetic reading. Continually reading plurality where singularity has been is both a highlighting of the gaps and spaces in a term like 'woman' and a kind of slippage in terms infused from the contexts in which the discourse is placed (fourth and fifth strategies). In the recognition of plurality in apparent singularity, there is an overt acknowledgment that 'woman' is never just one neat subjectivity. The intertextuality inherent in the act of reading, arising from both prior discourses to the text itself and prior discourses to/for the women who approached the text in the Gathering process, exposed nuances and variations in the reading of the focal text and hence in the self-understanding of the community engaged in that reading. Noting the ambiguous interpretations of the focal text already began the process of placing different textual interpretations alongside each other (seventh strategy of the second stage of the method of poetic reading): a process that was to continue throughout the Gathering.

Diffusion of Sources

As part of the process of valorizing difference, the concept of having a keynote speaker was eventually rejected by the Programme & Liturgy Task Group, a subgroup of the Planning Group, on 20 August 1994. An earlier planning day for the whole Planning Group had suggested the possibility of a keynote speaker (9 July 1994). The avoidance of a keynote speaker was an attempt to avoid any specific voice being set up, either as an authority or as a position to react against in the Gathering process. Some members of the Planning Group who had attended previous conferences on women in the Uniting Church were wary of this possibility. It was also an attempt to emphasize the role of participants in the Gathering rather than any identified 'experts'. In place of the notion of a keynote speaker was an emphasis on participants reflecting on and sharing their own stories and hearing and reflecting on the stories of others.

There was a deliberate attempt to facilitate this process using groups and individuals from various parts of Queensland and with differing interests. For example, the five key 'spaces' planned around the five key images drawn from the Revelation story were facilitated by women from Rockhampton (a coastal regional city relating to a

large inland rural area in central Queensland), Maryborough (a
hinterland city with both a rural and industrial economic base),
Toowoomba (an inland city relating to a broad rural base), Inala (a
low socio-economic area in the southern suburbs of Brisbane, the
capital city of Queensland) and Unicare (a Uniting Church agency
supporting people with disabilities). The Congress women declined
to develop their own space or to coordinate a theme space, opting to
attempt to have at least some input from Aboriginal and/or Torres
Strait Islander women in every aspect of the programme. Remarkably,
this aim was achieved to a very high extent although because the
input was not always marked as belonging to Aboriginal and Torres
Strait Islander women specifically, some participants would have been
unaware of its source.[10]

Sources were not only identified as linguistic. A strong focus on
the experiential, including the provision of an 'Artspace' and various
non-written activities in the journaling process, pointed to an
otherness within and around participants which could not be accessed
merely through linguistic means.

Re-visiting Symbols

The five key images from the Revelation story around which the
theme of the Gathering was structured were visited in at least three
ways by participants at the Gathering. The expectation was that
participants would visit their own stories, that of the text, and those
of others in different ways, thereby coming upon their own
subjectivities, that of the text and those of others in their expressions
of multiplicity. In this strategy, the assumption was made that any

10. Indeed one or two evaluations of the Gathering from Gathering participants
reflect this probability. A couple of people indicated concern about what they
perceived as the lack of input from Aboriginal and Torres Strait Islander women.
Aboriginal and Torres Strait Islander women were 10 per cent of the participants at
the conference. (Aboriginal and Torres Strait Islander people form about 2 per cent
of the Australian population.) The two official representatives from the Congress
were significantly involved in the planning of the program and liturgies of the
conference. They particularly made substantial contributions to the content of
reflection/celebrations (liturgies for the whole community). All facilitators of 'spaces'
were asked to include content from Aboriginal and Torres Strait Islander women.
This inclusion was achieved in various ways such as the use of storytellers present
among conference participants and the use of stories from Aboriginal and Torres
Strait Islander women local to facilitators' areas. The stories of the interactions involved
in arranging this content are significant in their own right.

visiting of a particular symbol would be different from any other visiting of that same symbol. The five key images were used chronologically throughout the Gathering in a series of 'Reflection/ Celebrations' or modified liturgies, two of which were Eucharistic. They were also visited spatially in that five areas of the venue were set aside for each of the images. Participants had the opportunity to visit a planned programme in four of these 'spaces' at some time throughout the Gathering. At other times, the spaces were open for personal reflection. The third method of visiting the images was through journaling. Journaling formed a specific part of the reflection/ celebrations and some of the spaces, but the journal also contained material that invited participants to reflect on the thematic images outside of these contexts.

In this process of visiting and revisiting the same symbols, the seventh of the strategies in the second stage of poetic reading was enacted: the placing alongside each other of differing interpretations of the discourse under consideration, offering different readings of the textual dualities. This multiplicity was contributed to by readings of the text which reflected other strategies of the method.

Ambiguous Descriptions

Two of the five key images used in the sub-themes were deliberately described in ambiguous terms: 'The Birthing Experience'— 'Recognizing the Pain and Joy of Women's Creativity'; and 'The Desert Experience'—'Recognizing the Emptiness and Nourishment of the Dry Times'. Such descriptions were deliberate pointers to the ambiguity of symbols themselves as well as to the ambiguity of women's experiences as those experiences were able to be named as having both positive and negative connotations associated with them. This deliberate recognition of ambiguity was in part a placing of different interpretations alongside each other (seventh strategy of the second stage of poetic reading), but it was also a way of highlighting gaps in interpretations that take an either/or stance (fourth strategy), and because of this a way of introducing the possibility of playing with slippages in terms (fifth strategy).

Emphasis on Speaking and Listening

The articulated vision for the Gathering was:

- That those who dwell in silence may find a voice.
- That those who have a voice will find a place to speak.
- That those who deny the voice will realize its authenticity.

This vision was put into words by Colleen Geyer Cooper, the Gathering Liaison Person or official contact person for all Gathering matters. The vision was supplemented by a strong emphasis on listening to each other's stories already identified as part of the Gathering process. This dual visionary emphasis was important in both encouraging women to speak from their silences, and inviting women to listen to other women speak from their silences. The two incidents that particularly stand out for me as evidence of both the importance and the effectiveness of this vision, are one which relates to the participation of Aboriginal and Torres Strait Islander women and a second which relates to the participation of non-feminist women.

The Gathering was held over a long weekend in January 1996 which included the Australia Day public holiday (26 January). Australia Day commemorates the arrival of the so-called 'First Fleet' of convicts and their keepers from Britain to establish a settlement in Australia. For many non-indigenous Australians, Australia Day is a time of celebration of the nation of Australia and its apparent advantages. However, for many indigenous Australians, Australia, Day is not a day of celebration but one of mourning over the invasion of the land. Because of the variety of approaches to Australia Day and the whole strategic context of the Gathering where stories and experiences were expected to be shared in their multiplicity, the Planning Group in consultation with the Congress representatives on that group determined that no formal recognition of Australia Day would be made during the Gathering, but that this decision itself required recognition. A statement to this effect was included in the Programme Notes and read out on the morning of 26 January in the announcement section prior to the Day Opening Reflection/Celebration. The reading of the statement was followed by a minute's silence in recognition of the indigenous people of Australia.

Because of the chronological liturgical process, the theme of the Day Closing Reflection/Celebration for that day was 'The Loss of a Child and the Threat of the Dragon: Remembering the Struggle and Grief of Women's lives'. This liturgical event included a number of women telling their stories of loss, struggle and grief. These stories were divided into three groups: stories from experiences in the church;

stories from experiences as indigenous women; and stories from experiences of women outside Australia. The stories of Aboriginal and Torres Strait Islander women included events related to the State-sanctioned forced removal of indigenous children from their parents. These children are known colloquially as 'the stolen generations'.

Unfortunately, because of an oversight involving the arrangement, timing and number of the various groups of stories, the very significant stories of the stolen generations were overshadowed by the stories of experiences particularly related to women's experiences in the church. Since Australia Day was already a day of mourning and the recollection of the stories of the stolen generations had added to the grief of indigenous women present, the overshadowing of these stories was a very painful occurrence for the Congress women present. The process of addressing this concern was also a very significant encounter between different Gathering participants: one of the most significant of the Gathering.

The Congress women met to discuss their concerns. Through a 'doula', one of the designated 'listeners' or 'chaplains' in the Gathering process, and the Congress representatives on the liturgy subgroup of the Programme and Liturgy Task Group, they communicated their grief, disappointment and concern with the liturgy subgroup. Following a process of discussion, a series of changes and additions to the following days' liturgies were negotiated in response to the expressed concerns of the Congress women. This negotiation depended on the willingness for the Congress women as a group, the Congress representatives on the liturgy subgroup and the members of the liturgy subgroup to speak from their understandings of the experiences that had led to the development of the liturgies and the hopes each had for the continuing liturgical process; and to listen to the perspectives and responses of each other.[11]

The second incident I wish to relate in connection with the strategy of encouraging both speaking and listening is a brief conversation between me and an older woman from a fairly conservative congregation in the hinterland to the north of Brisbane. This conversation took place after the workshop where I attempted to communicate some of the theory behind the Gathering process. The

11. The work of Lurleen Blackman as coordinator of the Congress women's presence, Elizabeth Law and Tamara Cassady as the Congress representatives on the liturgy subgroup, Ann Hobson as key doula, and Christine Gapes as convenor of the liturgy subgroup should be acknowledged here.

key element of the conversation that I remember quite vividly was this woman's expression in words of a feeling of acceptance of herself as a woman who had fulfilled the socially accepted role of women in her generation: looking after family, being involved in church activities. For her the possibility that other women, particularly feminists, could value what she had achieved although they might not choose that path for themselves was a moment of freedom.

There were some people who found themselves in a position where they were unable to hear the stories of others or to speak their own. The evaluation forms reflect this small but important group. It is difficult to know what were the issues involved here. Undoubtedly, some stories were too painful and private to share; some people did not or could not hear some stories; and some people did not find the process safe. For the sake of the Gathering emphasis on speaking and listening, it is important that the stories of being unable to tell or to hear stories are recognized also.

Valuing of Unconscious Processes of Meaning-Making

Throughout the Gathering process, there were implicit and explicit recognitions that there are unconscious processes involved in meaning-making. The importance of music, dance, art and visual display in all aspects of the Gathering was testimony to this recognition, as was the focus on journaling and meditative reflection. Because of the context of the Gathering in a religious environment contributed to by Christian, indigenous and feminist spiritual traditions which overtly recognized an 'otherness' outside our linguistic expressions, and/or because of the recognition by many women present of the importance of expression that did not necessarily 'put things into words', the sense that there was more going on than was available in the public or linguistic realm was an easily assimilable concept within the group. While it may be true that, at one level, there was a lack of political analysis being done in formal theoretical categories by Gathering participants (an observation offered on one evaluation form), the negotiations between the Congress women and the liturgy subgroup as just one significant example show a clear ability for women to analyse the unstated elements of human communication using sophisticated categories (which may not be named in official theoretical terms), to critique the results of these and to work towards better ways of 'speaking' not only in words. The Gathering process itself encouraged each participant to participate in their own analysis of the images, programme, ideas etc. presented throughout.

Self as Reader

There was a clear emphasis on individual participants taking responsibility for their participation at the Gathering. The initial Programme Notes invited participants 'to take responsibility for your own journey throughout this Gathering' as they engaged in an 'action/reflection' process. This invitation to 'be intentional' and 'take responsibility' was a key aspect to the Gathering process. Participants were invited to be participants and to reflect on their participation and the programme elements which they encountered: to read themselves and their environment. In line with the understanding of the role of the reader as analyst which undergirds the method of 'poetic reading', this invitation asked participants to create an identity from a position of non-identity. It was an encouragement to active involvement in, rather than passive receipt of the programme as a whole. Because readers were also being read by themselves, there were at least two identities assumed by the invitation. A tension sited in the self was produced: which identity is the 'other'; is there an element of 'otherness' to both? Singular identity was shattered because it was multiplied, and the multiplication was multiplied by the various interactions of other selves and other readers with each other.

Re-Presenting Subjectivity

The re-presentation of this shattered identity, the moment(s) of *jouissance* encountered in the Gathering process, occurred in that process itself. To a certain extent, it is no longer available, if it ever was. It is now a moment in time and space, a blink that might have been missed. Nevertheless, an enduring image that remains with me as evidence that the Gathering process did achieve something of the celebration of the multiplicity of women's identities that it set out to achieve relates to the Gathering Closing Reflection/Celebration. This event was a composite event semi-planned by the liturgy subgroup and completed by various groups developed over the period of the Gathering e.g. drama, dance and art groups; groups formed around interests in the various thematic spaces. Within this event, which was already a celebration of diversity, the moment which most effectively enacted or at least acted out a *jouissance* which was experienced in the Gathering process came in a dance segment. The group of dancers included women of all shapes and sizes, some trained dancers and some people who had never danced in front of other people before. After following a set routine together, they each broke off from the main group into individual and self-devised movements. That moment was a moment of *jouissance* for me personally too, as I saw enacted the results of the strategies developed and set in place for the Gathering as a whole. This 'identity' that was the programme strategy, so much a part of my own identity as Programme Convenor, had been taken over by others: it was no longer what it had been; it was no longer mine; and it was no longer 'one'.

That personal experience causes me to reflect then on those for whom the Gathering strategy did not succeed. A moment of *jouissance* was missed by some Gathering participants. In particular, the strategy was not as successful for women who had already discovered an identity of a certain kind in the feminist movement in the Uniting Church as it was for those women who were exploring new territory or had no particular status in the movement. This lack of success may have been due in part to the fact that the invitation for their participation in this process as readers alongside other readers was an invitation to loss of identity: an invitation to become just another participant alongside participants with the attendant loss of status as speakers, knowers and doers in this particular realm (and the corresponding relegation of other women to the categories of non-speakers, non-knowers and non-doers).

The Gathering strategy had assumed that it was the development of different women's identities and the differences which women found within those identities that would contribute to an overall expression of women's subjectivity as diverse, multiple and ambiguous. That is, it assumed that generally it was space to create and express identity that was required by women, not space to divest oneself of an identity already acquired in order that further aspects of one's own and other identities might be explored. Another way of expressing this assumption would be to suggest that while the Gathering addressed the shattering of the singular, unitary identity 'woman', it did not address as effectively the shattering of the singular, unitary identities of women who had been able to establish such an identity for themselves as individuals in the context of the women's movement in the Uniting Church. While listening to the stories of each other's identities was emphasized, there was no specific strategy to cater for those who found it difficult to give up something of their own identity in order to be able to participate in this process. That is, there was a clear focus on empowering women to speak and to listen, but not as clear an addressing of the need to moderate the use of power in relationships with other women in order to allow that empowerment. If this was the possible dynamic as I suspect it was, then I confess there was little account taken of it in the development of the programme concept.[12]

Upon reflection, this failure to address loss of individual identity in developing notions of diverse, multiple and ambiguous subjectivity as well as the gaining or expression of various identities was a problem for the planning process as well as for the Gathering process. Women of a generation who had struggled hard to gain a personal identity found it difficult in the planning process to give up the strategic concepts to other people to implement in their own ways. Indeed, this perceived 'lack of control' in the planning process led one woman to resign from the Planning Group within weeks of the Gathering actually occurring. Such a dynamic is also demonstrated in certain participants' reactions to the Gathering process.

Anne Ryan, former chairperson of the Uniting Church's National Commission on Women and Men, the sponsoring body for the Gathering, expresses what I think is the same dynamic in a different way. Ryan characterizes the Gathering as 'noticeably less radical' than the previous two conferences, while noting that 'the conflict between the more radical women in the church and the conservative (or at least non-feminist women) was at the same time more obvious'. She attributes the obviousness of difference to the provision of 'a space where women can freely express themselves and their spirituality' and implies that such provision was a compromise that allowed the loss of 'any noticeable feminist edge'. Ryan expresses her disappointment in 'the generally covert nature of the radical feminine insight' while acknowledging a gentle accessibility to the approach. Her dominant response is one of frustration at a 'slowness' she perceives from her self-defined position as someone who has been

12. The analysis of internal power dynamics within oppressed groups can be easily overlooked because of the contextual necessity of the gaining of some kind of identity by that group in a broader society.

involved in the women's movement for 'a while' (Ryan 1997: 47). Ryan's critique with its patronizing overtones and highlighting of the discomfort of her identified 'radical' women in the Gathering process is illuminating, although I suspect that I would dispute Ryan's assessment of what 'radicalism' might be and certainly I reject her definition of the Gathering as being 'less radical' than the first conference on women in the Uniting Church either in programme format or in content.

The Gathering relied upon the presence of a variety of participants to validate the multiplicity of its community. For a variety of reasons, many of those women whom Ryan would identify as 'radical' from southern Synods in the Uniting Church were unable or chose not to attend the Gathering, and therefore were unavailable in the process to be part of the hearing and speaking of stories. This phenomenon is itself interesting. For while it does reflect economic constraints to some extent, I believe that it also reflects a degree of difficulty for those who have gained identities, often after considerable struggle, in being able to give up some of that subjectivity so that other identities might emerge. It points to the difficulty that any identity faces simply because it is created in language, the phallologocentric realm. Such a difficulty is inherent in this project as well as in any other piece of communication. The *jouissance* of the 'other' is found in an entry into subjectivity. When the other is no longer other, but has gained an identity in the symbolic realm, the strategy for *jouissance* is an entirely different one: the need for the identity to give itself up to otherness—Kristeva's poetic language, rather than my poetic reading.

The inability for the moment of *jouissance* implicit in the Gathering to be replicated outside the Gathering (except in another similar, entirely different event) is both problematic and effective. It is problematic because this inability means that its communication (and indeed its verification) is virtually impossible except in the replication of *jouissance* itself, not by speaking about it, but by experiencing it. It is effective because *jouissance* cannot be spoken about because it is a moment that exists outside the constraints of language. All that is left of the Gathering are the anecdotes and remembrances now well and truly ensconced in the symbolic. For myself, the enduring evidence of the significance of the Gathering as a trial attempt at poetic reading in and of community are the stories of women who do feel that something significant happened there: such as that of the woman who spoke to me after my workshop. I like to think that we did provide a space for participants to find a subjectivity which is aware of the illusive creation of identities and capable of playing with that creativity as an indispensable tool for living, and that is my own self-chosen illusion.

Chapter 3

DUALITY: THE GENESIS OF AMBIGUITY

Whence Poststructuralism?

It is the structuralist background to poststructuralism which establishes the case for the existence of a profound dualism in human systems of meaning and, therefore, activity. It is this dualism which feminism identifies and defies, and poststructuralism plays with and flouts. Such poststructuralist play is a source of hope for bringing notions of ambiguity into discourse (in my case, theological discourse), and for breaking the categories which have made feminist reforms so painful and painstaking, and social systems so recalcitrant in their response to feminist critique. From a feminist perspective, dualism has functioned to maintain women and all that is identified as 'feminine' as the lesser term in the duality within human systems of constructed meaning. This chapter does not explore the specifically feminist implications of the inherent duality identified by structuralism in human language and meaning. It does, however, show the way in which structuralism develops the concept of that inherent duality as intrinsic and persistent to human meaning structures in terms of linguistic construction. In the following chapter, the gender implications of this duality are made clearer via an exploration of the work of poststructuralist language theorist Jacques Derrida and psychoanalyst Jacques Lacan, who inhabits the shifting ground between structuralist and poststructuralist theory, language and psychosomatic human experience.

Poststructuralism is *post*structuralist. Because poststructuralism both continues and supersedes structuralist principles, it is important that these principles are identified at the beginning of a theoretical project such as this book. Edith Kurzweil while regarding the 'age of structuralism' as all but dead, emphasizes its importance for understanding the advent of poststructuralism (Kurzweil 1980: 2). In this respect also, Elizabeth Grosz engages critically with the conceptual impact of structuralism on notions of human subjectivity (Grosz 1989: 10), a major issue for poststructuralism and for feminism. Both Kurzweil and Grosz are interested in the foundation that structuralism lays for the succeeding speculations of French poststructuralist theory. For Grosz, the focal construction on the structuralist base is the work of some of the 'French feminists', notably Julia Kristeva, but also Luce Irigaray and Michèle Le Doeuff. For Kurzweil, the focal construction on the structuralist base is the work of some poststructuralist theorists of language and psychoanalysis, notably Julia Kristeva, but also Gilles Deleuze and Jacques Derrida among others.

Failure to recognize the structuralist underpinning of post-structuralism can result in misinterpretations of the intentions of poststructuralist strategies. It is crucial that the nexus between meaning and language assumed by structuralism is understood as forming part of the poststructuralist agenda so that the poststructuralist deconstruction of ideas is not mistaken for denying the existence of concrete objects in any sense other than a conceptual one. That is, to deconstruct the concept 'table' does not deny that there is an object made of wood, metal or another substance which has a flat surface and supporting legs etc. Rather, it is to reveal the concept that this object is a 'table' for the linguistic construction that it is. Such an example might similarly use the word 'God' for a concrete entity, although, because the concept 'God' is essentially metaphysical rather than concrete, the existence of the entity is vicariously questioned. Nevertheless, this questioning does not occur because of any 'destructive' process or denial of the existence of a 'real' reality. Rather, the concept is 'deconstructed', i.e. its existence as a concept is questioned and, thereby, the conceptual system of which it is a part, i.e. a belief system focussing on a metaphysically present God. This distinction is a fine one, but nonetheless significant.

Similarly, with the notion of subjectivity, the deconstruction of the so-called Cartesian subject invalidates neither the existence of persons nor their social operation as subjects. Rather, it questions the way in which that subjectivity has been and is continually constructed. Similarly, with notions of the subjectivity of women, questioning the way in which women's subjectivity has been constructed does not automatically imply a surrender to the patriarchal order through an acquiescence to an apparently imposed lack of women's agency. Explicitly addressing the structuralist foundation of poststructuralism counters arguments from both theological and feminist sources against the validity of using poststructuralist theory because of its supposed rejection of God and subjectivity *per se*. Exploring the structuralist underpinning of poststructuralism provides a ground for understanding the intentions of poststructuralism as an essentially linguistic and highly politically provocative group of theoretical perspectives.

In Chapter 1, I suggested that the following four assumptions were important aspects of the structuralist underpinning of post-structuralism:

1. Human meaning systems are arbitrarily constructed according to certain structures, albeit deeply unconsciously embedded ones.
2. These structures are essentially binary or dualistic.
3. The construction process of meaning systems governs the nature of the constructed meanings within them, i.e. the unconscious binary structures produce dualistic systems of meaning; and thus.
4. There is no real referential relationship between language (and other symbols) and the 'objects' which they purport to represent.

In this chapter, I use these four points to outline the significance of the structuralist background to poststructuralist theory for a poststructuralist theology. Ferdinand de Saussure (1857–1913) and Claude Lévi-Strauss (b. 1908) are used as the chief exponents of structuralism for this purpose.[1]

Ferdinand de Saussure is generally regarded as the 'father' of linguistic structuralism.[2] Saussure's thought is most methodically

1.   Saussure and Lévi-Strauss do not represent the full range of theoretical work available within the structuralist paradigm, nor do they represent the sole sources of innovation within that schema. In the context of a project which relies heavily on the work of Julia Kristeva, the contribution of 1930s Russian formalist, Roman Jakobson, among others, might equally have been chosen as a useful focus for establishing the parameters of the theoretical background. Indeed, Edith Kurzweil regards the work of Roman Jakobson as an important bridge between the work of Saussure and Lévi-Strauss (Kurzweil 1980: 15). Lévi-Strauss himself attributes the foundation of structural linguistics to another Russian formalist writing in the 1930s, N. Troubetzkoy (Lévi-Strauss 1968: 33).

2.   While, as Kristeva indicates through her historical study of linguistic theory (1989: 43–261), elements of Saussure's approach are evident in prior philosophical systems, the particular collation, arrangement and enhancement of such precedents is usually attributed to Saussure as unique.

expressed in *Course in General Linguistics* (1966),[3] a transcribed and edited version of his lectures. Similarly, anthropologist Claude Lévi-Strauss is regarded as the 'first to adapt Saussurean linguistics to the social sciences" (Kurzweil 1980: 1). Social structures, understood as systems like languages, became the focus of a renewed structuralist method with Lévi-Strauss as demonstrated in the two-volume set *Structural Anthropology* (Lévi-Strauss 1968, 1977).

Saussure and Lévi-Strauss have been chosen as the paradigms for this exposition of the important tenets of structuralism relating to poststructuralist theory because of the reputation of their archetypical applications of the tenets of structuralism, first to linguistics in the case of Saussure, and second to the social sciences, or more specifically anthropology, in the case of Lévi-Strauss. Settling on the work of Saussure and Lévi-Strauss allows the two movements of structuralism—linguistic and social scientific—to be clearly highlighted. In the context of a poststructuralist project, this focus is a useful act of clarification because of the eventual incorporation of psychoanalytic concepts with linguistic ones in the poststructuralist agenda. With the work of Saussure, the specific linguistic base of structuralism is made explicit. With the work of Lévi-Strauss, the adaptation of an essentially linguistic system to other systemic structures is demonstrated.

Assumption 1

Human meaning systems are arbitrarily constructed according to certain structures, albeit deeply unconsciously embedded ones.

The exposition of this tenet in relation to its significance for poststructuralism and poststructuralist theology demands an analysis of several components of the assumption:

1. Human meaning is a systemic phenomenon.
2. Manifestations of this phenomenon are arbitrarily constructed.
3. This arbitrary construction is premised on unconscious processes.
4. Such processes imply a structural relationality between systemic components.

Human meaning is a systemic phenomenon

The theoretical focus of structuralism is on systems: systems of language, symbols, meaning and culture. Structural linguistics shifted

---

3.   Henceforth cited as *Course*.

the focus of language study from individual components in language to language systems as a whole, and language as a whole system (Lévi-Strauss 1968: 33). A basic assumption of structuralism is that systems, not their components, are the foci of analysis (Grosz 1989: 11).

Course (Saussure 1966) is clearly concerned with language as a whole system. This is explicitly stated in part one: 'Language is a system whose parts can and must all be considered in their synchronic solidarity' (Saussure 1966: 87). Later, in the discussion on synchronic linguistics which is the prime strand of linguistic investigation for *Course*, this principle is reiterated in a variety of ways. Synchronic linguistics is the study of any one language at any one point in time. Language is understood as 'a system of interdependent terms' in which the role of each term is affected by the role of all of the other components found in the same system (Saussure 1966: 114). The importance of chains and progressions of components in languages is asserted (Saussure 1966: 127). The relevance of linguistic context for the worth or value of linguistic components remains a constant theme throughout this discussion (Saussure 1966: 101–39). According to *Course* then, words or signs, as components of language systems, must be considered in the context of those systems in any effort to understand their significance. The value of a word is very closely allied to its relation to other words, i.e. to other components of the same system. The function and significance of any individual component in a system is established by the nature of the system to which it belongs. Systems are thus seen to establish the context for any evaluation of their individual components.

From a social scientific viewpoint, Lévi-Strauss asserts emphatically that the 'social facts which we study are manifested in societies, each of which is a *total, concrete, and cohesive entity*' (1977: 14). Here again, the importance of attending to the whole context of any given phenomenon is stressed, although this time the system is a society and, therefore, its components include not just elements of language but also actions, both ritual and mundane, and the characterization of individual people. For Lévi-Strauss, 'Structuralism uncovers a unity and a coherence within things which could not be revealed by a simple description of the facts' (Lévi-Strauss 1977: ix).

Such bold statements about unity, coherence and systems from Lévi-Strauss open the gate for criticism of the structuralist approach. When Lévi-Strauss defends himself against the attack of D. Maybury-Lewis over his approach to 'dual organizations', he asserts that a focus on the underlying social system enacted in specific 'segments' or 'symbolic representations' is justified as having 'a better explanatory value, although—or rather, because—empirical observation never apprehends it as such' (Lévi-Strauss 1977: 81). While this statement obviously raises the issue of the speculative nature of structuralism, it is the prior focus on systems that requires attention in this discussion. It is precisely the goal of determining anthropological universals through a focus on underlying social systems that requires the speculative proposals of structuralism. Thus, one of the significant critiques of structuralism as a study of systems concerns the attention to detail or rather lack of it which structuralism exhibits.

While Saussure and Lévi-Strauss spend much time giving examples and offering details of linguistic and social activity, their tendency to systematize such detail is generally critiqued. After all, it is possible to treat details as abnormalities if they do not coincide with the assumed systemic operations or to delve further into abstraction in order to determine the underlying system which would encompass them. Lévi-Strauss' analysis of North American Indian myth and ritual provides an interesting example of progressive abstraction in order to achieve the goal of enunciating a clear system. 'Structure and Dialectics' (Lévi-Strauss 1968: 232–41) notes that myth and ritual do not always coincide within the one social group (1968: 232). Asserting that their relationship is dialectical (1968: 233), Lévi-Strauss introduces evidence from neighbouring social groups to suggest that this dialectical relationship only makes sense when considered in relation to the 'symmetrical and inverse ritual' of neighbouring tribes (1968: 236). Via this approach, Lévi-Strauss establishes a system of binary oppositions with reconciling ambivalent third terms. His work is highly speculative. Its goals are absolute universals.

Edith Kurzweil, who describes structuralism as 'the systematic attempt to uncover deep universal mental structures' (Kurzweil 1980: 1), regards this universalistic aim as the death-knell of the methodology. According to Kurzweil, the universal structures have not been and can not be found. Hence, nobody bothers to look for them any longer (Kurzweil 1980: 10). Such an assessment highlights two aspects of the structuralist impact on poststructuralism. First, poststructuralism intensifies the search for a universal system. This intensification is particularly evident in Julia Kristeva's analysis of language and subject acquisition. Second, this intensification is an exposure of the failure of systemic theories to comprehend the complexity of 'reality'. In this way, poststructuralism juggles both an interest in systems and a wariness about systematization. In a theological context, such a juggling image is particularly apt. Theology, as an apophatic exercise, is constantly plagued by the paradoxical nature of the attempt to discuss a subject, namely God, which cannot be discussed in the terms available. Mark C. Taylor expresses this intersecting poststructuralist and theological dilemma in the following manner: 'Writing books, after having absorbed the insights of Deconstruction, is as difficult as writing theology, after having interiorized the death of God' (Taylor 1982: xx).

The discovery of universal laws is the stated intention of the structuralist methodology as conceived by both *Course* and Lévi-Strauss. One of the three declared aims of linguistics in *Course* is the determination of permanent and universal forces 'at work in all languages' and the deduction of 'the general laws to which all specific historical phenomena can be reduced' (Saussure 1966: 6). Similarly, Lévi-Strauss announces the aspiration of discovering the 'universal laws' of the unconscious mind (Lévi-Strauss 1968: 65). The accusation regarding universalism and its attendant failure is an apparent foundational delimitation of the extent and significance of structuralism. Yet, the criticism of universalism is a critique which can be understood to arise self-reflectively from the very enterprise of structuralism itself which implicitly questions the establishment of any definitive form of human knowledge. This particular critique impels exploration beyond the structuralist enterprise to poststructuralism.

Manifestations of systems are arbitrarily constructed

An important element of the focus on systems is the prior assumption that the components of systems, the words or signs, are arbitrary by nature. They are accidental. In shape, form and content, they could have been otherwise as is obvious from the profusion of human languages.[4] This arbitrariness is apparent in two ways: first, via the

---

4. *Course* will admit to the possibility of only two exceptions to this assumption of the unmotivatedness of language: onomatopoeia, words which are presumed to sound like their referents, and interjections, words which are presumed to be purely motivated by emotion. Nevertheless, even in these two cases, *Course* asserts that their variations from language to language suggest that any possibility of a natural internal relationality between concept or intent and word or sound-image cannot be sustained in debate (Saussure 1966: 69–70).

adherence of the components of the system to certain conventions prescribed by each system and second, in the relation of the form of the sign or component to its presumed underlying concept. The latter is actually the first of Saussure's general principles of linguistics: 'The bond between the signifier and the signified is arbitrary' (Saussure 1966: 67).

Saussure makes use of three key terms in relation to the concept of the sign: 'sign' (Fr. *signe*), signified (Fr. *signifié*), and signifier (Fr. *signifiant*). The signified is the presumed concept for which the signifier, the form, sound-image or word stands. The signifier and signified together form the sign. The signifier and signified stand in a type of opposition to one another, an opposition of form and content. Yet, it is an opposition united in the whole entity of the sign (Saussure 1966: 67). The construction of language, however, is not simply a naming process, a matching of a sound-image or form with a particular object, concept or person. It is also an ordering of human perception via the formation of conceptual entities through the process of giving them a tag. The assumptions that 'ready-made ideas exist before words' and 'that the linking of a name and a thing is a very simple operation' are 'anything but true' (Saussure 1966: 65). While the premise of the arbitrariness of the sign indicates that there is understood to be no 'natural connection' (1966: 69) between signifier and signified, it does suggest that the construction of language follows given patterns and plays a significant role in organizing human consciousness. This distinction is formulated in *Course* as a distinction between the 'absolute' and the 'relative' arbitrariness of the sign.

The 'absolute' arbitrary nature of the internal relationality of the sign means that the choice of relation does not belong to an individual speaker. Language is essentially a communal enterprise undertaken via tacitly agreed conventions and some not so tacitly as in the case of the production of dictionaries, grammars and media guidelines on the use of spoken language (Saussure 1966: 69–70). 'The signifier, though to all appearances freely chosen with respect to the idea that it represents, is fixed, not free, with respect to the linguistic community that uses it' (Saussure 1966: 71). Language is acquired and constructed in relationships between users. Components are added, deleted and modified in relation to other components within the same system. In comparison to the 'absolute' arbitrariness of the internal relationality between the signified and the signifier, Saussure refers to this external relationality as 'relative' arbitrariness (1966: 131–34). This produces

the paradoxical assertion that 'Because the sign is arbitrary, it follows
no law other than that of tradition, and because it is based on tradition,
it is arbitrary' (1966: 74). The necessity of approaching language as a
system is thus reinforced by the presumption of the two-fold arbitrary
nature of the sign.

Lévi-Strauss retains this dual concern for the proper understanding
of the arbitrariness of signs. In 'Structural Analysis in Linguistics and
Anthropology' (1968: 31–54), he maintains elements of Saussure's
notion of the 'absolute' arbitrariness of signs when he asserts that
kinship systems are not premised on blood ties but in the construction
of 'an arbitrary system of representations' in the consciousness of
humans (Lévi-Strauss 1968: 50). Lévi-Strauss argues this position
throughout the chapter, principally via an examination of varying
attitudes towards the relationships assumed between maternal uncles
and their nephews within different societies. He is more circumspect
in the use of the term 'arbitrary' in response to a critique of his work
made by A.G. Haudricourt and G. Granai who accused him of
reducing society and culture to language (Lévi-Strauss 1968: 55–66;
67–80; 81–97). According to Lévi-Strauss, one of Haudricourt's and
Granai's key errors is the rigid contrast of the arbitrary nature of
language and the intrinsic relation of society to nature (1968: 89–90).
Lévi-Strauss defends his own work not by stressing the arbitrary
nature of society but by noting what Saussure would have called the
'relative' arbitrariness of language. Lévi-Strauss prefers to speak of
signs being arbitrary *a priori* but not *a posteriori* (Lévi-Strauss 1968:
90–91). Via this distinction, as in the case of Saussure's distinction
between absolute and relative arbitrariness, the role of relations
between signs is emphasized (1968: 93). When language is considered
as a complete entity after the fact, the function of individual
components is dependent on the presence or absence of other
components and the relations which exist between them. Arbitrariness
is, therefore, both absolute and relative in the context of the systemic
study which is the basis of structuralism.

The assumption of the arbitrary nature of system components raises
the criticism of structuralism being characterized as 'non-
materialistic'. In effect this is a twofold criticism of structuralism's
tendency to be both ahistorical and non-physical. Structuralism is
criticized on the grounds that it pays little attention to the relevance
of historical detail and physical objects in the study of systems since
the characterizations of these elements, as components of the system

themselves, provide only surface layer evidence of the assumed underlying unconscious relations operating within the system. That is, for *Course*, linguistic structuralism is a study of abstract entities (Saussure 1966: 138) which, although in a relationship of 'complementarity' with concrete entities (sounds and letters), determine the meaning and function of the 'material unit' with which they are associated (Saussure 1966: 139). The material element (in this case, sound) cannot belong to language as a single entity since its role is secondary. As an element of language, able to be sensed, it supports the intangible elements of language which carry the effective meaning (Saussure 1966: 118). Thus, the 'sensible' or tangible elements of language are recorded as less significant and less determinative in their function than the intangible, speculated relationships.

Kurzweil addresses this element of Lévi-Strauss' structuralism via her analysis of his use of Marxism. Suggesting that Lévi-Strauss departs from the Marxist maxim that 'life is not determined by consciousness, but consciousness by life', Kurzweil accuses Lévi-Strauss of focussing only on social relations and not on the economic tangibles of the 'means, mode, and relations of production'. This tendency, together with his ahistorical use of myth apart from its material context, afforded Lévi-Strauss a great deal of criticism from contemporary philosophers such as Jean-Paul Sartre. It also assisted the accusation against structuralism of a lack of concern for political agendas and implications (Kurzweil 1980: 234–35).

Neither Saussure nor Lévi-Strauss were unconcerned by contextual factors. Saussure's idea of relative arbitrariness indicates this concern, as does Lévi-Strauss' distinction between similar cultural practices in different cultural contexts, e.g. his distinction between 'primitive' and 'scientific' methods of thought as a matter of environment, not of rigour, application or even possible intent (Lévi-Strauss 1968: 230). Yet, structuralism, with its assumption of the construction of human experience by systems of language and socio-cultural expression, questions the relationship between such expressions and the concrete, tangible realities of life. Structuralism, in effect, says that everything is experienced through a predetermined framework of language and culture. It is the relations between arbitrary units of expression which determine the structure of human society, not the relations between material units. The recognition of the role of systems of meaning in determining human perceptions is a major claim and consequence of the structuralist method.

The relation between material units and meaning constructions is problematic in structuralism. That it is problematic is precisely the point of structuralism: there is no intrinsic meaning associated with any material item. Rather, the meanings associated with any particular material unit are constructed. This interest in the construction of meaning later brings poststructuralism back to an investigation of the material source of such meanings—the human body, but not before the rigorous deconstruction of linguistic meaning. In the meantime, in Kurzweil's words, structuralism, particularly that of Lévi-Strauss, has been 'vulnerable to accusations of being based on "faith" or "metaphysics"' (Kurzweil 1980: 25). It is precisely this ability to play with meanings not intrinsically tied to concrete objects that makes structuralism, and its heir poststructuralism, attractive to a theological setting.

Arbitrary construction is premised on unconscious processes
The relations between systemic components are mediated unconsciously. For Lévi-Strauss, structural linguistics shifted the focus of language study from the accidence of conscious phenomena to the substance of their underlying unconscious organization (Lévi-Strauss 1968: 33). Consciousness and experience are mediated through such 'complex, unconscious relations' (Grosz 1989: 11).

Perhaps the most vulnerable element of structuralism to accusations of metaphysics is the concept of the construction of consciousness via the human unconscious. Since the arbitrariness of system components is tempered by the system itself, the system plays a role in establishing a framework of meaning and organization. This framework is dependent on the relations which exist between system components latently or *unconsciously*. This assertion has two implications for structuralism as a methodology. First, consciousness itself is not regarded as a necessarily self-reflective exercise. As the result of 'the unrecognized effects of complex, unconscious relations', consciousness and experience are regarded as constructs. This idea is related to the notion of the absolute arbitrariness of signs. According to Grosz, it also ensures that structuralism is considered to be 'antihumanist' (Grosz 1989: 11). Understanding consciousness as a construct allows human perception no inherent truth or knowledge value. The second implication of the unconscious/conscious distinction for structuralism is that consciousness is the result of a collective activity. Consciousness, as a construct, is communally developed.

The conscious/unconscious distinction is not specifically developed in *Course*, although the notion of the collective construction of a system and the difficulty of identifying and proving relations between components are. The 'Introduction' (Saussure 1966: 1–5) stresses this communal aspect. A brief survey of the history of linguistic studies from the ancient Greeks to late nineteenth century Europeans concludes that 'language is no longer looked upon as an organism that develops independently but as a product of the collective mind of linguistic groups' (Saussure 1966: 5). This collective construction is the producer of meaning since, 'Without language, thought is a vague, uncharted nebula. There are no pre-existing ideas, and nothing is distinct before the appearance of language' (Saussure 1966: 112). From a structuralist perspective then, language can be regarded as both producing consciousness and defining experience via a communal process. That this process is presumed to be unconscious is significant.

The assertion that the production of consciousness occurs via unconscious processes is the successor to Saussure's observations about the development of meaning and value resulting from relations between components and not from any particular assignment of concept to sound-image. The study of synchronic linguistics concerns 'the logical and psychological relations that bind together coexisting terms and form a system in the collective mind of speakers' (Saussure 1966: 99–100). Language, as essentially 'a confused mass', requires 'attentiveness and familiarization' in order to identify its 'particular elements' (Saussure 1966: 104). Since ideas do not precede language, concepts and values as they are formed by language are essentially 'differential'. That is, they are defined not by the 'positive content' of a preexistent idea but by the negative relation of their existence within the system in association with other components of that system. 'Their most precise characteristic is in being what the others are not' (Saussure 1966: 117). The abstract and illusive quality of the relations of the system are thus advanced by Saussure even if the conscious/unconscious distinction is not yet clearly delineated in the systematic presentation of linguistic structuralism in *Course*.

In the 'Translator's Preface' to *Structural Anthropology*, Claire Jacobson asserts that Lévi-Strauss, as an influential structuralist, focuses on the relations which exist among phenomena; the systems which contain them; the necessity of considering both unconscious and conscious 'social processes'; and the occurrence of all of these in 'the major aspects of culture—language, kinship, social organization, magic, religion, and art' (Lévi-Strauss 1968: x). Lévi-Strauss himself claims that he seeks to move beyond the distinctions made between 'the collective nature of culture' and its individual manifestations since both are expressions of the 'unconscious activity of the mind' (Lévi-Strauss 1968: 65). Anthropology's focus on the unconscious basis of society is what, for Lévi-Strauss, distinguishes it from the discipline of history which records and interprets conscious social phenomena (Lévi-Strauss 1968: 24). While earlier expressions of structuralism as exemplified by Saussure's *Course* had not yet specifically made the distinction between the conscious and the unconscious, the groundwork had been laid for this later distinction made in particular by social scientific structuralists such as Lévi-Strauss. This distinction is also an important development in the further move towards poststructuralism (and its use of psychoanalytic theory) as well as a prime target for critical attack against structuralism.

Grosz suggests that 'structuralists such as Claude Lévi-Strauss...criticize the notion of the pregiven subject and the sign as the bearer of a self-constituted meaning' (Grosz 1989: 10) in contrast to the humanistic belief that 'all values, meanings, history and culture are the products of human consciousness and individual activity' (Grosz 1989: 6). By asserting that the concept of the subject or individual human identity is conflated with the notion of consciousness, Grosz defines a humanistic approach as that which gives 'primary value to consciousness in making choices, and judging, creating and transforming social relations' (Grosz 1989: 7). In this way, Grosz establishes humanism as the inevitable champion of the Cartesian subject and the assumption that human identity relies on human conscious thought. By advancing the position that structuralism is antihumanistic, Grosz suggests that, from a structuralist perspective, there is 'no human essence and no pregiven, universal identity' but rather humanistic beliefs in such are the results of 'particular social/historical contexts and powers' (Grosz 1989: 39). This suggestion does not ignore the structuralist attempts to establish apparently universal notions of the construction of language and meaning systems. Rather, it reinforces that such underlying structures are *unconscious*. They are neither immediately apparent to the conscious processes of human thought; nor do they produce meanings that are intrinsically related to an essential 'reality'. Human identity itself is far more complex than immediately apparent and, as a product of those same unconscious processes, equally as vulnerable to the vagaries of arbitrary construction.

In this manner, structuralism engineers a major collision in epistemology between humans as knowing/thinking beings and knowledge as constructed/fabricated thought. While the actual impact is felt more fully in the poststructuralist arena, it is structuralism that provides the preconditions for the questioning of all human thought processes and, therefore, all human knowledge. If our knowledge is governed by the way in which we have organized it unconsciously, is it knowledge at all and, if so, of what? Can we in fact know only that we do not know or are other knowledges still possible? For structuralism, other knowledges are possible although no currently available knowledge is absolute (Lévi-Strauss 1977: ix).

A self-reflective engagement with the structures in which one finds oneself is possible although somewhat precarious. In this respect, structuralism is apparently at the one time both very humanist and extremely antihumanist. Humans may not know that their knowledge is governed by certain predetermined organizational tools; nevertheless, they do have the capacity for such knowledge. The structuralist enterprise itself is thus placed in the highly compromising position of continuing to work for something which may not be possible given the constraints of its own assumptions. It is not surprising that linguistic theorist Deborah Cameron suggests that the 'proposal that meaning does not arise from experience initially strikes most people as running entirely counter to common sense' (Cameron 1985: 117). Such a position heralds the necessity of further exploration and constant review of this theoretical stance. It foreshadows the ambiguous position of poststructuralism, and its concern with ambiguity. In a theological context, the paradox of the emerging structuralist (later poststructuralist) subject offers a philosophical grounding for the simultaneous optimism and pessimism of the traditional Christian views of humanity as both good creation and fallible being, both redeemed and sinful—in Reformation terms, *simul iustus et peccator*.

A structural relationality between systemic components
Structuralism focuses on the relations between system components. For Lévi-Strauss, structural linguistics shifted the focus of language

study from the incidence of independent terms to the relations which exist between those terms (Lévi-Strauss 1968: 33). The individual components of systems are not reliable indices of reality, but symptoms of 'latent relations' within the system (Grosz 1989: 11).

As a study of systems, structuralism is not so much interested in the individual components of the systems as in the relations which exist between components, characterizing the nature of each system. The signs or 'facts' of a system are treated more like symptoms or indicators of underlying realities than attributes holding any innate significance of their own. In Grosz's words, the 'individual element, given to observation, is not a reliable index of reality'. The focus of attention is thus on the 'deeper non-observable' structure of the system (Grosz 1989: 11). *Course* establishes this principle via a discussion of the value of words in relation to their presumed meaning. Again, the importance of the relationship between the individual components of a system is emphasized as it is asserted that the value of words comes not from any associations with pre-existing ideas but rather via their differential relationship to other words. 'Their most precise characteristic is in being what the others are not' (Saussure 1966: 117). These 'latent relations' (Grosz 1989: 11) between components of a system are a better indicator of the nature of the structure of that system than the individual components themselves. For *Course*, these latent relations are also internal to the sign itself, existing between the two components of the sign, the word or sound-image and its presumed meaning content. It is the internal relationality of signs which gives them their nature as concrete, observable entities (Saussure 1966: 102–103).

Lévi-Strauss also emphasizes the necessity of a focus upon the relations which exist between system components. In a postscript to two pieces focussing on the relation between linguistic and social analysis, Lévi-Strauss makes reference to the work of Karl Marx and suggests that *relationships* between systemic components should be regarded as entities in their own right since it is these structural elements which have the ultimate significance for anthropological investigation (Lévi-Strauss 1968: 95). Lévi-Strauss is particularly interested in a number of binary relations which he perceives as existing between system components. For example, he discusses the relations of dialectic, dualism, binary opposition, complementarity and even triadism in this respect. Two key essays for these discussions are 'Do Dual Organizations Exist?' (1968: 132–63) and 'Structure and

Dialectics' (1968: 233–41) but this interest permeates the whole of both volumes of *Structural Anthropology* (Lévi-Strauss 1968, 1977).

Despite the fact that Kurzweil (1980: 14, 229–30, 234–35) is somewhat scathing in her assessments of Lévi-Strauss' understanding and use of Marxism, especially in connection with his conception of component relations, Lévi-Strauss' emphasis on the relations between components of social systems cannot be ignored. In a structuralist context, such relations are treated as the real elements of any system and, therefore, the 'concrete' focus of study. Nevertheless, Kurzweil's critique of Lévi-Strauss' 'debatable conception' (1980: 229) serves to highlight again the critique of the speculative nature of structuralism. Kurzweil accuses Lévi-Strauss of transforming 'speculative ideas into facts and past reflections into current assumptions' as well as of justifying 'the mixing of personal experience with intellectual interpretation' by claiming a threefold theoretical foundation of 'geology, psychoanalysis, and Marxism' (Kurzweil 1980: 14). Lévi-Strauss' interest in relations between elements of systems existed not only within his own application of a structuralist perspective to anthropology but also in his characterization of his own theoretical genealogy. It is no wonder that the accusation of speculation against structuralism is an often repeated and profound one.

The accusation of speculation is a major point of critique for structuralism. To some extent, this accusation serves to challenge the deeply held hope of both Saussure and Lévi-Strauss that linguistic and anthropological structuralism respectively could be recognized as legitimate sciences. Saussure envisaged a linguistic science as part of a broader context of a science of signs or semiology (1966: 16). Lévi-Strauss defended the place of structural social analysis as a science in the context of the linguistic method established by Saussure (Lévi-Strauss 1968: 55–66). While Kurzweil cautions that 'the French use of the term "scientific" is not linked to empirical proof in the same way as its [Anglo-] American equivalent is' (Kurzweil 1980: 14), the broad claims of structuralist methodology leave the method quite open to the speculative critique.

Jacobson recognizes this critique and defends Lévi-Strauss in the face of it. Acknowledging that Lévi-Strauss 'proposes bold and at times frankly speculative hypotheses', she points to his constant use of 'empirical observation' both in working from specific examples towards theoretical proposals and vice versa (Lévi-Strauss 1968: x). Unfortunately, this defence only lends itself to the possibility of further accusations of circular argumentation being levelled against Lévi-Strauss. The enterprise of structuralism is speculative as are all inductive ventures, even those of the so-called natural sciences. Lévi-Strauss does not avoid this apparent limitation, preferring to confront it directly and deny its relevance. By asserting that the hypotheses of human sciences can neither be verified nor falsified, Lévi-Strauss presents this feature of the human sciences as one of the inevitable limitations of social scientific disciplines. Nevertheless, by claiming for such hypotheses a 'relative value', Lévi-Strauss affirms that this does not render the social scientific method null and void. Rather, in the acknowledgement of the limitations of the method and thereby the status of any hypotheses, Lévi-Strauss finds the necessary justification for continuing to advance and maintain hypotheses of 'relative value' until new ones are suggested which are found to have greater plausibility (1977: ix). Kurzweil is somewhat sceptical of Lévi-Strauss' tendency to 'refute criticisms by pointing to his own awareness of the problem'. Nevertheless, she recognizes the legitimacy which such an approach also gave continuing structuralist explorations (Kurzweil 1980: 230). Speculation thus proves to be both an asset and a limitation for structuralist methodology.

Speculation implies exploration into areas of human thought, experience and knowledge which are not yet regarded as fully investigated or understood. While this critique does compel caution about the permissible claims of a structuralist method, it also positions structuralism as an attempt to deal with one of the current frontiers of human knowledge and experience, that of language and culture. Unable to be isolated from their contexts as physical objects may be isolated in a laboratory, language and culture present illusive subjects for analysis. According to Lévi-Strauss, this presents the unusual scientific situation of experiments in language and culture always preceding observation and the construction of hypotheses. Experiments are continually in progress in human life. They cannot be controlled; neither can they be detached or set apart from their environment—human society. This is the major subjective limitation of the study of language and culture, the 'boldness' of which can only be tempered by 'humility' (Lévi-Strauss 1977: 15). Since humility is probably as equally illusive as the possibility of isolating language and culture, the criticism of speculation offers an important caveat upon the methodology of structuralism and its successors, no matter how important the method may be considered to 'the attainment of a general science of man [sic]' (Jacobson in Lévi-Strauss 1968: x). Nevertheless, structuralism as a basis for further poststructuralist investigations provides another movement into the exploration of ambiguity by highlighting the speculative enterprise of the 'sciences', recognizing itself within that speculative enterprise, continuing its explorations despite this position, and, thereby, claiming its own position as a contributor to the construction of human knowledge. This combined exploration, recognition of limitations and claiming of perspectival validity is one of the features of poststructuralism which I have already identified as holding a particular attraction for feminism and theology.

Assumption 2

Structures are essentially binary or dualistic
The relations formed between systemic components are inherently dualistic both in their construction and in their organization within systems.

One of the key aspects of the unconscious processes referred to by Lévi-Strauss and anticipated in the unrecognized relations accented by Saussure is the notion of an inherent duality in the construction of language and society. For Saussure, this duality existed in the 'nature of the linguistic sign'. The construction of a sign as a combination of a signifier and a signified establishes a binary opposition: a pair separated from themselves and from the whole of which they are parts (Saussure 1966: 65–67). This binary opposition forms the basis for subsequent divisions in structuralist thought. For example, *Course* distinguishes between the study of language (Fr. *langue*) and the study of speaking (Fr. *parole*).

Both *langue* and *parole* are parts of human speech (Fr. *langage*) but quite distinct components of it, just as the signifier and the signified are quite distinct components of the sign. Language (*langue*) is both the product of speech and the 'collection of necessary conventions that have been adopted by a social body to permit individuals to exercise that faculty' (Saussure 1966: 9). Speaking or *parole* is the 'executive' function of speech. It refers to the individual utterances made by individual people in the shared social context of language (1966: 13). This separation of language and speaking moreover forms the basis for the distinction between the study of the socio-psychological aspect of human speech, i.e. language, and the individual and psychophysical aspect of human speech, i.e. speaking (1966: 18).

An additional distinction is made in *Course* between the diachronic study of language and the synchronic study of the same. Synchronic study of language focuses on *a* language at *a* particular point in time, in order to extrapolate general principles for the underlying substantial form of all languages (1966: 87). Diachronic study of language observes linguistic change within one language over time and, potentially, between a number of different languages or registers. In this distinction, change is actually the product, although not an aspect, of speaking. Static conditions, the focus of synchronic study, are the social norms to which speakers adhere.

For Saussure, the linguistic phenomenon always has two related elements (1966: 8). These two related elements, having been equated in a single unifying entity, are necessarily placed in confrontation with or opposition to one another (1966: 79). This understanding of an inherent duality in the structure of language provides the basis for the explorations of Lévi-Strauss as he attends to anthropological 'relationships of opposition and correlation and permutation and transformation' (Jacobson in Lévi-Strauss 1968: x).

While Lévi-Strauss specifically distinguishes his own thinking from the synchronic and diachronic distinctions of *Course*, he maintains the 'dialectical' character of the process of structural transformation. The definitive quality of the separation between synchrony and diachrony, and hence speaking and language, individual and collective, is attributed by Lévi-Strauss not to Saussure but to the editors of *Course*. Saussure's own position, Lévi-Strauss assures, would have been far closer to that expressed by French sociologist Emile Durkheim (1858–1917), where the difference in such structural elements is only one of 'degree'. Interestingly, Lévi-Strauss goes on to assert that 'the nature of the facts' which are the focus of social anthropological study necessitates the division of their characters into that which belongs to the 'order of structure' and that which belongs to the 'order of event'. This division is required by the scientific imperative of the observation of a structure via its transformations from one system to another (Lévi-Strauss 1977: 16–18). Kurzweil suggests that the distinction between synchronic and diachronic study is still an important one for Lévi-Strauss (Kurzweil 1980: 231). The distinction between the 'order of structure' and the 'order of event' suggests this importance.

Elsewhere Lévi-Strauss walks a similar tight-rope between the necessity of the use of binary oppositions in the exploration of social phenomena and the rejection of the concept of a rigid dualism as a sufficient explanation for them. For example, in 'Do Dual Organizations Exist?' (1968: 132–63), Lévi-Strauss attempts to show that the theory of 'dual organizations' contains 'so many anomalies and contradictions' that it can not be treated as a serious explanation for the 'real nature' of social phenomena (1968: 161). Much of Lévi-Strauss' argument for this position consists of pointing out the multiple overlays of binary oppositions in examples of such contradictory and anomalous phenomena. The only logical conclusion to be drawn from this essay is that, while Lévi-Strauss rejects the notion of societies being organized on one single, simple binary opposition which governs all social divisions, he does not reject the assumption of the inherent duality of social relationships, even if such dualities are understood as being constantly in search of a third term and always multiple. Even Lévi-Strauss' postulated triadic structure is described as a third form of dualism (1966: 150), and his suggested ternary structures are underlaid by binary oppositions (1968: 159–60). If Lévi-Strauss is cautious in describing the nature of the duality of structures, it is because of the recognition of their complexity. Nevertheless, for Lévi-Strauss, there is inherent duality in social organization.

Lévi-Strauss cross-correlated examples from a variety of cultures and times in order to explore the universal structures, not simply of language, but of human activity in general, and therefore of human mental processes themselves (1968: 65). His concern with the full range of cultural expressions from any and every era of human existence should not be taken as an interest in the history or progression of human communication strategies, since history is regarded as being reinvented in each repetition of prior cultural forms such as those of myths (Lévi-Strauss 1968: 23). Rather, it is a concern with the universals of the human mind, the all-pervasive 'givens' of human existence which transcend both history and material particularity. Duality looms large in these patterns.

For Lévi-Strauss, duality constantly seeks reconciliation and is, therefore, dialectical or ternary in its expression. For example, he argues that any individual case of dualism may be regarded as a 'simplification' and a 'limit' of a broader triadic system which can be explained in terms of underlying binary oppositions (Lévi-Strauss

1977: 73). Since Saussure's, or at least *Course's*, binary oppositions underpin unitary structures, the focus on the resolution of dichotomous concepts is also maintained in these two examples of structuralism albeit with diverging projected solutions. This concern for a movement towards the resolution or reconciliation of opposites becomes an important hub for later poststructuralist explorations beyond the assumption of the inherent duality of meaning constructions.

Structuralism establishes a binary pattern underlying all human thought and activity. That pattern is an unintended consequence of language itself. In one sense, it is the absolute given of the structure of human language and therefore consciousness. Nevertheless, as an assumption about the universalist structure of human language and culture, it provides an important opening to a major critique. This critique, which I have called the accusation of dualism, can be divided into two components: first, a questioning of the imposition of binary opposition onto the structure of language and culture; and second, a concern about the tight separation of the oppositional concepts established via the use of a binary classification system. The first aspect of this critique raises again the issue of the overburdening of linguistic analysis with speculative assumption. The second aspect simply suggests that wherever dichotomy or binary opposition is used as a tool, it has the capacity to suggest a far stricter and more prescriptive division than is intended, via a division of the indivisible pair into two separate entities.

Cameron raises the first issue in a twofold format. In two questions addressing the validity of the binary oppositional formula, she asks whether such oppositions actually exist in language or whether they are 'invented as a handy way of analysing language'; and whether, given the assumption that humans tend to think in binary oppositions, that tendency is the result of physiology or environment (Cameron 1985: 58). This coincides with an assessment by T.K. Seung (1982) of two different rationales which underlie Lévi-Strauss' structuralist programme: linguistic and psychological. The linguistic approach asserts that all human culture and activity is governed by binary oppositions because it is an 'extension' of language and language is founded on a basic binary oppositional structure. The psychological approach suggests that binary opposition is the foundational structure of language and culture because it is the foundational structure of the human mind. While Seung suggests that Lévi-Strauss and his followers have not always been clear on this division, he regards it as an important one, since the two approaches represent two different sets of assumptions and goals. The linguistic approach implies that 'the structure of language determines even the structure of mind' whereas the psychological approach maintains that 'the structure of mind determines that of language' (Seung 1982: 7–8). This distinction still leaves the underlying question as to the nature of the analysis of linguistic and cultural structures as binary: is it purely a description of the state of human institutions or is it the prescription required by a particular tool of analysis, namely structuralism? Is structuralism itself determining its own context through its own system of meaning? This is a major dilemma for structuralism given its own concern with the role of language and social organization within human culture.

Seung's work introduces the association between structuralism and hermeneutics, and hence that between poststructuralism and hermeneutics. Like Grosz and Kurzweil, Seung is interested in structuralism as a precursor to poststructuralism. The stated objective of his book is to examine the nature of the theoretical movement from the scientific intentions of structuralism to the anti-scientific reactions of poststructuralism (Seung 1982: xi). Seung is a strident critic of the anti-rationalism of poststructuralism (1982: xii) and also critical of the structuralist enterprise. He attributes the poststructuralist reaction to the failure of the structuralist search for universal cultural forms (1982: xi). Seung's work provides an interesting account of structuralism as a hermeneutical tool, not simply for the examination of texts but also for the analysis of 'a whole age or culture' (1982: ix). It raises useful questions about the possibility of the use of poststructuralist methodology in a similar way, although such a possibility may not be envisaged by Seung.

The second issue, that of the excessive polarization of binary oppositions, is one to which Lévi-Strauss was obviously sensitive as shown in the discussion above. He asserts that the number of 'anomalies and contradictions' in relation to theories on the existence of these organizations requires the treatment of their 'apparent manifestations' as 'superficial distortions of structures whose real nature is quite different and vastly more complex' (Lévi-Strauss 1968: 161). In this way, Lévi-Strauss rejects the notion of absolute dualisms while retaining the necessity of binary oppositions as underlying organizational arrangements. This paradoxical position is obviously another case where 'humility' and a self-conscious process are required by the structuralist method which itself suggests the difficulty of attaining such an 'objective' position. The issue of binary patterns and their possible reconciliation and/or disruption remains a captivating issue for poststructuralism as it does for theology.

Assumption 3

The construction process of meaning systems governs the nature of the constructed meanings within them, i.e. the unconscious binary structures produce dualistic systems of meaning.

This assumption concerns the direct relationship posited by structuralism between the construction process and the meanings constructed. The assumption involves a notion of determinism, but at a very specific level of the meaning construction process.

Recognizing that 'the Saussurean position' has been considered to be deterministic, Cameron defends Saussurean linguistics while suggesting that linguistic determinism is better attributed to the work of American structuralists Edward Sapir (1884–1939) and Benjamin Whorf (1897–1941). In the eyes of Cameron, the Saussurean assertion is that language is 'an intermediary between brute reality and human perception' while the implications of the work of Sapir and Whorf is that language is a 'mode of action' and 'words are things' (Cameron 1985: 96). There are clear distinctions between the French structuralists and their American counterparts, although whether such a difference exists in the level of determinism proposed is debatable. More probably, the difference in deterministic attitudes lies in varying interpretations of the level of language where such determinism is seen to take place rather than in the amount of determinism which is suggested to operate at those varying levels.

Sapir and Whorf, for example, are best known for their association with what has become the Sapir-Whorf hypothesis. The principle proposed by that hypothesis suggests that language encodes and therefore shapes our experience and perception of reality: 'people act about situations in ways which are like the ways they talk about them' (Whorf 1956: 148). Kristeva traces this theory to the work of philosopher-linguist Wilhelm von Humboldt (1767–1835) via its reconfiguration by L. Weisgerber. She characterizes it as a theory of 'linguistic relativity' and makes it clear that the hypothesis, in her view, is concerned with particular languages and their particular effects. In this scheme of events, 'there would therefore be as many types of signifying organizations of the universes as there are linguistic structures' (Kristeva 1989: 47, 202–203). This assessment of the hypothesis is confirmed by sociolinguist Peter Trudgill who suggests that the interest of Sapir and Whorf is far more in language particulars than language universals. Trudgill attributes the concentration of the Sapir-Whorf hypothesis as being on 'a speaker's native language' as it is seen to set up 'series of categories which act as a kind of grid' through which the world is perceived (Trudgill 1983: 24). While this account of the hypothesis may be overstating slightly the emphasis on particulars by Sapir and Whorf, there still remains a clear contrast between such an interest and the clear focus by Saussure and Lévi-Strauss on linguistic and even mental universals. Determinism may be understood as occurring at somewhat different levels of the language spectrum.

Both Saussure and Lévi-Strauss are very much aware of social and linguistic change and indeed of theoretical change. The issue perhaps is at what level this change takes place. As has been suggested, the duality of the sign is a crucial given for Saussure, as is binary opposition for Lévi-Strauss. Yet, neither has denied the individual cultural variations exhibited by various human populations. This situation, I believe, is largely because the constitution of the sign is still regarded as arbitrary although its structure may be predetermined. If structuralism is deterministic, it is not at the level of signs, in the externals of language and culture, it is at the heart of their formulation and perhaps even prior to their construction, as poststructuralism will come to suggest. The profound depth of the level of determinism in the language construction process and in human meaning itself is a powerful contribution by structuralism to the poststructuralist fascination with duality and its subversion.

The accusation of determinism is a critique which also raises the issue of the political stance of structuralism. If structuralism is simply concerned with uncovering universal structures, what concern with movement, change and revolution can it be seen to exhibit? This criticism is one which is poignantly carried through to poststructuralism where a concern with deconstruction is rendered as an attack on the inability to envisage anything new or different, while pulling apart the extant.

Kurzweil suggests that structuralism has had a general conservative bias although this was not apparent in the methodological development of Lévi-Strauss with whom she begins her investigation of the structuralist programme (Kurzweil 1980: 4). For Kurzweil, 'the limited political consequences of most structuralist theory' did not prevent the work of Lévi-Strauss containing the promise of 'a new theory of nature and culture' along with 'political and ideological unity'. Kurzweil understood the socio-political upheaval of 1968 to have sidelined the structuralist endeavour (1980: 27–28). Even with the protestations of Kurzweil, it is easy to see the dangers envisaged in a structuralist method by those concerned with socio-cultural change. If indeed structuralism is concerned with ascertaining the universalities of human nature, be they genetically or environmentally determined, then a large part of the aim of structuralism could be said to be descriptive. When structuralism purports to describe, it seems to offer no antidote to its description. In this respect, Kurzweil suggests that the assumption of the existence of 'certain invariable natural laws which govern humanity' was the focus of an important critique of Lévi-Strauss (Kurzweil 1980: 24).

Is structuralism apolitical? Is there any human activity which could be said to be so? Description does not necessarily reinforce the status quo. Reinforcing the status quo is not necessarily apolitical. Certainly, statements such as that found in *Course* to the effect that 'language presupposes the exclusion of everything that is outside its organism or system' including 'ethnology', 'politics', 'institutions', 'geography and "dialectical splitting"' (Saussure 1966: 20–21) would appear to support the accusation of apoliticality. Nevertheless, when the implications of the linguistic model for the structural analysis of societies and institutions are realized, it is hard to reconcile these with any notion of apoliticality.

Even if such an accusation is about whether structuralism promotes change, it is difficult to understand. Description, analysis and critique seldom end with their own outcomes, but are often the spur to movement and change in the phenomena under study. *Course* includes some notes on the nature of change in language in its understanding of diachronic linguistics (1966: 93). Lévi-Strauss is concerned with change, particularly that beyond duality (Lévi-Strauss 1968: 159–60), which is a key movement for poststructuralist analysis also.

Assumption 4

There is no real referential relationship between language (and other symbols) and the 'objects' which they purport to represent.

Signs, i.e. the components of structuralist systems, are arbitrary constructions within the arbitrary constraints of the systems to which they belong. There is no inherent referential value between them and the entities they purport to represent.

This final assumption has, in part, been addressed in the discussions above. What remains to say is that structuralism is clearly concerned with human meaning, recognizing that the construction of that meaning is, in at least certain respects, entirely independent of the 'reality' of the objects etc. about which meaning is constructed. That is, 'reality' for humans as sentient beings is essentially the meaning(s) which are created, not the intrinsic actuality of anything about which such meaning is made. In this respect, structuralism is a meta-discourse: a discourse about discourse. It is concerned with what we think we know, rather than what we might be able to know about. Poststructuralism pursues this concentration on discursive meaning even further when it seeks to expose even more vividly the dynamics of meaning creation through the processes of deconstruction. For theology, the 'meta-' viewpoint is consistent with the theological use of sources—the primary ones being Scripture and tradition; the focus on the received revelation of God through such sources and the primary motif of the Christian faith, the person of Jesus Christ; and the important place of hermeneutics or interpretation of both the sources and this central motif. The element in this assumption which remains unaddressed by the discussion above is the validity of the use of a linguistic model for extra-linguistic, e.g. socio-cultural, explorations.

Via his systematic structuring of the phenomena of language into one coherent, if not irrefutable, theory and by the firm linking of that linguistic structure to the content of all human culture and activity, Ferdinand de Saussure laid an unmistakable foundation for the work of Claude Lévi-Strauss. In his positing of the possibility of the science of semiology, the study of the 'life of signs at the heart of social life' (Saussure 1966: 9), Saussure indicates that language is simply one possible aspect of semiological investigation. Rites and customs, among other things, can also be the focus of systemic studies of signs.

Language has *a* place, albeit highly significant, among a whole range of 'human facts' (1966: 15–17). The model of linguistic structuralism because of its emphasis on systems and its characterization of systemic components as signs could thus be applied to other areas of systematic enquiry by Saussure's followers.

To a large extent, all of the previous discussion has assumed this last significant principle of a structuralist perspective, i.e. that the structuralist method applied to language can be translated to other forms of cultural or social expressions such as ritual and myth. Here the concept of sign is dramatically broadened from that represented by a sound-image or word and its presumed referent to anything that can be an expression of the human construction of reality. A statue, a story and a method of cooking or eating are just a few of the myriad of possibilities. This assumption is the foundation for the anthropological work of Lévi-Strauss as well as for the literary and cultural explorations of the focal theoretician of this project, Julia Kristeva.

Seung claims that, in *Structural Anthropology* (1968), Lévi-Strauss 'adopts two premises':

1. that 'structural linguistics has established a set of structural universals for all languages'; and
2. that 'the entire human culture is an extension of language'.

The human or social sciences can thus be regarded as an extension of structural linguistics (Seung 1982: 8). Lévi-Strauss actually appears slightly more cautious in at least one of the essays contained in the volume indicated. In 'Linguistics and Anthropology' (1968: 67–80), Lévi-Strauss concedes that there is not a one hundred per cent correlation between language and culture and hence between linguistics and anthropology but that neither is there no correlation. This ensures that the relationship between linguistics and anthropology has the potential to be mutually beneficial (1968: 79) with the ultimate aim of conceiving a new broad anthropology or study of humanity which 'incorporates all the different approaches which can be used' and provides 'a clue to the way according to which our uninvited guest, the human mind, works' (1968: 80). It will come as no surprise that Lévi-Strauss' audience on the occasion of the first delivery of this paper in 1952 was populated by both linguists and anthropologists (1968: 382). Nevertheless, the point is clearly made: the new human sciences are envisaged as following in the footsteps of the systematic approach of linguistic structuralism, a pilgrimage which is expected to be both status-enhancing and scientifically fruitful.

The concern for the status of the human sciences as scientific is a favourite anthem of Lévi-Strauss. He argues that when language is acknowledged as a tool for understanding the 'fundamental characteristics of social life' (1968: 64–65), the argument that the social sciences are unmathematisable, and therefore unscientific, can be counteracted (1968: 55). While Seung is not as confident that such an argument for the scientific nature of the human sciences can be maintained, since the processes of each are unavoidably different (Seung 1982: 2–5), there is no doubt that the issue of the sciential possibilities of structuralism are strongly linked with the hope of its interdisciplinary suitability. In the words of Grosz, structuralism as an interdisciplinary method suggests that 'Social, religious, cultural and economic relations are amenable to a scientific analysis, not on the model provided by the natural sciences, but because all are, in some sense, "structured like a language"' (Grosz 1989: 11).

Chapter 4

BEYOND DUALITY: ALTERITY AND THE EXODUS OF IDENTITY

Post-Structuralism

As an epithet, the term 'poststructuralism' indicates more faithfully the precedents of the group of writings positioned within that category than their intentions. For Kurzweil, 'the failure of Parisian structuralism itself...prepared the ground for the various "post-structuralisms"' which would follow (1980: 10). Nevertheless, relying implicitly on structuralism, 'poststructuralism' is not 'anti-structuralist'. Its profound questioning of the organization of language identified by structuralism affirms the significance of the insights of its precursor, particularly in relation to the issue of duality. In some respects, 'poststructuralism' is 'ante- structuralist'. It concerns itself with that which exists prior to, in and around acknowledged and alleged social and linguistic structures. Poststructuralist writer, Jacques Derrida, describes 'poststructuralism' as 'ultrastructuralist'. For Derrida, poststructuralism accentuates socio-linguistic structures to the point where even the aberrations and the deficiencies within and around the dualities are embraced in an analysis of their workings (Derrida 1978: 26).

Poststructuralism is not content simply with the binary structures presumed by structuralism. This sense of there being something beyond the picture of socio-cultural duality left by structuralism is a key aspect of poststructuralist theory. While not denying the usefulness of interpretative principles such as the notion of the inherent duality found within language and culture, poststructuralism suggests the parallel possibility of a precursor and internal subverter of such forms and categories. This contradictory emphasis on structure and its subversion produces the extraordinary situation where binary oppositions may be upheld, reversed, subverted and denied in a simultaneous process of apparent theoretical destabilization. The concept of alterity, a particular notion of an 'otherness' that exists outside the restraints of dichotomy, provides a useful device for exploring this important aspect of poststructuralism: the movement beyond duality.

In this exploration of alterity, as it relates to both language and identity, a recognition is made of the two major theoretical strands from which poststructuralism emerges: linguistics and psychoanalysis, or, as Kristeva suggests, 'semiotics' and psychoanalysis. The term 'semiotics' refers to the 'study of signs' or the interpretation of 'the diversity of modes of signification', among them, literary forms, symbols and images. The use of this term alludes to the broader socio-cultural context affected by the structure of language and dependent upon it (Kristeva 1989: 328).

With the intention of highlighting the contribution of each strand—linguistic and psychoanalytic—to the continuing emergence of poststructuralism as a methodological force, the work of literary philosopher, Jacques Derrida, and psychoanalyst, Jacques Lacan, is considered. The locus of interest in their work within this chapter concerns their conceptualization of a place or entity both within and beyond the socio-cultural duality established by structuralism. For Derrida, the term *différance* provides an entry point into this conceptual ambiguity; for Lacan, *jouissance*. These two signposts in their associated contexts provide a useful background to Julia Kristeva's synthesis of semiotics and psychoanalysis and her notion of *jouissance*.

Alterity

Mark C. Taylor describes alterity, or in his spelling, 'altarity', as 'a slippery word whose meaning can be neither stated clearly nor fixed firmly'. He suggests that the complexity of his notion of 'altarity' may be approached through a network of linguistic associations: 'altar, alter, alternate, alternative, alternation, alterity' (Taylor 1987: xxviii). In Taylor's context, the spelling 'alterity' is reduced to its dictionary definitions: the English word 'alterity' as 'the state of being other or different; diversity, otherness', and the French term '*altérité*' as the 'contrary of *identité*', specifying 'otherness or that which is other' (Taylor 1987: xxix). It is the conceptual profusion and lively wordplay of Taylor's altarity which falls closer to my use of the term 'alterity' in the context of this exploration. This profusive play, in my opinion, is the alterity or otherness that is the outcome of poststructuralist investigations beyond and around the duality of language and culture.

The concept of alterity is perhaps most easily signified when it is described in the algebraic terms of logic, a type of sign-play in itself. Clarification of my use of some terms in relation to binary divisions will assist this explanation: binary opposition, polarization, dichotomy, duality, and dualism. The binary division envisaged within the sign by structuralism is a duality, i.e. it is a division which does not assume that the dividends are adversarial to each other, merely two components of a larger entity. Nevertheless, these two components, often envisaged as discrete entities, present the inevitable temptation to polarization, i.e. to placing them antagonistically at opposite ends of a continuum, or simply in opposition to one another. Either situation of binary opposition, continuous or broken, is, in my terms, a dichotomy. Dichotomy may, therefore, be cast in two forms—A/B or A/Not-A: the former representing the poles of the continuum; the latter, the opposition of entities which are presumed to be discrete. It is the A/Not-A paradigm which provides the pattern for my understanding of dualism.

In an article entitled 'Gender and Dichotomy', Nancy Jay refers to the contrariness of A/B as distinct from the logical contradiction of A/Not-A (Jay 1981: 44). The purpose of Jay's article is to suggest the necessity of moving back from the A/Not-A paradigm to take seriously the A/B distinction. The A/Not-A paradigm assumes that only one term in the dichotomy is positive; the other is designated negatively in relation to the positive term. For Jay, this type of dichotomy is controlled by three basic rules of logic: (1) 'the Principle of Identity (if anything is A, it is A)'; (2) 'the Principle of Contradiction (nothing can be both A and Not A)'; and (3) 'the Principle of the Excluded Middle (anything, and everything, must be *either* A *or* Not-A)' (Jay 1981: 42). Thus, in Jay's understanding of the A/Not-A paradigm, there is only one positively identified term and no possibility of confused identity, continuum or a mediating term. In contrast, for Jay, the A/B distinction allows for the positive identity of both terms, a continuum of identity rather than discrete entities, and the introduction of third, fourth, fifth etc. terms, which move the paradigm beyond a situation of dichotomy. The A/B pattern is, for

Jay, a more realistic and flexible way of characterizing binary distinctions than the A/Not-A paradigm. For example, in the 'dichotomous distinction' which exists 'in every society', 'that between male and female', 'biologically, sex is a continuum', even if 'it is not one socially' (Jay 1981: 43). Similarly, Jay asserts that 'Everything that exists (including women) exists positively' (1981: 48). Jay's primary illustration of the usefulness of A/B over A/Not-A concerns Emile Durkheim's 'radical separation of, the total opposition between, the sacred and the profane' (1981: 39). For Jay, the complete inadequacy of such a distinction is profoundly revealed by the absence of 'objective features' that 'necessarily distinguish it [the sacred] from the profane', and by the destruction of distinctions between the sacred and profane achieved by their 'mere proximity'. The sacred/profane distinction is also clearly linked with the male/female dichotomy by Jay (1981: 40).

While Jay's A/B distinction appears to open itself to the possibility of something 'outside the restraints of dichotomy', it is precisely the powerful attraction of the A/Not-A paradigm which renders this attempted movement inadequate. Jay herself asserts that the male-female dichotomy is 'particularly susceptible' to an A/Not-A characterization although such a distinction is not necessary (Jay 1981: 43). Alterity, therefore, cannot be equated with Jay's attempted introduction of third, fourth, fifth etc. terms into a dichotomy envisaged as A/B. It must arise from the A/Not-A paradigm which is the socio-culturally susceptible formulation of dichotomy. For, while all dualities are not necessarily dichotomies, their mere characterization as pairs or binary divisions lends itself to socio-cultural dualism. Since it is very difficult to move back from this position, the concept of alterity is necessarily a movement beyond it. Given, then, that dichotomies are often, even generally, characterized dualistically, alterity is necessarily a movement beyond both duality and dualism.

Grosz defines alterity as a 'form of otherness...outside the binary opposition between self and other' (Grosz 1989: xiv). For her, dichotomy is completely in the province of A/Not-A perceived relations. The two elements of the dichotomy are envisaged as 'discrete', 'self-contained', 'mutually exclusive', and 'mutually exhaustive'. They are arranged in 'inherently non-reversible, non-reciprocal hierarchies' (Grosz 1989: xvi). Despite the apparent impossibility of such an enterprise, alterity is precisely the philosophical approach/tool which seeks to destabilize this clearly identified dichotomy, defying its logical rules of control. This approach does not necessarily obliterate the dichotomy, but it does seek to break its socio-cultural power by making its constructed nature obvious and by positing alternative constructions. Such alternatives include the reversal of the dichotomy, the movement of the negative term to be the condition of the positive term, and the subsequent envisaging of a term existing outside of the dichotomy, and being both A and Not-A, and neither (Grosz 1989: xv, xvii). Alterity is thus envisaged as a position, or more accurately, a multiplicity, which is simultaneously A, Not-A, both and neither: a 'form of otherness irreducible to and unable to be modelled on any form of projection of or identification with the subject'; 'outside of, unpredictable by and ontologically prior to the subject' (Grosz 1989: xiv).

Any definition of alterity is inherently tenuous because of its radical heterogeneity. As a position of heterogeneity, it has some links to the 'opposition itself' that occurs between dichotomous terms as identified by Jay in Durkheim's account of the distinction between the sacred and the profane. Even Jay uses this heterogeneity as an aspect of her argument for rejecting the dominance of the A/Not-A paradigm of dichotomy, albeit because of its apparent indescribability (Jay 1981: 40). Alterity is, in many senses, indescribable. It is a circumstance of generally unacknowledged and uncontainable diversity, and its 'existence' outside of established categories challenges even the very notion of that existence. Indeed, alterity challenges concepts of knowledge, identity and subjectivity as well.

Taylor asserts that the 'ceaseless oscillation' of 'altarity' calls into 'question every word and all language' (Taylor 1987: xxix). This destabilization of subjectivity, identity and knowledge is a key aspect of any attempted definition of the illusive nature of alterity for, in Grosz's words, alterity is 'outside of, unpredictable by and ontologically prior to the subject' (Grosz 1989: xiv). It is via the medium of the assumed autonomous subject that knowledge has been constructed in a modern Western framework. If alterity, as underlying or conditional to dichotomy, precedes the formation of identity or subjectivity, this destabilizes not only dichotomy but also meaning itself. Such a destabilization lays open the metaphysical and theological question of 'Truth'.

The terms *différance* and *jouissance* represent attempts by Jacques Derrida and Jacques Lacan respectively to approach the notion of alterity, first from a linguistic and second, from a psychoanalytic point of view.

Derrida and Différance

Différance is a Derridean neologism. Derived from the nouns, différence (difference) and différance (deferral), and the ambiguous verb, différer (to differ in space and to defer in time), différance is assigned a multi-layered meaning by Derrida (Bass in Derrida 1978: xvi). Derrida suggests four possible nuances to this multiplicity of layers. First, *différance* is a deferral of presence which simultaneously announces presence (Derrida 1981: 8). Second, *différance* is a differentiation between things which also exposes their similarity. Third, *différance* is the 'production' of the differences or divisions required for meaning or signification to be established (1981: 9). Fourth, *différance* is the 'unfolding of difference': the deconstruction of the distinctions which have been made, together with their 'ontico-ontological' significances; the unpacking of the meanings which have been constructed (1981: 10). This succinct fourfold statement of *différance* provides a useful framework for examining a broader exposition of the term which particularly concerns itself with the 'temporization' and 'spacing' of *différance* (1981: 18). The use of the terms 'temporization' and 'spacing' alludes, in part, to the defer/differ ambiguity.

First, *différance* is a deferral of presence which simultaneously announces presence (1981: 8). According to Derrida, the 'classically determined structure of the sign' is a substitute 'in place of the thing itself', be it either 'meaning or referent'. Initially, this assessment seems to reflect an equivocal use of the word 'sign'. It would seem far more appropriate to speak about the 'signifier' as standing in place of the 'signified'. This apparent, if not actual, equivocation signals Derrida's movement through and beyond structuralist categories where one entity stands in place of another. Indeed, for Derrida, such a 'classical semiology' makes 'the substitution of the sign for the thing itself...both *secondary* and *provisional*': secondary because it purports to refer to some original presence, and provisional because it somehow promises the reinstatement of that original presence. Yet, if the sign in its totality 'represents the present in its absence', it is the sign which establishes presence and it does so from a position of non-presence or a 'deferral of presence' (1981: 9). If presence is established through our linguistic arrangements, the moment of deferral contained in the act of signification is not the deferral of 'the originary and indivisible unity of a present possibility that I could reserve, like an expenditure that I would put off calculatedly or for reasons of economy'. It is a 'delay, delegation, reprieve, referral, detour, postponement, reserving' of something other than presence. Thus, what appears to defer presence 'is the very basis on which presence is announced' (1981: 8). *Différance*, the moment of deferral, can thus be regarded as the 'origin' of the sign as matched signifier and signified, and its presence presenting appearance (1981: 10).

The paradox of this element of deferral in *différance* is essential to its alterior nature. *Différance* is not a presence, nor is it an absence of something which could be present. Rather, it is a pre-existing moment/space of suspension which both challenges and makes possible the construction of any system of meaning. It is, therefore, presence, absence, both and neither: essentially indescribable and, thus, nonexistent, although its effects are evident.

Second, *différance* is a differentiation between things which also exposes their similarity. *Différance* produces differences which allow for the duality necessary for the establishment of meaning through the act of signification. The moment of deferral is a space which produces separations or divisions. This spatial moment is 'the common root of all the oppositional concepts', e.g. 'nature/culture' (1981: 9). As a common origin, *différance* exposes the similarity of the entities produced by separation and signification. It calls into question all notions of presence (1981: 10), exposing their sameness (1981: 9) in their dependence upon non-presence. Language is revealed as a system of 'only differences *without positive terms*': 'every concept is inscribed in a chain or in a system within which it refers to the other, to other concepts, by means of the systematic play of differences'. This play is *différance* (1981: 11).

In exploring this aspect of *différance*, Derrida suggests that, since presence is only established through signification, the basis of signification can only be a game of creating distinctions between signs. The process of signification is not one of definition based on a comparison with some real thing, e.g. person, place or concept. It is a conceptualization based on a comparison with other signs and their perceived meaning content. For example, the concept of 'love' is not simply an allocation of a group of letters to a pre-existing entity, it is the shaping of that concept as an entity by the other word-concepts with which it is contextually associated e.g. 'hate', 'like', 'prefer', 'want'. In the recognition of this process, all distinctions are exposed in their similarity as distinctions or differences.

The notion of language being an arrangement of terms which derive their meaning solely from their negative relations with, or differences from other terms, is an important aspect of the theoretical apparatus around Derrida's concept of *différance*. Language as dependent on the play of differences is 'a system in which the central signified, the original or transcendental signified, is never absolutely present outside a system of differences'. This 'absence of the transcendental signified', i.e. an absolutely defined or present entity, 'extends the domain and the play of signification infinitely'. For Derrida, the absence of the absolute brings about the rupture of the structurality of structure (1978: 280). It reveals the transient and tenuous nature of the arbitrary constructions of language. For example, in relation to the nature-culture opposition pursued by Lévi-Strauss, once the limitations of that opposition are recognized, two responses are possible: the systematic and rigorous questioning of these concepts; and the maintenance of them as disposable tools. Derrida attributes the latter course of action to Lévi-Strauss (1978: 282–84). Within the former, the recognition of the play of differences constituted in language becomes the basis for deconstructing the processes of language production and, thereby, language itself. 'Play is the disruption of presence' (1978: 292).

Third then for Derrida, *différance* is the 'production' of the differences or divisions required for meaning or signification to be established (1981: 9). *Différance* is the play of differences. This play called *différance* is the 'movement according to which language, any code, any system of referral in general, is constituted "historically" as a weave of differences' (1981: 12). Differences are the 'effects of *différance*'. They are the primary, negative relations which produce images of identity. Presence and identity are thus understood to exist on the basis of absence and difference or distinction, i.e. on the foundation of 'all that is *not it*' (Grosz 1989: 27). Differences and their resulting systems of signification are 'neither inscribed in the heavens, nor in the brain' (Derrida 1981: 9). They are neither ontologically nor biologically determined. They are produced 'historically' although this does not mean that *différance* is 'simple', 'unmodified' or 'in-different' (1981: 11).

'*Différance* is the non-full, non-simple, structured and differentiating origin of differences.' Indeed, its complexity is such that the designation 'origin' for Derrida is problematic (1981: 11): 'To say that *différance* is originary is simultaneously to erase the myth of a present origin'. *Différance* as origin cannot be understood as a concrete place, point or thing from which all else emerges. In a sense, it is an origin which has been '*crossed out*'. This 'crossing-out' signifies that *différance* is not an 'original plentitude'. 'It is a non-origin which is originary' (Derrida 1978: 203).

The word-play of Derrida's explanations attempts a mimicking and parody of the play which is *différance*. Via this word-play, the processes of language and meaning construction are interrogated and exposed. *Différance* is revealed as the producer of differences and therefore signification, and as the production process itself, but its own fragility as construction is also recognized in the assertion that, in a certain sense, it 'is not' (Derrida 1982: 21). *Différance* has no existence of its own and cannot be confused with any attempt to define an absolute, e.g. 'Truth'. The play of differences, the play that is *différance*, does not seek to decipher 'a truth or an origin which escapes play and the order of the sign'. Rather, it 'affirms play and tries to pass beyond man [sic] and humanism', rejecting the dream of 'full presence, the reassuring foundation, the origin and end of play' and opting for 'a world of signs without fault, without truth, and without origin' (Derrida 1978: 292). The play of *différance* rejects the metaphysical or 'theological certainty' of truth (1978: 10), decentring the notion of absolute presence (1978: 292). In this respect, it is a 'pre-opening of the ontic-ontological difference', Derrida's fourth definition of *différance* (1978: 198).

The radical nature of this 'non-originary origin' is remarkable. As the site of the production of that which is necessary for meaning, *différance* is given an identity. Yet in the positing of this 'site' prior to meaning, its identity is removed. There is a sense in which *différance* is a place, an entity, and a process which is none of these because such descriptions rely on the very construction processes for which *différance* is the apparent source, unidentifiable as it may be. The moment that the concept of *différance* appears to be well-described is the moment when *différance* will have slipped from the describer's grasp. Such is the illusive and arbitrary nature of any description. Logically, therefore, *différance* is not simply the source of differences and meaning, but also the site of the deconstruction of these.

Hence, fourth, for Derrida, *différance* is the 'unfolding of difference': the deconstruction of the distinctions which have been made together with their 'ontico-ontological' significances; the unpacking of the meanings which have been constructed (1981: 10). *Différance* is a movement beyond (and before) the established ontological difference between Being and being. This movement seems a large 'metaphysical' jump. Nevertheless, it directly arises from the thinking which precedes it about signification and differences. A philosophical and metaphysical distinction between Being and being, or 'presence and the present' (Derrida 1982: 23) is established in the process of signification based on the '*differential character* of the sign' (1982: 10). Signs make present aspects of a presence which is presumed to be preexisting. This 'ontological difference' (1982: 23) is the product of the play of differences which occurs in the process of signification. *Différance*, as outside of, originary to and somehow preceding and exceeding these differences, calls into question this metaphysical presupposition: 'it is the determination of Being as presence or as beingness that is interrogated by the thought of *différance*'. All notions of the present and of presence are called into question by the play which is *différance* for '*différance* is not. It is not a present being' (1982: 21). Neither is *différance* the 'truth of Being' for, 'in a certain and very strange way', *différance* is 'older' than the truth of Being (1982: 22), '"Older" than Being itself'. *Différance* 'is not a name'. It is 'not a pure nominal unity' since it 'unceasingly dislocates itself in a chain of differing and deferring substitutions' (1982: 26). *Différance* is a 'radical alterity' (1982: 21). 'Not only is there no kingdom of *différance*, but *différance* instigates the subversion of every kingdom' (1982: 22). *Différance* is 'not an ineffable Being'. In this sense, it is not 'God' (1982: 26). Technically, it is unnameable, although this 'unnameable is the play which makes possible nominal effects' (1982: 26–27).

Derrida's concept of *différance* challenges all notions of absolutes and ideals. Specifically, therefore, it challenges notions such as 'Truth', the 'Good' and the 'Right'. Such concepts are deeply embedded in Western philosophy. A confrontation with their validity is also a confrontation with the entirety of the socio-linguistic structures which have cast them as 'eternal' presences or discernible entities. This confrontation is, naturally, a major challenge to Western epistemology and the ontology implied therein.

Différance *and Deconstruction*

In an attempt to paraphrase the complexity of Derrida's concept, Taylor describes *différance* thus: 'Though *différance* is the condition of the possibility of presence and absence, as well as being and nonbeing, it is neither present nor absent, neither is nor is not' (Taylor 1987: 277). In Derridean terms, this radical alterity of presence, absence, both and neither is indicated by a graphical play on the word 'is'. *Différance* is both 'i̶s̶' and 'i̶s̶' crossed out.[1] *Différance* is 'what makes possible the presentation of the being-present', although 'it is never presented as such'. In this manner, it 'exceeds the order of truth', 'but without dissimulating itself as something, as a mysterious being, in the occult of a nonknowledge or in a hole with indeterminable borders' (Derrida 1982: 6). Jean-Louis Houdebine, one of the interviewers in *Positions* (Derrida 1981), reflects on Derrida's notion of an 'irreducible alterity' as a 'motif of heterogeneity', the 'basic dialectical materialist contradiction' where 'any reappropriation-interiorization-idealization-*relève* in a becoming of Meaning' is exceeded (1981: 92). The ambivalent nature of this Derridean 'irreducible alterity' destabilizes assumptions about meaning, perspective and truth. It thereby questions the nature of human subjectivity, identity and knowledge. In Grosz's words, 'To recognize that identity depends on difference, and that presence relies on absence is to disturb the very structure of knowledges' (Grosz 1989: 27). The acknowledgement of alterity disturbs the duality identified by structuralism by exposing duality as a construction based on something which precedes and indeed exceeds its follower.

When the structure of knowledge, which is potentially subverted by *différance*, is understood to be 'implicitly patriarchal' by reason of its differential play, i.e. 'the oppositional structure' 'between men and non-men', *différance* presents the possibility of a deconstruction of that ideological domination as well (Grosz 1989: 37) and other ideological dominations based on varying dualities, e.g. racial distinctions such as white/non-white.

---

1. While this negation and double negation of 'i̶s̶' and 'i̶s̶' crossed out appears inaccurate, when the concept of the 'non-originary origin' is retained, the necessity of the double negation is apparent. There is no primal 'isness' which requires crossing out, only an 'i̶s̶' that must be negated as soon as it is posited for fear that it might be mistaken for an 'is'.

For Derrida, this deconstruction occurs through the critique of logocentrism or idealism (Derrida 1981: 51). Logocentrism is the ideological domination of the order of language and meaning, the *logos*. Such domination is achieved by a process of repression. The 'deconstruction of logocentrism' requires 'the analysis of historical repression and suppression of writing since Plato' for it is this repression which has established 'the origin of philosophy as *epistēmē*' and 'truth as the unity of *logos* and *phonē*' (Derrida 1978: 196). The act of writing, which for Derrida embodies within itself the multiplicity of *différance*, offers the possibility of challenging this nexus established between the spoken word and truth. The 'repression of writing' is the 'the repression of that which threatens presence and the mastering of absence' (p. 197), the repression of *différance*. The representation of writing as a possible disrupter of ideological domination and liberator of *différance* presents the possibility of a type of writing that will expose dualistic sociolinguistic constructions by showcasing the 'otherness' of language and patriarchal ideological domination by a privileging of the 'other' in the men/non-men and parallel dichotomies.

Grosz describes logocentrism as the presumption 'that being, language, knowledge are self-evident, neutral and transparent terms'. Deconstruction attempts to problematize 'logocentric discourses' (Grosz 1989: 28) by both explaining the nature of their binary structures and seeking to displace their effects (Grosz 1989: 29). For Derrida, such a 'general strategy of deconstruction' seeks to avoid the false neutralization of binary oppositions which merely allows for a continued residency 'within the closed field of these oppositions' (Derrida 1981: 41). Such a strategy can only be managed from within the discourse of logocentrism itself (Grosz 1989: 29). 'The incision of deconstruction ... does not take place just anywhere, or in an absolute elsewhere.' Necessarily, 'it can be made only according to lines of force and forces of rupture that are localizable in the discourse to be deconstructed' (Derrida 1981: 82). While the deconstructive potential of *différance* challenges the product of signification, it is only from within the process of signification that such a challenge is able to be attempted.

Grosz describes this strategy of deconstruction as a 'three-fold intervention into the metaphysical structures of binary oppositions' (1989: xv). For Derrida, it is a 'double gesture': '"*La double séance*," a double science'. This 'double gesture' consists of two movements: a reversal and a displacement (Derrida 1981: 41). For Grosz, Derrida's twofold movement is really threefold because of the advent of a third term in the process of reversal and displacement (Grosz 1989: xv). For Derrida, the nature of this third term, a variation on the theme of *différance*, is such that it does not exist. Hence the double play is the key motif of deconstruction, not any posited material outcome. This double play is described by Derrida as 'a writing that is in and of itself multiple' (1981: 41).

The first dimension of this double play is in Grosz's words 'the strategic reversal of binary terms' with the negative term becoming the positive term and vice versa (Grosz 1989: xv). For Derrida, this process of reversal or 'phase of *overturning*' is necessary in order to 'do justice' to the 'violent hierarchy' of 'classical philosophical opposition[s]'. 'One of the two terms governs the other.' Therefore, the deconstruction of the opposition must first 'overturn the hierarchy'. For example, using the men/non-men dichotomy, the term 'non-men' is highlighted in a context where logocentric patriarchy prevails. 'To overlook this phase of overturning is to forget the conflictual and subordinating structure of opposition.' The danger of such an overlooking is a too quick procession to the type of false neutralization previously mentioned, where the issues of ideological power remain unaddressed. The overturning of an established hierarchy leaves a point of 'hold on the previous opposition'. This hold allows for the possibility of intervention in the field of signification in which that opposition participates (Derrida 1981: 41). Since 'the hierarchy of dual oppositions always reestablishes itself', the necessity of operating 'on the terrain of and from within the deconstructed system' is evident (Derrida 1981: 42). The strength of the tendency towards dualism is a constant force against deconstruction. It is thus only by a programme of subversion from within the paradigm of signification that any opening of that system may be attained. By focusing on the term 'non-men' and exposing its arbitrary positioning, the duality of which it is a part is addressed within its own system in a manner which both pays homage to the *logos* and calls into question its results.

The second procedure in the process of Derridean deconstruction as described by Grosz is the displacement of the originally negative term 'from its dependent position' by revealing it to be 'the very condition of the positive term' (Grosz 1989: xv). This displacement exposes the construction of concepts as an exercise in delineating differences and as an activity founded in *différance*. For example, in the men/non-men dichotomy, the construction of 'men' is shown to rely on the construction of what is 'non-men', i.e. what is 'other'. In the process, the arbitrariness of such constructions, based in differentials, is revealed and the 'truth' of language is disclosed. For Derrida, this 'biphase' is 'the interval between inversion, which brings low what was high, and the irruptive emergence of a new "concept"'. It occurs outside the logocentric text. It is, therefore, 'impossible to *point* it out' (Derrida 1981: 42). It is a moment of suspension outside of signification that exists between one order of signification and the next which re-asserts itself in the vacuum of the disruption caused by deconstruction, re-establishing the same principles of sociolinguistic construction, if with slightly different nuances. Exposure of the arbitrary construction of concepts produces a moment where all meaning is momentarily lost. This moment exists outside signification, i.e. constructed meaning.

The 'irruptive emergence of a new "concept"' is in some senses the revaluing of the 'Not-A' term of the dichotomy, the absence which establishes the presence of the apparently positive 'A' term. In other ways, this is an inadequate description of the peculiar complexity of *différance*. It is easy to understand Grosz's division of this second aspect of Derrida's framework of deconstruction. Yet, the new or third term described by Grosz as being somehow created or discovered in the process of deconstruction is for Derrida not a third term at all. This non-existent third term is '*both* and *neither* of the binary terms' (Grosz 1989: xv). It 'exists' outside of the order of signification in the moment of suspension made possible by the second gesture of deconstruction.

One of the words used for this third term by Derrida is *différance*, a position of both and neither identity and difference (Derrida 1981: 30). Other partially equivalent terms include '*pharmakon*' which 'is neither remedy nor poison, neither good nor evil, neither the inside nor the outside, neither speech nor writing'; the '*supplement*' which 'is neither a plus nor a minus, neither an outside nor the complement of an inside, neither accident nor essence, etc.'; the '*hymen*' which 'is neither confusion nor distinction, neither identity nor difference, neither consummation nor virginity, neither the veil nor unveiling, neither the inside nor the outside, etc.'; and the '*gram*' which 'is neither a signifier nor a signified, neither a sign nor a thing, neither a presence nor an absence, neither a position nor a negation, etc.' (Derrida 1981: 43). This list is not exhaustive although it does give some indication of the variety of ways in which Derrida seeks to explore the complexity which is for him *différance*. A further name for alterity in Derrida's work is 'woman' (Grosz 1989: 29). Certainly, the type of writing envisaged as participating in the disruptive process is somehow 'feminine' in the face of the 'masculine' logocentric domination of the order of signification. These gender/sex nominations are implicitly related to the psychoanalytic roots of poststructuralism. For that reason, they are considered further below.

Différance, as the moment and space preceding the construction of meaning, is entirely elusive to full description and entirely necessary in the construction process. Yet, its exposure exposes the arbitrary and fragile nature of the structures of meaning by uncovering the non-existent base upon which they are understood to stand. This is the peculiar nature of the alterity of *différance*.

Lacan and Jouissance

In Lacanian terms, *jouissance* is more the indicator of the presence of alterity, than alterity itself, although the possibility of *jouissance* presents the potential (if not actuality) of the alterity of both discourse (spoken)[2] and subjectivity (human agency) being recognized, claimed and enjoyed—albeit transiently. According to Kurzweil, *jouissance* is the goal of Lacanian analysis (1980: 153). For Lacan, *jouissance* is the 'motive' of the 'being of *signifiance*' (Lacan in Mitchell & Rose 1982: 142). It is that which underlies the whole of the activity of signification and its identity-producing results.

Signification

Signification, for Lacan, is more than the process of forming language, it is also the process of gaining identity or subjectivity. The process of gaining subjectivity mirrors the process of developing language because of a split in subjectivity which parallels the split which is established in language between the signified and the signifier. This

2.   Lacan, as a psychoanalyst, privileges speech, particularly the speech of the psychoanalyst's client or analysand. This privileging of speech by Lacan in part reflects the emphasis on the spoken word assured by the psychoanalytic process. It also signifies the variant interpretations of the functions of speech and writing as envisaged by Lacan in contrast to Derrida.

split is achieved in human subjectivity via a two-stage process: the mirror stage and the Oedipus Complex which introduces the notion of castration.

The 'mirror stage' is a phase which occurs very early in a child's development, somewhere between the ages of six and eighteen months. This early period of development is also described by Lacan as the '*infans* stage', a time when the child is 'still sunk in his [sic] motor incapacity and nursling dependency'. During the mirror stage, the child begins to assume the basic elements necessary for establishing its own subjectivity or presence in the human world. This subjectivity is achieved by the child first procuring for itself an image of itself in its context. Significantly, the child recognizes its own body-image in a mirror. It also recognizes an image of its own identity in the behaviour of its primary caregiver, usually the mother. The child thus assumes a 'specular' or intermediate identity by assuming an image, an *imago*, received from a process of reflection (Lacan 1977: 1–2). This experience is preparatory and related to the 'social determination' (1977: 2) of a child's individual agency via its identification with the image of a 'counterpart' or 'other' outside of itself (1977: 5). In identifying its own image, the child separates that image from the other images which share the reflection. The child does not, however, separate itself from its own image, but experiences itself as somehow divided or fragmented (1977: 6). Lacan refers to this fragmentation as a 'pregnancy' since the identity of the child has not reached 'its alienating destination' (1977: 2). The subjectivity of the child is still in the process of gestation. The mirror stage is an important stage in this process but it is only a stage.

One of the key aspects of the mirror stage, for Lacan, is the development of an imaginary 'I' or 'Ideal-I' by the child through this early process of reflection and identification. This 'I' is retained by the child as its self-conscious image. Through this retention, 'the agency of the ego' or self-concept is established. The ego is destined to carry the child's subjective identity but, at this point, it represents a 'primordial form' of identity which occurs before the advent of the functional subject. It is however an 'irreducible' element of the process of signification or the gaining of identity and language (1977: 2). This preliminary development of a self-concept introduces a fragmentation into the child's experience. The fragmentation or alienation is necessary for the development of a socially workable identity.

The fragmentation, which is described by Lacan as being of the 'body', is observed by him to surface in the dreams of his clients in the form of 'disjointed limbs' and hybrid images of internal body organs sprouting arms or wings. The 'formation of the *I*' is symbolized in the language of dreams through the imagery of 'two opposed fields of contest', e.g. 'a fortress, or a stadium—its inner arena and enclosure, surrounded by marshes and rubbish-tips'. The inner fortifications stand for the 'id' or subconscious/preconscious from which the emerging subject is alienated by the advent of the 'I' and its instigation of 'a relation between the organism and its reality' (Lacan 1977: 4–5). In the mirror stage, then, a distinction is created between the Imaginary world of the ego or self-concept, and the Real world of the id or impenetrable preconscious and undivided self. This distinction, for Lacan, is 'a temporal dialectic that decisively projects the formation of the individual into history'. The mirror stage 'manufactures for the subject' a 'succession of phantasies' which moves from the 'fragmented body-image' towards the 'assumption of the armour of an alienating identity': from 'insufficiency to anticipation' (Lacan 1977: 4). The mirror stage is anticipatory of the full subjectivity of the individual.

That the period of the mirror stage is also the period of the child's emerging separation from its mother is also significant for Lacan. The separation occurring in the child's subjectivity mirrors the separation which occurs between mother and child. This mirroring explains in part why the fragmentation of the child's body-image is aligned with the image of pregnancy. It also sets the scene for Lacan's identification of 'the woman'.

In the second stage of Lacan's process for the development of human subjectivity, the rupture is more (although not completely) permanently achieved. This is also the stage where sexual identities are determined by their relationship to the split. Before this second stage is outlined, it is useful to note that in the mirror stage, according to Lacan, the child perceives its identity as separate enough from the mother to perceive that she 'contains' something and desires something. This something is, for Lacan, the phallus. The child, in attempting to retain its relationship with the mother, tries to become the phallus, its perceived concept of that which its mother desires. The child's identity is governed by its perception of what the mother wants (Lacan in Mitchell & Rose 1982: 83). This question of what the mother wants, what 'the woman' wants is a key psychoanalytic question which puzzles Freud and fascinates Lacan. It is this question which guides Lacan's examination of feminine *jouissance* (Lacan in Mitchell & Rose 1982: 151) and causes him to raise questions about the characterization of the relation between girls and the Oedipus Complex (Lacan in Mitchell & Rose 1982: 86–98).

The Oedipus Complex represents the termination of the mirror stage and the subsequent 'deflection of the specular *I* into the social *I*'. This 'drama of primordial jealousy' (Lacan 1977: 5–6) is inaugurated via the intervention of a third term into the duality perceived between mother and child, and the subsequent 'castration', 'split' or 'rupture' which is achieved by this intervention. Lacan's parental and biological references should not be understood too concretely. The 'mother', as much as anything, is the presubjective state from which the child's subjectivity is emerging; similarly, 'father' is a concretized image of a more generalized concept. The third term introduced into the previous duality is variously described as the Father, the Name of the Father, the Law, the Symbolic Order, or simply the Symbolic. The 'necessity of the myth underlying the structuring of the Oedipus complex' for characterizing this process of developing subjectivity shows, for Lacan, the impossibility of reducing the psychoanalytical terminology to 'biological factors'. The use of the story itself betrays any possibility of the biological references being overly concretized (Lacan 1982: 75). Essentially then, the image of the father represents the realm of socio-cultural and linguistic meaning, the 'order' of being into which the child as subject is born (Lacan 1977: 103). The sexual identity of this subject is determined by its relation to the phallus, an imaginary rather than a biological organ.

The Phallus

Lacan acknowledges the difficulty that the term and the image interpose into analytical discourse. The phallus as 'signifier' can be regarded as being 'chosen as what stands out as most easily seized upon in the real of sexual copulation'. It is the '(logical) copula' or link as well as 'the most symbolic in the literal (typographical) sense of the term' (Lacan in Mitchell & Rose 1982: 82). Its relationship to the penis, metaphorically and metonymically, is both necessary and problematic. It is necessary because of the very clear split in sexual identities which is observed to occur during the process of the development of human subjectivity. For Lacan, this clear split is governed by a distinction between having and being the 'phallus': the male identity 'has' the phallus; the female identity is the 'phallus' (1982: 84). The 'unconscious castration complex has the function of a knot': 'by installing in the subject an unconscious position without which he [sic] would be unable to identify with the ideal type of his [sic] sex' (1982: 75). The rupture in subjectivity which allows the individual to acquire a position in the realm of signification via the phallus also accords a sexual identity to the newly cut subjectivity via its relation to the phallus. The male identity has that which is required for operation in the realm of subjectivity, i.e. the phallus. The female identity will 'masquerade' as the phallus. The phallus thus becomes the key signifier of the split subjectivity which is necessary for identity in the socio-cultural realm.

As an imaginary organ, the 'phallus' is definitively related to the realm of signification. For Lacan, 'the phallus is the privileged signifier of that mark where the share of the logos is wedded to the advent of desire' (Lacan in Mitchell & Rose 1982: 82). The term 'logos' in this context is a broad reference to the whole of the linguistic or 'symbolic' order: the complex construction of language and culture which provides an individual's meaning context. The entry into, or 'sharing' of, this symbolic order is a necessary stage in the development of identity, i.e. of human subjectivity. This entry however is marked by a split which institutes a state of desire for a return to the pre-ruptured condition. This desire, which is insatiable, is displaced onto objects which come to represent, without making present, the realm of pre-signification. Alan Sheridan describes Lacanian desire '(fundamentally in the singular)' as the 'perpetual effect of symbolic articulation'. It is not to be coordinated 'with the object that would seem to satisfy it', i.e. the signifier of that from which it is separated, 'but with the object that causes it', i.e. the split or rupture signified by the phallus (Sheridan in Lacan 1977: viii).

But signifiers do not have referential signifieds. The phallus, like all signifiers, is without a signified. As the primary symbol of the phallologocentric order, it stands for nothing other than that the realm of signification exists: 'For it is to this signified that it is given to designate as a whole the effect of there being a signified, inasmuch as it conditions any such effect by its presence as signifier' (Lacan in Mitchell & Rose 1982: 80). The phallus as signifier is empty because the subjectivity it purports to represent is non-existent. The phallus thus represents a lack. The split subjectivity that permits the individual to participate in the realm of signification institutes the desire to overcome that lack and the phallus becomes the 'signifier of the desire of the Other' (1982: 84). The order of the phallus is signified by the phallic 'I'. The subjective position of the 'I' is achieved through a process of 'fundamental alienation' or separation, which leaves a sense of lack (Lacan 1977: 42). That lack, and the desire to relieve it, is represented by the term which also represents the separation, the pronoun 'I' or the phallus. For Lacan, the 'whole of human knowledge' is mediated through this state of desire. This makes the position of the 'I', a very vulnerable situation (Lacan 1977: 5) although it always maintains for itself 'the illusion of autonomy' (1977: 6).

~~The~~ Woman

The 'I' is an imaginary position predicated on a subjectivity far more complex than can be recognized in the realm of signification. This complexity is symbolized in the Lacanian concept of ~~the~~ woman. For Lacan, 'there is woman only as excluded by the nature of things which is by the nature of words'. ~~The~~ woman is that which is outside the realm of signification. This is the Real, the preexistent unruptured subjectivity which is nonexistent because it cannot be signified. The 'status of *the* woman' is as 'being not all' (Lacan in Mitchell & Rose 1982: 144). Jacqueline Rose suggests that Lacan shows how the 'status of the phallus' defines the woman as 'simultaneously symptom and myth', fundamentally relegated outside of the Symbolic. This relegation is the source of much criticism of Lacan's position, although Rose defends Lacan by asserting that psychoanalysis 'does not produce that definition' but rather 'gives an account of how that definition is produced' (1982: 57). It is also the source of some hope for challenging the logocentric dominance of the Symbolic sphere.

If the Symbolic is dominated by the phallus (and all of its related masculine constructions), but predicated on the Real (which is constructed in language as the feminine other), then the 'non-existence' of ~~the~~ woman is a means by which the Symbolic is challenged through the transgression of the Real into the Symbolic in the various gaps and spaces available. This transgression, a movement between two brinks which produces the Imaginary, results in the cry of *jouissance* of the pain and pleasure of such a transgression. This movement both participates in the Symbolic, and reminds the Symbolic of its underside. In so doing, it challenges the identities created within the Symbolic, suggesting that there is always more to that which is constructed. In one sense, this movement from the Real into the Symbolic is the process of signification itself. In another, it is a challenge to signification by its exposure of that process. The 'I' is always split, divided, more than '1'. Subjectivity is challenged. In Mark C. Taylor's interpretation of Lacan, the 'beyond' or the '*au-delà*' of the pleasure principle is the cry of 'The Woman', a transgression that produces *jouissance* (Taylor 1987: 112). *Jouissance*, i.e. the *jouissance* of the woman, is thus defined as the fundamental motivation or impetus for the development of human subjectivity or the being of signification. Because of this, it is also the site of the exodus of identity: 'To experience *jouissance* is to suffer loss—the loss of desire that exposes the impossibility of satisfaction' (Taylor 1987: 113).

Jouissance is that by which 'we are played' (Lacan in Mitchell & Rose 1982: 142). It is the painful enjoyment of the oscillation underlying signification and subjectivity which ensures an engagement in the realm of signification predicated on an awareness of the realities of signification. Such an aware engagement arises from an encounter with the radical alterity which withstands constant attempts at representation because it stands outside the realm of signification. It is an encounter sited in the very unconscious processes which structuralism identified as being so crucial to the formation of language and therefore meaning.

Alterity, the Woman and Jouissance

The primary meaning of the French term '*jouissance*' is pleasure or enjoyment. This pleasure is associated with the enjoyment of action (e.g. pleasure in serving another), the use of privileges or rights, and the possession of property or position, i.e. 'tenure'. A further emphasis extends the enjoyment of property connotation by reference to the benefits forthcoming from the possession of property, e.g. financial dividends. Jane Gallop refers to one of the alternative definitions of *jouissance*, 'usufruct', to suggest that the key element of *jouissance* for Lacan is not ownership, but use and enjoyment of something which cannot be exchanged (Gallop 1982: 50). In the context of language and identity, *jouissance* is the outcome of the use of the various elements that produce meaning and subjectivity.

Significantly, *jouissance* is not *pure* pleasure. Freud relates pleasure and unpleasure to 'the quantity of excitation': 'unpleasure corresponds to an *increase* in the quantity of excitation and pleasure to a *diminution*' (Freud 1955: 8). Other 'forces or circumstances' work to delay the receiving of pleasure (1955: 9). For example, the 'reality principle', a concept related to the 'ego's instincts of self-preservation', effects the postponement of pleasure: 'the abandonment of a number of possibilities of gaining satisfaction and the temporary toleration of unpleasure as a step on the long indirect road to pleasure' (1955: 10). Following from this, he points to a notion of something 'beyond the pleasure principle' which coincides with elements of the Lacanian notion of *jouissance*. Freud notes the presence of 'a peculiar tension' which may be either pleasurable or unpleasurable. This note is coupled with an observation that 'life instincts' seem somehow related to the production of tensions while 'death instincts' seem to be served by the pleasure principle (1955: 63). The distinction between the 'beyond pleasure' life instincts and the 'pleasure' of death instincts relates to a correlation between pleasure, fulfilment, stasis and therefore death. For Freud, the remarks about something 'beyond the pleasure principle' heralded a new area of exploration in psychoanalysis (1955: 64). Kristeva specifically develops the notion of *jouissance* post-Lacan as something which traverses a passage between the 'two brinks' of pain and pleasure indicating not simply an enjoyment of use but a 'mastery' (Kristeva 1980: x).

That such a mastery is specifically associated with 'the Woman' and an experience of excess which is 'supplementary' and 'beyond the phallus' (Lacan in Mitchell & Rose 1982: 144–45) presents the very clear possibility that attending to it will challenge the phallologocentric order of meaning and signification via a confrontation with something that exists outside of that order, thereby introducing into identity and subjectivity a recognition of ambiguity and multiplicity. Thus, 'Woman' functions 'as a point upon which the text turns upon itself...a metaphoric textual infrastructure that displaces, defers and delays the various logocentric commitments to an identity, substance or identity' (Grosz 1989: 33).

Alterity is both that on which subjects are predicated and that which challenges the very notion of subjectivity. In the realm of the Symbolic, it is often cast in feminine imagery. This casting affects not only the non-subjectivity of women in language, but also the possibility that the entry of women/woman into language is a transgression which has the capacity to disrupt the Symbolic and bring about certain alterations, albeit momentary, to the dominant order. A focus on the subjectivity, or more accurately subjectiv*ies*, *multiple* subjectivity and *non*-subjectivity, of 'woman' challenges the dominant, universalistic and patriarchal subjectivity, demanding an understanding of identity that encompasses ambiguity, and is attentive to the cry of *jouissance*.

Such an attentiveness requires an attendance to the gaps and spaces in language and identity where the vacillation of the unconscious processes of meaning and subjectivity are manifest. Discontinuity in discourse—'impediment, failure, split', something which 'stumbles' in a 'spoken or written sentence'—is where the unconscious is revealed (Lacan 1978: 25). For Lacan, it is through such gaps that contact 'with a real' may be made (1978: 22) and the 'dealienation of the subject' is conceivable (1977: 90). In these gaps, 'desire' is uncovered (1977: 28) as premised on the split or rupture of identity and the corresponding sense of 'lack' associated with subjectivity (1977: 26). Through such an uncovering, alterity emerges and subjectivity as unitary and singular is challenged.

Conclusion

The concepts of *différance* and *jouissance*, and the term associated with both, alterity, raise a number of issues in relation to poststructuralist theory and its application to philosophical/theological problems:

1. The nature of subjectivity as envisaged in a poststructuralist context.
2. The constitution of sexual identity within such a framework.
3. The role and value of the practice of signification.
4. The differential basis of the ideology of patriarchy.
5. The ideological subversive possibilities of a radical alterity.
6. The implications of all this for any understanding of epistemology.

Poststructuralism challenges a number of foundational aspects of Western philosophical and theological thought. Its confrontation with established categories of presence is epitomized in the concept of alterity and the concomitant encounter with that which exists beyond dichotomy and dualism.

Chapter 5

THE CRY OF AMBIGUITY:
JOUISSANCE AS HERMENEUTICAL BIRTH

Introduction

Poststructuralism shatters the notion of singular and unitary subjectivity by its attendance to the alterity or 'otherness' of language and identity. A key aspect of the process of such shattering is the deliberate intention to move beyond the dualities identified by structuralism, and further explored by poststructuralism, in language and culture. In the context of poststructuralism, *jouissance*, the painful enjoyment of the movement beyond duality and singular, unitary identity, is the product of a confrontation with alterity, the unconfined 'other' component of language and identity which underlies all signification. Because such otherness is 'abjectified' in language, a confrontation with alterity entails an encounter with the 'abject' in language. Such a confrontation produces a disruption of phallologocentrism, 'a singular and unified conceptual order' predicated on the masculine subject as normative (Grosz 1989: xix, xx). It presents the possibility of a type of discourse that openly displays the oscillating manufacturing processes of signification, and the ambiguous nature of subjectivity. *Jouissance* is thus achieved through certain kinds of discourses.

This chapter argues that *jouissance* is not only the product of certain kinds of discourse, but also an appropriate hermeneutical goal for the interpretation of discourse where the aim of that interpretation is an interaction with the otherness embodied within the discourse being interpreted. That is, *jouissance* can be the outcome of a particular kind of re-production of discourse where the otherness or alterity of the original discourse is highlighted. In order to pursue this argument, I develop the notion of *jouissance* as the product of a confrontation with an abject alterity using the work of Julia Kristeva. For Kristeva, *jouissance* is a 'joying in the truth of self-division' (Kristeva 1982: 89): a discursive expression which hovers between/beyond identity and non-identity via an implicit recognition of the dual forces of language and subjectivity—the symbolic and semiotic modalities of language. As a hermeneutical goal, such an expression would be the aim of a hermeneutical method which seeks the presence of alterity within a discourse, e.g. a biblical text. Because Kristeva's description of discourses which exemplify *jouissance* is 'poetic language', such a hermeneutical method might be called 'poetic reading'.

A hermeneutical method of 'poetic reading' seeks to articulate a subjectivity within a text which is neither singular nor unitary, but rather conforms to Kristeva's notion of *le sujet en procès*: a subjectivity in process/on trial rather than solidified or singularly represented. Kristeva specifically regards such subjectivity as belonging to the discourse of early Christianity and to the texts of Louis-Ferdinand Céline. Both these examples achieve such expressions of subjectivity via confrontations with an otherness which is at first described as 'abject' and then incorporated into the concept of the self in order that a new kind of subjectivity is produced: one which does not require the rigid distinctions that ensure the maintenance of an identity for 'one's own clean and proper body' (*le corps propre*), but which produces a type of subjectivity which is 'changed, adulterated', a 'being for the other' (*un être altéré*) (Roudiez in Kristeva 1982: vii-viii; Kristeva 1982: 53-54, 101-103); a subjectivity that is aware of its own fragility and the 'otherness' on which it is dependent.

In developing an argument for *jouissance* as a hermeneutical goal rather than a discursive product, I will offer some suggestions on reading a biblical text identified by Kristeva as *not* embodying *jouissance*. These suggestions attempt to identify something of the ambiguous subjectivity of *le sujet en procès* within that text, thereby rendering an interpretation which seeks *jouissance* although the text itself may not be regarded as expressing it without such reading strategies. The text under consideration is the biblical book of Revelation. Revelation is identified by Kristeva as belonging to the discursive genre of apocalypse. The strong dualities of the genre of apocalypse are contrasted by Kristeva with the paradoxical cry of 'apocalyptic laughter': an expression of a subjectivity which confronts the abyss threatened by apocalypse but, recognizing the arbitrary nature of the construction of its horror, is unafraid to face the chasm of apparent meaninglessness for the sake of its own 'truth'. This laughter is an expression of the discourse of the 'abjection of self': 'the culminating form of that experience of the subject to which it is revealed that all its objects are based merely on the inaugural *loss* that laid the foundations of its own being' (Kristeva 1982: 5). I will suggest that the identified text may be read in such a way that its 'otherness' will be highlighted and its meaning shattered and multiplied to allow for interpretations that legitimize the diversity and ambiguity of identity, rather than uphold the rigidity of the dualities embodied therein as a feature of its status as an apocalypse—the account of a cataclysmic confrontation between the forces of good and evil in the face of the threat of violent destruction.

The movement from the use of *jouissance* as an evaluative measure to its use as an interpretative goal is both feminist and Kristevan. It is in keeping with Kristeva's framework since:

1. The dual elements of language, the symbolic and the semiotic, are regarded as present in most, if not all, discourse;
2. Kristeva herself suggests that once the play of these elements has been identified in certain discourses, it may also be identified in others;
3. The reproduction of discourse is, in fact, simply another discursive production; and
4. It can be argued that the process in which Kristeva is engaged is itself interpretative not simply evaluative.

It is feminist because:

- The suggested method of poetic reading seeks to disrupt the phallologocentric order; and
- Whereas, in Kristeva's assessment of the exemplary discourse of poetic language, the examples are the products of male authors confronting the 'otherness' of language characterized as feminine, in the context of poetic reading, it is necessarily the 'other' sex who must be introduced into the reading of a phallologocentric discourse in order that *jouissance* might be achieved.

The Jouissance *of Poetic Language*

Conceptually, *jouissance*, for Kristeva, is a balancing act between 'two brinks' (1980: x). These two brinks are the dual modalities of language and identity—the semiotic and the symbolic—developments of the

Lacanian concepts of the Real and the Symbolic. The semiotic is the prelinguistic, presubjective realm which precedes and undergirds all identity and meaning: it is alterity. It is a place of oscillation, fluctuation and potential but unattained identity—the 'site' of the 'drives' and their contradictory operations of life and death (Kristeva 1984: 27-28); the 'genotext' or generative site of meaning and subjectivity (1984: 86). The symbolic is the force towards the use of signs and their appropriate ordering—the regulator, not just of language, but also of identity. It establishes the 'law' by which language and identity are managed. It governs the signifying process by ensuring the possibility of a phenotext: a 'structure' which follows the rules of the symbolic, presupposing the possibility of communication between a sender and receiver—'a subject of enunciation and an addressee' (Kristeva 1984: 87).

The double helix of the DNA or RNA molecule provides a convenient model for the oscillating interaction between the semiotic and the symbolic, a mirroring of the underlying oscillation of the drive economy. Just as the DNA strand determines genetically the biological nature of human life, the fluctuation of the drives and its mirroring in the twin twist of the semiotic and the symbolic determines human life linguistically and subjectively. The entry of the oscillation of the drive economy into the 'thetic phase' is crucial to the gaining of subjectivity. The semiotic is the place from which the subject must emerge, but in which subjectivity is thwarted by the oscillation of drive charges and stases (Kristeva 1984: 27-28). The thetic phase is the site of the advent of subjectivity and discourse.

As the 'threshold between two heterogeneous realms', the thetic phase marks the boundary between the semiotic and the symbolic (Kristeva 1984: 48). The name of the thetic phase refers to its role as the portal to meaning. As the moment in the linguistic order when meaning becomes possible, the thetic is the place where 'theses', however simple, are proposed. The primary thesis is that of the positing of the 'I' or subjectivity itself. The thetic phase marks the movement from the drive economy, where subjectivity and meaning are lacking, to the symbolic order, where identity and discourse are possible. This movement is achieved via a rupture in the semiotic, the drive economy. Through this rupture, the heterogeneity of the prelinguistic economy is translated into the world of language and identity. In the process, a split in the characterization of the oscillation of the drives occurs, and identity is established in dualistic terms

(Kristeva 1984: 27-28): the drive towards identity and the drive away from identity (life and death in linguistic terms); the symbolic and the semiotic; the self and the other.

The 'thetic phase' is crucial to the development of language and identity, but it is not without its legacy of division. The symbolic order, the site governed by the symbolic but dependent on the semiotic, is always a 'split unification': an apparent homogeneity which is predicated on heterogeneity, and governed by dualities because of the thetic rupture. The integral role of these governing dualities in the symbolic order is represented by the signifying split between the signifier and the signified in the sign, the primary element of signification. The illusion of homogeneity is maintained by the suppression of the heterogeneity of the semiotic: the otherness outside of the dualities constructed in language and identity (Kristeva 1984: 48–49). In a sense, the elements of the symbolic always stand in place of the heterogeneity of the semiotic rather than any specific signified. However, in the necessary split made in the thetic phase, this heterogeneous signification is disguised by a homogeneous facade. Thus, meaning, language and subjectivity are assumed to be singular and unitary in communication when in reality they are multiple, ambiguous and heterogeneous.

Discourse which exhibits *jouissance* exposes that heterogeneity, ambiguity and multiplicity. The exemplary mode of discourse which demonstrates the illusive 'mastery'[1] and ambivalent proprietary[2] over the tools of language and identity that is *jouissance* is 'poetic language'. Poetic language is not simply poetry. It is a form of discourse that calls upon and reveals multiple meanings and significations in the one process by openly displaying the oscillation on which language and identity is based. Poetic language refuses to hide the 'process that produces' language and meaning, thereby preventing the subject in discourse being 'reified as a transcendental ego' (Kristeva 1984: 58–59). Where the thetic position is the point of acquisition of language and subjectivity, and the semiotic is the alterity which undergirds all language and subjectivity, poetic language 'maintains and transgresses thetic unicity by making it undergo a kind of anamnesis,

1. The term 'mastery', clearly associated for Kristeva with *jouissance*, is indicative of the characterization of subjectivity in the Kristevan schema as masculine, and the evaluation of texts by male authors as key examples of discourses which exhibit *jouissance*.

2. Juridically, *jouissance* indicates the enjoyment of rights, particularly to the usage of property (Grosz 1989: xix).

by introducing into the thetic position the stream of semiotic drives and making it signify' (1984: 60). Poetic language puts the subject 'on trial' by exposing its manufacturing process (1984: 58). Such exemplary discourse recognizes, albeit not necessarily consciously, the 'basic incompleteness' which pertains to the subject because of its origins (Kristeva 1982: 89).

For Kristeva, the 'transcendental ego' or the Cartesian, unitary subject is merely a 'liminary moment of the process' of signification (1984: 30). The illusion that 'I' am and 'I' know is fleeting. The sense of a stable and unitary subject is a mirage. *Le sujet en procès*, the subject in process/on trial, uses the 'linguistic network' to reveal the process underlying the illusion of representation created within that network. Language is exposed in its lack of correlation with 'something real posited in advance and forever detached from instinctual process'. The subject in process/on trial 'experiments with or practices' the linguistic process 'by submerging in it and emerging from it through the drives', i.e. through elements that are essentially non-linguistic but which still may be apparent in language, e.g. rhythm, gaps, silences. In this traversal of the dual elements of language and identity, *le sujet en procès* reveals itself to be unafraid of the boundaries of language and subjectivity by facing the very 'otherness' of language itself. It also has the capacity to cause alterations in the system of signification and the 'historically accepted *signifying device*' by suggesting different ways of representing the 'relation to natural objects, social apparatuses, and the body proper' in the sociolinguistic realm through its play with the dual modalities of language and meaning (Kristeva 1984: 126). As a subjectivity which shows its mastery of the oscillating interaction between the semiotic and the symbolic, *le sujet en procès* is a particular manifestation of the speaking subject or subject of enunciation that exudes *jouissance*.

As an adept balancing act between the two brinks of language and subjectivity, *jouissance* is a 'joying in the truth of self-division'—an ambivalent and risky recognition of both the subject's complicity in the use of the tools of meaning construction, and the limitations of such tools in exploring the complexity of an identity which defies them (Kristeva 1982: 89). In this respect, *jouissance* is the result of the clearly intensified process of language and identity revealing their boundaries (Kristeva 1984: 17). If *jouissance* for Lacan is the 'motive' of the 'being of *signifiance*' (Lacan in Mitchell & Rose 1982: 142), for Kristeva, it is the result of a heightened form of the common process of *signifiance*.

Abjection of Self as Poetic Language

Kristeva develops the notion of 'abjection' in *Powers of Horror: An Essay on Abjection* (1982). In *Powers*, the term is used somewhat ambiguously. First, abjection is the process of separation demanded by language and subjectivity from the prelinguistic other. Second, it is the determination of certain objects as abject, i.e. as totem and/or taboo, the 'others' to the self. Third, abjection is the recognition of the self as divided, i.e. as an incomplete, non-static, non-definitive, non-entity. *Jouissance* properly belongs to the third of these definitions, although this third manifestation is predicated on the first two. In the first case, the 'other' is alterity. In the second case, other signifiers are treated as substitutes for this lost alterity. In the third case, the discourse of the abjection of self, as an exemplary discourse, produces *jouissance* based on its recognition and 'enjoyment' of the shattering of identity, language and meaning through an acknowledgement of an 'otherness' within the self. This recognition involves an implicit acknowledgement of the process of separation required for the development of language and identity, and of the abject identity of alterity. Such 'enjoyment' contrasts with the rigid discourse of apocalypse and the transgressive discourse of carnival.[3]

Separation

Following from and building on the work of Jacques Lacan, in the early pages of *Powers* (Kristeva 1982: 2–3), Julia Kristeva describes the violent separation of parental and infant subjectivity which occurs in the course of the development of individual identity. Using the imagery of food loathing, she depicts a process that must occur in order for the child to become an 'I'. This process is identified by

3. Carnival involves the transgression of boundaries, often through the reversal of dualities. While such activity has the potential to precipitate *jouissance*, it also has the capacity to reinforce the original dualities as an exercise in cathartic release of tension in order that the 'proper' order can be maintained. Carnival, for Kristeva, is not simply parody, an activity which strengthens the law because of its reliance upon it. It is a revolutionary action which precipitates the kind of discourse that embodies ambivalence. But its role as precipitator ties it, as precedent, to the very law which it seeks to transgress (1980: 80). It remains the 'only discourse integrally to achieve the 0–2 poetic logic' by precipitating the discourse of *jouissance* but it does not embody *jouissance* itself (1980: 70).

Kristeva as the process of abjection. It is particularly symbolized in an infant's apparent act of rejection of an offered parental gift of milk. The involuntary physical reaction signals, for Kristeva, the separation of the child from the parent. The act of offering food is a symbol of parental desire for the child. The act of rejection of the offering is a symbol of the infant's refusal to be subsumed in that desire, i.e. in the parental identity. The involuntary action is an attempt to establish difference and therefore identity. But, because the infant does not yet have an established identity, this exchange is not the rejection of one subject by another. It is the attempt to create a subjectivity from a position of unformed heterogeneity. The infant symbolically rejects an aspect of its prior, unformed self, i.e. its mother, in its rejection of the milk, in order to establish its own subjectivity. It determines part of its self as 'other': 'I expel *myself*, I spit *myself* out, I abject *myself* within the same motion through which "I" claim to establish *myself*'. The process of abjection, thus, involves a separation from that which the subject determines as its 'other', but which is also part of itself. Identity is achieved at the expense of the rejection of that aspect of the self which is determined as other: '"I" am in the process of becoming an other at the expense of my own death' (Kristeva 1982: 3). The subject 'I' is born from the death of the unformed, heterogeneous pre-subjectivity which, in a sense, was also self.

Abjectification

In this process of separation, the conceptual notion of the 'abject' is formed. The abject is the other: neither in the sense of a simple object, nor in the sense of something which is utterly dissociated from self. The abject is that which is part of 'me' but from which I must separate in order to gain my identity (Kristeva 1982: 1–4). It is what I create as the 'other' in the process of creating my own identity and entering into the realm of meaning. The food rejected by the child is not in itself abject, or *the* abject, rather it stands arbitrarily for the indefinable heterogeneity that precedes and underlies all subjectivity, and from which the emerging subject attempts, with limited and illusionary success, to distance itself. The subject's relation to the abject is displaced on to identifiable objects such as food because of the indefinability of the abject. This displacement reveals the true nature of the abject, indicated by the play in the word itself, to be Lacan's '*l'objet petit a*': the object of the displaced desire for reunification with the 'other' which is beyond language and identity. The abject is 'the "object" of primal repression' (Kristeva 1982: 12), both that to which the subject is drawn and from which the subject is repulsed. Any object the subject desires or fears is yet another substitute for *l'objet petit a*: the alterity repressed in the process of the formation of language and identity (Roudiez in Kristeva 1982: x). The existence of desire is a recognition of dissatisfaction with the original, necessary separation—an awareness that there is more to myself than 'I'.

In understanding the discourse of abjection, the notion of the abject plays a key role. That which repels, horrifies and, conversely, fascinates provides the focus for Kristeva's explorations of the depiction of alterity within sociolinguistic structures. These fascinating, repulsive concepts are the 'abject' objects of language and subjectivity. They reveal a hidden boundarylessness from which the sociosymbolic attempts to distance itself. Images of the abject, for Kristeva, revolve around three key categories which can be succinctly described as food, death and sex: 'food taboos', e.g., certain meats including human flesh which are forbidden to be consumed; 'corporeal alteration and its climax, death', including urine, faeces, tears and other bodily excretions, which may not be reincorporated into oneself; and, 'the feminine body and incest', i.e., images of the 'other sex' as abnormal and certain sexual acts as inappropriate (Kristeva 1982: 93). Key among Kristeva's images of the abject are food loathings, corpses and the 'other sex', i.e. 'woman'. The characterization of alterity as the abject reflects Kristeva's identification of the resurfacing of elements which have been repressed in the necessary process of separation that precedes and precipitates the formation of human language and identity. The repressed reappears in language as the abject. Such images of abjection present the possibility of approaching the radical otherness of alterity. When objects of taboo, such as those mentioned above, are confronted within discourse in a certain manner, the alterity of language and subjectivity may be revealed in a play of expression which approaches *jouissance*.

Abjection of Self

Separation of the self from the other is essential to the development of language and, hence, of communication. But by its very nature, this separation is an ambivalent act: an action which is desired but which also leads to a corresponding desire for re-connection, re-fusion with the other; an action which results in impossible and unsustainable delineations as well as necessary and persistent ones. The discourse of abjection is the discourse of the recognition of that unsustainability despite its persistence: the recognition that 'I' am also part of the other, the other is also part of 'me'. In exploring such a discourse, it is necessary to consider the separation which it recognizes and, in the process of that recognition, moves beyond.

The type of discourse that recognizes the process of abjection as separation, and confronts the 'abject', not as 'other' but as part of self, is an 'abjection of self', both in the sense of the 'self' having abjected that which it construes as 'other' than itself; and of the 'self' recognizing its basis in that process of impossible and illusory separation. For Kristeva, the 'abjection of self' is the 'culminating form' of the revelation that 'all abjection is...the recognition of the *want* on which any being, meaning, language, or desire is founded' (1982: 5). The abjection of self is the recognition of the fundamental split on which my subjectivity is based, and the acknowledgement, albeit perhaps unconsciously, of the complexity of my 'real' subjectivity. Primal repression, the process of separation whereby subjectivity in all its ambiguity is established, belongs to the first meaning of 'abjection': 'the ability of the speaking being...to divide, reject, repeat' (1982: 12). The second meaning of "abjection" represents the production of the by-product of that division: the abject representations of the 'otherness' of language and identity—alterity. The third meaning of 'abjection' belongs to the discourse that recognizes the process and revels in its ambiguity—that of the process, the discourse and the discursive subject. It is specifically the type of discourse that produces *jouissance*.

Exemplary Discourse: Louis-Ferdinand Céline

For *Powers* (1982), the genre of abjection is definitively that of the novels of Louis-Ferdinand Céline (1894–1961). Céline wrote in the context of the European desolation of World Wars I and II. His novel writing is characterized by a style which is speechlike: syntactically and grammatically broken. In this enterprise, his trademark eventually became the insertion of the pregnant pause, in the form of an ellipsis, i.e. three periods '...', between dislocated phrases and half-formed sentences.[4] It is precisely this style that reveals for Kristeva the ambiguous subjectivity of *le sujet en procès* in the work of Céline: 'The site of Céline's scription is always that fascinating crest of decomposition-composition, suffering-music, and abomination-ecstasy' (Kristeva 1982: 153). This oscillating style renders both the establishment of dualities and their destruction in a rhythm that remains indebted to the original binaries only because it seeks to move beyond their confines.

The choice of Céline's work as an example of the discourse of abjection is controversial. The content of Céline's overall literary work is characterized by political ambivalence. Céline revealed anti-Semitic sentiments and misogyny as well as a pacifist approach and anti-fascist rhetoric. His experiences of regimes identified variously as communist, fascist and democratic left him with a similar attitude towards the people who espoused each of them (Kristeva 1982: 154). This experience ensured that his ideological position was always shifting, and thus ambiguous or ambivalent. Ruth Ostrovsky, Céline's first English language biographer, describes this ambivalence as 'his drive for contradiction' (Ostrovsky 1971: 314). Mixing analysis of Céline's life and of his work, Ostrovsky attempts to document examples of the ideological conflicts apparently encompassed in Céline's words and actions. In the account of an extraordinary life, Céline features as pacifist and attempted enlistee; Nazi and French Leftist; tender of the wounds of Gestapo torture victims and friend of an eminent doctor in the Third Reich; anti-Semite and protector of Jews (1971: 149).

It is this ambivalence which Kristeva pursues, intrigued by its sources and its place as a discourse of human experience. For Kristeva, Céline's writing is intimately connected with a confrontation with suffering and horror, and a loss of previously established boundaries between self and other. Even Céline's adherence to Nazism 'ambivalent and paltry as that action was' is regarded as evidence of 'the disintegration of identity' that is manifest in his novels: a clinging to an identity (as abhorrent as such an identity is) in the face of the threat of the loss of all identity (a horrifying prospect) via the violent delineation of the 'other' (1982: 136) through political polemics.

The transgression of established boundaries and, through this transgression, the loss of a unitary subject is symbolized for *Powers*

4. See, for example, Céline, *Castle to Castle*.

in the identity which Céline develops for himself as a writer. Destouche is actually Céline's birth name: the name he used in his profession as a doctor. Céline, one of his grandmother's given names, is the name Destouche uses as a writer. *Powers* expresses the significance of this feminine authorial identity on behalf of Céline: 'Where that other who writes and is not my familial ego is concerned, "I" go beyond, "I" shift, "I" am no longer' (Kristeva 1982: 174–75).

The significance of Céline's identification with the feminine in the activity of writing is a signal of both his confrontation with the abject and the ambiguous subjectivity which is embodied in the writing itself because of the confrontation. For Kristeva, the unitary, singular subject, as a product of the symbolic order, is characterized as masculine: a legacy of the Lacanian phallic 'I'. Consequently, it is avant-garde male writers who approach the feminine in their writing, thereby transgressing the boundaries of subjectivity, who become the key examples for her exemplary discourses of poetic language (1982: 18–26, 134; see also Kristeva 1984). Conversely, it can be argued that it is Kristeva's personal entry into the logocentric discourse of theory that produces a similar result from an alternate position[5]— another entry of the feminine into the masculine realm—and that the introduction of interpretations of phallologocentric texts from an 'other' perspective might achieve a similar result.

For Kristeva, the assertion of dualities is both starting place of and response to the threatened loss of identity (1982: 136) which Céline encounters in the face of the horror of the 'global catastrophe of the Second World War' (1982: 207). Céline is confronted by his own complicity in the 'otherness' which has been constructed in his fascist environment. This confrontation threatens the loss of identity. The dualities are re-asserted in an effort to avoid that loss, but it is the moment(s) of loss in the text that promise something more than scapegoating or diatribe. The syntactic rhythm (1982: 192) of brokenness and incompleteness in the text is a narrative which 'cries out' under the unbearable stress on the 'narrated identity' which can no longer maintain its unicity when confronted by the nature of the constructed dualities, their abjection and abject failure, and the shattering of identity which this failure entails: 'The Jew becomes

5. In the 'Preface' to *Desire in Language* (1980), Kristeva writes: 'It was perhaps also necessary to a *woman* to attempt to take up that exorbitant wager of carrying the rational project to the outer borders of the signifying venture of men.' (1980: x). See also Kristeva's discussion on 'Socratic Dialogue' (1980: 80–81).

the feminine exalted to the point of mastery, the impaired master, the ambivalent, the border where exact limits between same and other, subject and object, and even beyond these, between inside and outside, and disappearing—hence an Object of fear and fascination. *Abjection itself.'* (1982: 185). The confrontation with the abject is symbolized in the identification of the writer with the abject other which is 'feminized'.

What is *jouissance* here? It is the cry of a subjectivity which speaks even in a situation where identity is not available in a singular and unitary form. In this cry, there is both a determination to remain in the realm of language and identity without denying the presence of an 'otherness' within, under and through that realm, and a recognition of the arbitrary nature of meaning and subjectivity: a tearing of the 'veil of the communitarian mystery' (1982: 209). This recognition is a 'demystification of Power' (1982: 210) which exposes the abyss on which the powerful structures of language and identity have been laid. Rhythm remains within this cry as testimony to the oscillation of the drive economy and the powerful attraction of the tools of meaning-making. The cry of *jouissance*, as an expression of the impossible division of the subject is the cry of a subjectivity which knows itself to be in a perpetual and oscillating process of becoming, rather than in a static state of being. It is the cry of a lost pre-subjectivity which is characterized in language as feminine: 'the waste cut off the phallus' (1982: 166).

In this characterization, Kristeva more firmly identifies the Lacanian 'the Woman' as situated in the semiotic which is constituted as feminine in the process of language and subjectivity acquisition. The mother is an image of the ambiguous subjectivity which cries out in *jouissance*; pregnancy and motherhood, an analogy for the complexity of the heterogeneous process of signification. In this analogy, *jouissance* is found 'at the far limits of repression, whence bodies, identities, and signs are begotten' (1980: 269) in the womb of the semiotic: the heterogeneous site of the drives, the generative site of the '(m)other' from which the infant subject emerges. In written discourse, the confrontation with the semiotic is found 'in the beauty of a gesture that, here, on the page, compels language to come nearest to the human enigma' (Kristeva 1982: 206): that of an ambiguous or pregnant subjectivity where the 'I' is engulfed by its preceding heterogeneity.

Exemplary Discourse: Christianity

Interestingly, Christianity as a discourse is identified by Kristeva as belonging to the genre of the abjection of self also. Historically, for Kristeva, the rituals of religions have provided cathartic exercises where the abject could be 'purified': confronted and controlled. Rites of 'defilement and pollution', *'exclusion* or taboo' have enabled the abject to be confronted as 'always nameable, always totalizeable', and therefore always controllable. Such rites ensure that the essential repression contained within human language and communication continues. 'Abjection accompanies all religious structurings and reappears, to be worked out in a new guise, at the time of their collapse' (1982: 17). For example, the Judaic regulations from the Levitical and Deuteronomic codes about right conduct in relation to food, sex and death provide Kristeva first with an illustration of the careful maintenance of appropriate boundaries and the associated fear of the ambivalent or unbounded (1982: 90–112); and second with a prototype of a religious system which is disrupted and reformulated with the emergence of another system, i.e. Christianity. For Kristeva, the advent of Christianity brought a crossing of some previously established boundaries, e.g. dietary taboos and their associated Jew/ Gentile distinctions. The 'processes of division, separation, and differentiation' (1982: 117) did persist in a new form but, in the changeover, moments of instability occurred. At the birth of Christianity, the Judaic settlement was disrupted by transgressions which eventually resulted in the formation of the new religion, but the moments of instability presented the possibility of an alternate genre of discourse: one without resolution and not yet cathartic. Thus, the discourses of the early instability at the time of the emergence of Christianity are identified with the discourse of the abjection of self, and therefore with *jouissance*, while the later discourses (e.g. Revelation), which herald the new religious settlement, are discussed as parallels to the earlier discourses of the Judaic settlement (e.g. Leviticus and Deuteronomy).

For Kristeva, the Christian category of 'sin' brings about an internalization of boundaries which suggests the possibility of a recognition of the ambivalent position of humanity, at least until a new self/other distinction is made and 'a diabolical otherness in relation to the divine' (1982: 127) is established using another representation of the abject which can be treated as external. With the category of sin, the abject is internalized as the subject is confronted with its own complicity in the 'otherness' from which it would seek to delineate itself. With the establishment of a new external other (a new abject outside of a newly posited unitary subject), a new emphasis is placed on the 'rightness' of human action, particularly speech, and on the re-establishment of a unitary and singular subjectivity (1982: 131–32). Kristeva identifies Revelation with the texts of the Judaic settlement, for example, Leviticus, because of its apocalyptic struggle between good and evil envisaged as culminating with the triumphant victory of the good and proper singular subject, i.e. God. The discourse of early Christianity with its internalization of boundaries and implicit acknowledgement of an ambivalent subjectivity is identified with the rhythmic instability of the discourse of Céline.[6]

Analysis and Analysand

Thus far this discussion has highlighted exemplary discursive expressions of *jouissance*. In this section, I will show the move from *jouissance* as discursive expression to *jouissance* as hermeneutical outcome. This move is already implicit, if not explicit, within Kristeva's schema. In outlining this shift, I focus briefly on the type of analysand which Kristeva perceives as exuding *jouissance* and the

6. Such identification is controversial and problematic because of its characterization of Judaism and the consequent juxtaposition of the novels of the fascist Céline with the discourses of early Christianity as a transgressor of Judaism and politically revolutionary. Because of this problematic identification, it is helpful to keep in mind a distinction which Kristeva herself makes between religious experiences which may derive from art and literature and have the capacity for *jouissance* of a certain mystical kind (1982: 17); and the dogmatic expressions of religion which confirm old dualisms through cathartic transgressions with the explicit purpose of upholding the prevailing law. *Jouissance* is not cathartic: it 'transmits no fixed message except that itself should be "the eternal joy of becoming"' (1980: 84). The impetus of *jouissance* 'is destined to survive the collapse of the historical forms of religions' (1982: 17). It explicitly disrupts the 'theological' and 'monological' (1980: 70, 88) formulas of any ideology or belief system. Certain Christian forms exhibit as much inertia as certain expressions of Judaic legislation; just as the presence of a less rigid subjectivity may be perceived in the discourses of the Hebrew Scriptures. It is in the early stages of the development of any new religious forms (and at other times of instability) that one is most likely to discover the presence of *jouissance* denoting the precariousness of subjectivity.

response of the analyst in such an analysis. I will recall the inversive point made earlier about the in-breaking of the 'feminine' into the 'masculine' realm through more than one method or strategy.

The Borderline Analysand

The abjection of self is, for Kristeva, the condition of the borderline analysand, the subject of psychoanalysis (1982: 207). Here is a source of some of Kristeva's own ambivalence towards the position of abjection. For, indeed, the role of the psychoanalyst with the client in abjection is cure-oriented. Yet, there seems a truth about the position of the abjection of self that is unable to be attained by those who do not occupy it, by 'those that the path of analysis, or scription,[7] or of a painful or ecstatic ordeal has [not] led to tear the veil of the communitarian mystery, on which love of self and others is set up' (1982: 209). Abjection of self is, in some respects, a failure to distinguish one's self from the other, the abject. Yet, because these two posited entities are in fact inseparable, there is a certain attraction, 'truth' and even inevitability about the state of abjection (1982: 208). The boundaries of a moral[8] separation between self and other are

7.   Scription is the term that translator Leon Roudiez chooses to express what is described as the 'strong' meaning of the French *écriture* (Kristeva 1982: x) or writing. Similarly, John Lechte refers to a distinction between *écriture* and *écrivance* introduced by Roland Barthes. While *écrivance* is writing judged to be instrumental (e.g., scientific discourse), *écriture* 'engenders jouissance'. In so doing, such writing 'disturbs existing perceptions of the possibilities of writing'. It also has the possibility of engendering 'perversion', with the result that it 'does not *produce* anything' (Lechte 1990: 23). This analysis of *écriture* coincides neatly with the description of 'scription' which is contained within *Powers*: 'a *delirium* that literally prevents one from going mad, for it postpones the senseless abyss that threatens this passing through the identical'. It is a deferral both of the dissolution of meaning and of the succumbing to one type of meaning itself (Kristeva 1982: 136–37). The imagery of balancing in this description is an immediate reminder of Kristeva's concept of the tight-rope walk of *jouissance*.

8.   There is an important distinction made between morality and ethics by Kristeva. Morality is the type of delineation between self and other (good and bad etc.) which sees either side of the duality as discrete, identifiable and distinct. Ethics, on the other hand, struggles with the ambiguity of categories which are artificial and arbitrary, i.e. with the possibility that self and other (good and bad) co-exist and can never be neatly delineated. *Powers* (1982) displays the specific meaning aligned with the 'moral' when it distinguishes between the morality of apocalypse with its neat dualistic categories and the lack of morality in abjection where the boundaries of categories are blurred. A definition of the ethical is supplied in 'The Ethics of Linguistics' (1980: 23–35): 'ethics crops up wherever a code (mores, social contract) must

unsustainable. Because identity is formed in relation to others, all identities are implicated in the conspiracy of singular, unitary subjectivity and therefore in the economy which lies beneath it.

Abjection of self is a disturbance of the process of separation and delineation required for identity, language, communication and the positing of truth in logocentric terms. Separation must exist for disruption to occur. Abjection of self is thus a movement through and beyond the process of language and subjectivity acquisition. While it is generally imaged as a 'lack of cleanliness or health', an inappropriate connection with abject objects, sociolinguistically, it is a challenge to 'identity, system, order' through the disturbance of the same. That which 'does not respect borders, positions, rules' calls into question identity itself: the 'in-between, the ambiguous, the composite'; 'the criminal with a good conscience'; 'the killer who claims he is a savior' (1982: 4). The identity of the analysand going through the abjection of self is disturbed by images which do not conform to the dualities of the discourse of logocentrism: 'In the dark halls of the museum that is now what remains of Auschwitz, I see a heap of children's shoes... The abjection of Nazi crime reaches its apex when death, which, in any case, kills me, interferes with what, in my living universe, is supposed to save me from death: childhood, science, among other things' (1982: 4). The borderline analysand is a voyeur who sees the contradictions and finds in these the contradiction of his/her own identity. The loss of boundaries in such anomalous images at first repels, but then calls into question all boundaries including one's own. The abjection of self thus embraces a different kind of truth: an ambivalence where neither identity nor non-identity is sufficient since identity must be embraced in order to speak and the disruption of identity must be recognized in order to understand. Subjectively, this position between identity and non-identity is painful and exhilarating.

The Voyeur Analyst

The analyst too is a voyeur. In choosing to listen from/for a position of otherness outside/around/within the discourse of the analysand, the analyst discovers (perhaps even invents) a split subjectivity within

be shattered in order to give way to the free play of negativity, need, desire, pleasure, and jouissance, before being put together again, although temporarily and with full knowledge of what is involved' (1980: 23).

that discourse. In part, that discovery/invention occurs by virtue of the intrusion of the analyst into the analysand's discourse from a position of 'otherness'. Kristeva suggests that if analysts were able to listen to themselves as analysts in *'the void'*, they would hear the development of a discourse around that which threatens 'the speaking being', exposing the 'religious and political pretensions' of human meaning-making (Kristeva 1982: 209).

Both analyst and analysand are readers. In their reading, the discovery of anomalies splays open the reasonableness of their own identities. Perhaps because the analyst is familiar with this path, such a confrontation is less traumatic than it may be for the borderline analysand—perhaps because the analyst is one step removed from the confrontation with alterity or, more poignantly, has come to stand for alterity itself. Kristeva certainly reserves for herself 'the quiet shore of contemplation' in her reading of the discourse of abjection (1982: 210). But it is the act of reading which remains significant. Kristeva describes the 'true "miracle" of Céline' as residing in 'the very experience of one's reading': a liberation 'by means of a laughter without complacency yet complicitous' (1982: 133).

The Jouissance *of Reading*

If it is analysis as reading (or conversely reading as analysis) that is the key to the discovery of anomalies and the facilitation of such anomalies in the opening up of the split realm of subjectivity, then it would seem to be reasonable to propose an approach to *jouissance* that did not seek it in a text as such, but rather in the act of reading. Kristeva points to such possibilities in her reflections on her role as analyst in relation to the discourses of abjection (see, for example, 1982: 207–10) and in her recognition that, if the dual modalities of language are present in most, if not all communications, then once readers have learned to identify them in exemplary discourses they may discern them in discourses of all kinds.

The positing of *jouissance* as a hermeneutical principle coincides with the Kristevan recognition that all discourse is a mixture of the semiotic and the symbolic. This mixture necessarily leaves discourse open to variant readings produced via differing foci on these dual elements of language. Another way of expressing this observation is to say that there is already a multiplicity of subjectivity present in most (if not all) discourses, so that, once the nature of multiplicity and the goal of *jouissance* as the enjoyment of such multiplicity is identified, multiplicity may be detected in texts where it was not previously recognized and the reading of such multiplicity in(to) those texts may produce *jouissance* in the reader who has learned to enjoy non–singular, non-unity identity—both that of the text and the self. This movement neatly coincides with the assessment of *Revolution in Poetic Language* (Kristeva 1984) offered by Leon Roudiez in the introduction to that work. According to Roudiez, Kristeva presses 'large bodies of philosophical, linguistic, and psychoanalytic texts' into the service of her argument that 'the nineteenth-century post-Symbolist avant-garde' modelled a whole new literary form with the effect that, once such a form is identified, 'one is able to detect a similar ferment in the essential writings of other historical periods' (Kristeva 1984: 1–2). That is, the modelling of such an exemplary form highlights the places where the traces of that form can be found in other kinds of literary works.

The position of reader as a position of *jouissance* has an ambivalence of its own. The reader is one step removed from the abjection of self— the observer of the voyeur; a voyeur once removed. This position, in contrast to the position of the borderline analysand or avant-garde writer, is not a position of the loss of identity leading to an understanding of the subjective division, but a creation of identity from a position of non-identity in order to achieve a similar result, i.e. the reader enters the text as 'other' just as the analyst enters the discourse of the analysand as 'other'. Such an entry produces disruption in the discourse and confirmation of a subjectivity beyond it. But because the reader is always 'other', an identity for that subjectivity is never solidified. It is always ambiguous and multiple. For Kristeva, the goal of psychoanalysis is the carving out of a space for analysands to find a subjectivity which is aware of the illusive creation of identities and capable of playing with that creativity as an indispensable tool for living (Kristeva 1987a: 9, 51–52; see also Kernberg in Kristeva 1987a: xi). This goal is achieved by a confrontation with otherness—the role of the analyst. The goal of the analyst is to represent an identity which is not one—similarly, for a reader—provided that both seek a goal of *jouissance*: the enjoyment of a non-unitary, non-singular identity.

The *jouissance* of the 'other' is found in an entry into subjectivity. If it is maintained that discourse is essentially phallologocentric and that such phallologocentric discourse constructs the other as essentially feminine, then such entry into a text is a movement of the 'feminine' into the 'masculine' and a shattering of the subjective identity therein. Such a shattering conforms with an account of feminist processes and their aims as the breaking of patriarchal forms. This correlation has considerable implications for the practice of feminist hermeneutics in a theological context. In order to demonstrate some of the possibilities and introduce directions for the development of a reading strategy that seeks *jouissance*, I will tackle the problem of reading a discourse with the aim of achieving *jouissance* even when the discourse has not been identified as one which produces *jouissance*.

Reading Apocalypse

The Nature of Apocalypse

For Kristeva, the discourse of apocalypse is a discourse of delineation: 'An identical sacred horror for the feminine, the diabolical, and the sexual are expounded therein'. These distinctions are expounded in order to set up the scenario of 'an impossible future' in the event of such distinctions being transgressed. A scene of horror is depicted as a 'vision through sounds hallucinated as images' in order to establish the imperative of a particular 'moral' position where a singular, unitary subjectivity is asserted and an abject other determined. Such a singular moral position is not the result of philosophical reasoning but the goal of the seduction of 'a poetic incantation that is often elliptic, rhythmic, and cryptogrammic'. It is a discourse which invites *jouissance* but which defers it by its claim to a unitary, singular and definitive moral position of phallologocentrism. In its advocacy of such a position, apocalypse affords inspiration and hope 'in a flow of cataclysms, catastrophes, deaths, and ends of the world' as a reaction to the perception of an uncertain future and a disruptive and dangerous present. As a confrontation with suffering and horror, it emulates the preconditions for *jouissance*. Indeed, the discourse of apocalypse does present 'the incompleteness and abjection of any identity, group, or speech', but simultaneously allows 'a distance...for judging, lamenting, condemning' and the re-institution of the necessary distinctions between self and other. This is the key difference between the discourse of apocalypse and the discourse of the abjection of self: the re-institution of the dualities and the distinctions. The biblical Revelation to John is, for Kristeva, a prime example of the discourse of apocalypse, not least because an indebtedness to it is claimed by Céline. However, for Kristeva, 'With Céline we are elsewhere' (1982: 204–205).

Exemplary Discourse: Revelation

The book of Revelation is an 'apocalypse': an apparent revelation whose claimed source is divine and which discloses 'future events and/or transcendent reality' with the intent of affecting the behaviour of the reader/hearer (Talbert 1994: 4). As an apocalypse, it has an 'apocalyptic eschatology': 'the belief that the judgment of the wicked and the vindication of the righteous entails the destruction of the world and the resurrection of the faithful to a blessed heavenly existence' (Talbert 1994: 5). Such a message holds out the promise of a renewed (and perfected) subjectivity for the reader/hearer through a cathartic confrontational approach. So defined, the book of Revelation neatly fits the genre of apocalypse as described by Kristeva: a discourse which establishes a clear distinction between the self and an abject otherness via the threat of the loss of self and the dissipation of the distinction. It holds out the hope of catharsis—'the purgation of undesirable elements' in the reader/hearer (Pippin 1992: 17).

Reading Revelation

What kind of reading of such a text would produce *jouissance*: a subjective tension which does not embody a resolution in catharsis? What kind of injection of the reader as 'other' into the text might achieve a reading which celebrates non-unitary, non-singular subjectivity? In this section, I offer four readings which hold that possibility. All in some way or another introduce an 'identity' into the text which is unable to be resolved as a singular form. Such an introduction involves the identification, implicit and explicit, of certain dualities within the text, the transgression or disruption of those dualities in some way and consequently the re-presentation of a reading of the text which is aware of the ambiguity within it: the otherness that exceeds and underlines the identified dualities. The first and second readings take into account the reader's context. The third reading attempts to find the gaps and slippages in the characterization within the text itself. Finally, I offer a preliminary 'poetic reading' of a specific pericope from the book of Revelation: the story of the woman clothed with the sun in Revelation 12.

Reading 1: From the 'Underside' When You're Above

Feminist biblical scholar, Elisabeth Schüssler Fiorenza identifies two ways of approaching the text of Revelation: one from a position of dominance and power; the other from a situation of persecution and/ or injustice. For her, the 'language of divine kingship and royal reward' provides 'Christian groups excluded from political power' with a linguistic framework for challenging their disenfranchisement. In contrast, the same language provides Christians embedded in the 'power structures of their society' with the rhetorical tools to entrench their positions (Fiorenza 1991: 139).

By introducing a reading of Revelation from the 'underside' into a contemporary Christian context which, contrary to the book's probable original setting, represents a position of power and dominance, Fiorenza presents a reading which overturns the dualities of the text by reading them from a different position. It is no longer winners who win, but losers. For Fiorenza, this reading is clearly a 'fitting theo-ethical response' (1991: 139). More than that however, it is a disruption of the textual dualities (and their popular readings) by the introduction of an identity which is ambiguous (losers are winners) and heterogeneous (if winners are 'us' and losers are 'not us' then losers are whoever is 'not us', but 'I' who read the text must be assured that I am part of 'us' even when 'not us' is the 'us' I would prefer to be i.e. a winner who is a loser who is a winner). Both elements are crucial: ambiguity and heterogeneity. In the process of reading, it becomes impossible for the reader to identify with one side of the duality or the other because both are implicated in each other. The reader's own subjectivity is thereby called into question as is a singular, unitary interpretation of the text itself.

Reading 2: Emphasizing Ambiguous Human Nature

Adela Yarbro Collins reads Revelation as an emphatic articulation of a perceived crisis which precipitates the release of tension related to that crisis 'in a process similar to the phenomenon of catharsis which Aristotle discussed in connection with Greek tragedy' (Collins 1984: 165–66). She rejects the simple acceptance of this cathartic resolution, however, as a 'precritical response' to the text. This rejection occurs essentially because 'the experience of *tension* [my emphasis] is a perennial human experience' (Collins 1984: 166). She proposes the 'values of humanization, justice, and love' for evaluating the political and relational contribution of Revelation. Humanization, for Collins, relates to a concept of 'becoming fully human' as the recognition of the tension between limits and potential (1984: 167). Hence, the 'dualist division of humanity' in Revelation is 'a failure in love' and lacking in credibility because it 'is an oversimplification that eliminates not only the possibility of neutrality but also the complexities of life in which there are always shades of grey' (Collins 1984: 170). It is precisely such tension and complexity that a reading seeking *jouissance* must pursue. Collins provides an example of reading tension in the text when she plays with the violent imagery of Revelation as means of liberation, tool for overthrow of repression, and perpetuator of injustice, denier of human dignity (1984: 171–74). In this play, there is recognition of the invalid nature of tight dualistic categories which perceive a clear division between those who carry 'the mark of the beast' and those, 'the seal of God' (1984: 170). The text is brought into the ambivalent reality of human lives and experiences where the clear-cut categories are obviously arbitrary, yet powerful in their influence on meaning and identity.

Reading 3: Looking for Slips

The possibility of producing a *jouissant* reading of Revelation is related to the potential for interpreting the imagery contained within the text in multiple ways. This imagery is the 'evocative power inviting imaginative participation' (Fiorenza 1985: 22). It is imagination which Adela Yarbro Collins also sees as the means for humanizing the text: 'Since the book of Revelation is a book of visions and poetry, we should approach it first of all with our imaginations' (Collins 1984: 172). Hans-Ruedi Weber, a biblical scholar interested in imaginative corporate Bible study, focuses on the imagery content of Revelation, describing Revelation as visual and oral theology (Weber 1988: vii). He compares it with the arts of painting, sculpture, photography and cinematography, and with the literary genre of science fiction (Weber 1981: 260). It is a slippage in the text which fragments the images of Revelation that provides the motif for his production of an alternative reading of Revelation: one which highlights the transgression of duality rather than the many examples of its confirmation.

Weber observes that in Rev. 7: 10, when the reader may be expecting an acclamation of the salvation of the world, the words presented enjoin 'Salvation to our God and to the Lamb!'. This 'strange plea' causes Weber to ask 'Do God and the Lamb need to be saved?' (1988: 40).[9] While, at first glance, this observation seems minor, and even obscure, its ability to precipitate a deconstruction of the apocalyptic dualities staged in Revelation suggests the possibility that it is just such attention to gaps and slippages in the text that allows the multiplicity of the text and its interpretation to be exposed and approached. In this minor slippage, Weber perceives a major transgression across the careful delineations of God as ultimate conqueror and humanity as ultimately in need of a saviour to produce a reading of particular images in Revelation that is not content to reinforce the apparently strict dualisms of the text. A *jouissant* reading would pursue such a slippage, exposing the ambiguity of the imagery within the text, because the slippage itself has provided a glimpse of the arbitrary nature of the construction process which produced that imagery, so often interpreted in dualistic form only.

Reading 4: A Tentative Feminist 'Poetic Reading'

Catherine Keller, in an article entitled 'The Breast, the Apocalypse, and the Colonial Journey' which uses some Kristevan concepts in its analysis, observes the dual impetus of the text of Revelation when she comments: 'Whatever else is true of the apocalyptic tradition— and there is much to be said for its inspiration of anti-imperialist and ultimately revolutionary "protest and comfort"—it is militantly patriarchal' (Keller 1994: 68). Keller acknowledges a debt to Elisabeth Schüssler Fiorenza in making such an assessment. For both Keller and Fiorenza, the imagery of Revelation engenders injustice as much as it challenges it. That engendering is particularly highlighted in relation to the imaging of women as 'false prophets', 'whores or virgins' and never 'among the elite of the saved' (Keller 1994: 68; cf. Fiorenza 1985: 199). Keller's article makes connections between the apocalyptic hope of a return to paradise and the 'abjection of the

9. Elsewhere Weber acknowledges the variations in translation of the relevant text, see verse 10. He maintains the necessity of translating the simple dative case as 'to' via a comparison with translations of verse 12 where other attributes are indicated in a similar formula, i.e. 'Blessing and glory and honor and power and might be to our God forever and ever!' (1981: 265).

female' as both desirable object for conquering and acceptable object of exploitation (Keller 1994: 71). Such an assessment would appear to open the possibility of a *jouissant* reading of Revelation which attempted to defy such characterizations by a confrontation with the abject within the text: the feminine. In order to pursue this possibility, I offer a preliminary poetic reading of a text which focuses on one of the feminine figures in the book of Revelation, the 'woman clothed with the sun' (Rev. 12: 1–6,13–17).

A *jouissant* reading, by its unwillingness to accept dualistic categories at face value, refuses the catharsis offered by the text and, in so doing, rejects 'the act of scapegoating' which Tina Pippin perceives as the inevitable subconscious or conscious result of catharsis (Pippin 1992: 18). Such a rejection refuses to countenance any one-dimensional reading of the feminine imagery in the text, notably the figures of virgins and whores. It drags the fictional characterizations into an encounter with ambivalent experience: 'to face the divisions of women by the patriarchy and to face our [women's] own roles in the violence' (Pippin 1992: 107). While neither Pippin nor Kristeva envisages this encounter as embodied in the text itself, I would argue that there are still enough clues to the 'otherness' of the text of Revelation to allow such a *jouissant* reading to occur as an interpretation or re-production of the text. In the particular pericope of the story of the woman clothed with the sun, I wish to identify an ambiguity within the text which points to the possibility of an alternate reading where that ambiguity is highlighted. The identification of such an ambiguity involves first, the naming of a duality present within the text; second, the locating of a disruption or transgression of that duality; and third, the production of an alternate reading of the text that re-presents the otherness present within the text.

The woman clothed with the sun is clearly cast in the classic role of the 'virgin'. As a 'positive female image of Revelation', she is 'silent, passive, powerless, sexually controlled, and pure' (Fiorenza 1991: 13). Indeed, the superimposition of the figure of Mary, the mother of Jesus, onto the figure of the woman in the history of Christian interpretation of this text reinforces the casting (Collins 1979: 88). By implication, all that she is not is the abject other, the 'whore'. As the virgin, she is powerless and ultimately sidelined in the story. Once her progeny is delivered, her place is the wilderness. While she upholds the acceptable regime, she is never included within its bounds. Having identified this duality, it is possible to note an aspect of the text where the division between virgin and whore, sidelined feminine and abject other, is thwarted/transgressed.

In dogmatic Christians terms, the image of the woman clothed with the sun is not 'pure', i.e. it is 'adulterated' by its probable source— a 'pagan' goddess image. Fiorenza points out that this 'myth of the queen of heaven' or 'mother of the gods' is widely known in various cultures contemporary with the writer of Revelation (Fiorenza 1991: 80). The recognition of this source compromises the image, perhaps especially when the image of the woman clothed with the sun is also identified as a symbol of the emerging Christian community (Collins 1979: 88). The identity of the image is not clean, and so too the identity of the community which it represents. It is ambiguous, containing a suppressed element within its presented unitary and singular identity. Building from this tainted origin, it becomes possible to identify the figure of the woman clothed with the sun as one of repressed power within a virginal facade—an exile in the wilderness preparing for her return; a figure who cannot be sidelined by the neat categories of the dualistic text. In this reading, the pericope becomes the story of a repressed feminine which is returning imminently, having been 'nourished for a time, and times, and half a time' (Rev. 12: 14). This return is not achieved within the text of Revelation, yet the catharsis of the battle and victory within the book is dogged by a tension at its very heart—the exile of the feminine. It is this exile and the constant presence/absence of 'otherness' that it represents that makes an alternate and *jouissant* reading a possibility: one which enjoys the tension and seeks to explore it.

The valuing of ambivalence and multiplicity in the reading of the text introduces the possibility of a *jouissant* reading. In a sense, such a reading is the 'hope' envisaged by Tina Pippin of a movement beyond the utopian hopes of the straight dualistic readings of Revelation—a hope which is determined to face the division of self, to confront the horror of ambivalence and to sustain the gaze without resorting to the defence of the neat and impossible category of the clean and proper 'I' and its attendant abjectification of all that is other, i.e. that is not 'I'. Sustaining the gaze is crucial because the threshold for *jouissance* is narrow: if you blink, you miss it. *Jouissance* itself is a liminal moment. The hope promised by it is not Catherine Keller's vision of a 'counterapocalypse: a hope grounded in our mutual presences, in solidarity'—'a praxis of mutuality'. That hope too is utopian. Rather it is the type of hope which Keller rejects: a living 'in our time *hope-lessly* and *in the present*' (1994: 72). Such a hope can be equated with the 'apocalyptic laughter' of the discourse of abjection: 'the beauty of a gesture that...compels language to come nearest to the human enigma' (Kristeva 1982: 206) with 'no threats to offer, no morality to defend' (Kristeva 1982: 205). Merely, a 'gushing forth' (1982: 206) of the repressed revealing the ambiguity of subjectivity and its underlying heterogeneity. Pippin does not envisage this 'hope' as arising from the text itself, but from the attention to the text given by women, and the addition of the voices of women to the interpretative overlays of the text (Pippin 1992: 107). It is such a 'hope' that I have attempted to present here in this brief, tentative reading of the story of the woman clothed with the sun where the depth and complexity of the imagery contained in this pericope has barely begun to be addressed.

Conclusion

This chapter has outlined the theoretical underpinnings for Julia Kristeva's notion of *jouissance* as a 'joying in the truth of self-division'. Two elements of language and identity, identified by Kristeva as the semiotic and the symbolic, interact in *le sujet en procès*. This interaction is used by Kristeva to evaluate literary works. The evaluative process is a hermeneutical one. Readings of the biblical book of Revelation which interpret ambivalences in the text counter Kristeva's own assessment of that text which focuses on its rigidity. Such readings interpret the text as one of abjection rather than of apocalypse. Such an interpretation follows Kristeva's own claim that once a discourse of abjection is identified, the dual elements of language and identity which are present in most (if not all) discourses can be identified in other discourses which are not readily recognized as *jouissant* discourses. Because poetic language is the exemplary discourse which demonstrates the interplay of the dual elements of language and identity, a suitable epithet for an approach to reading that attempts to identify such interplay is 'poetic reading'. The following chapter outlines such a possible hermeneutical method more fully through the articulation of a series of strategies and their demonstration through a reading of another biblical text.

Chapter 6

ENUMERATING ALTERITY: THE TRANSGRESSIVE METHOD OF
POETIC READING

Unpacking a Method

If *jouissance* is a viable discursive aim for writing, then it is also an appropriate goal for reading. It is as much the product of the reproduction of discourse, i.e. of interpretative or hermeneutical action, as the product of certain types of discourses of the avant-garde or poetic kind. This argument is based on the observations of Kristeva about the two elements of linguistic and subjective formation—the semiotic and the symbolic; their exemplary combination in poetic language, discourse *par excellence* in Kristevan terms; and their presence in most, if not all, discourse. *Jouissance* is the celebration of the multiplicity of discourse, be it written text, oral utterance, subjectivity, or human community (collective subjectivity): a 'joying in the truth of self-division'. In this chapter, I outline a hermeneutical method for approaching such a goal by attending to the alterity or 'otherness' of language and subjectivity. I call this method 'poetic reading'. It relies on the possibility of reading discourse, which is not necessarily poetic language in Kristevan terms, as if it were, i.e. of reading discourse *as* poetic language. This move from identifying poetic language to reading language poetically is consistent with Roudiez's assertion that Kristeva's analysis of poetic language or discourse in an exemplary form, for example, 'nineteenth-century post-Symbolist avant-garde' literature, enables the further discovery of the multiplicity of other discourses in different settings (Roudiez in Kristeva 1984: 1–2). Kristeva herself asserts that all literature may well be a version of the apocalypse—a laughing one—that is on the border between identity and non-identity, i.e. ambiguous and *jouissant* (Kristeva 1982: 207).

The method of poetic reading involves a three stage process:

1. The identification of the dualities assumed by and contained within the discourse under scrutiny.
2. The recognition and highlighting of both the possible and actual displacement of the implied order contained within and promoted by those dualities, i.e. attention to the subversion of the dualities and the symbolic order which they advance.
3. The re-presentation of the focal discourse, highlighting its ambiguous nature and the alterity which underlies it.

The first stage of poetic reading is a direct corollary of the correlation between dualistic discursive structures and the processes of language and identity acquisition. The second stage of the method of poetic reading, as an expression of a deconstruction process, has a number of strategies:

1. The privileging of the lesser term of the duality, which may result in a reversal of the ordering of the dualities.
2. The treatment of the lesser term as the precondition for the dominant one, not vice versa.
3. The introduction of a third term outside and precedent to the dualities identified.
4. The highlighting of spaces or gaps in the discourse which undermine dominant and unitary interpretations and their assumed dualities.
5. The playing with the slippages of terms both contained within the discourse itself, and infused from the contexts in which the discourse is placed.
6. The paying of attention to the intertextuality of the discourse, the intersection between the focal discourse and other texts.
7. The placing alongside each other of differing interpretations of the discourse under consideration, offering different readings of the textual dualities.

These strategies may be identified within and around the focal discourse itself, or introduced as part of the reading process. They are essentially specific articulations of the Derridean deconstructive process of the reversal and displacement of dualities now redeveloped for this hermeneutical purpose of poetic reading in the context of Kristevan theory.

The third stage seeks the possibility of enunciating alterity: an impossibility except at the point that *jouissance* or a recognition of the fragility[1] of language and subjectivity is achieved. At such a point, enunciation is exceeded by the apocalyptic laughter that is the bitter-sweet response to the realization of the ambiguity of language as a constructive process or the recognition that language produces certain results based on its process alone, and not on the basis of any fixed reality.

Throughout the description of the method of poetic reading, an illustration of its use is made through an interpretative analysis of the story of the Canaanite woman (Mt. 15: 21–28) based on the textual work of Elaine Wainwright (1995).

Identifying Dualities

The identification of dualities is based on the assumption that language reflects its existential origins: the classic split between other and self, pre-linguistic and linguistic, semiotic and symbolic. It does not assume that the prelinguistic, semiotic or otherness is contained wholly within language. However, the lesser terms of the dualities mimic[2] the elements of language and subjectivity which are repressed in order for language and subjectivity to exist. This mimicking or representation is not a representation of presence, but of absence, as indeed are all linguistic representations through a poststructuralist lens. The presumption of the linguistic creation of meaning carries through the Saussurean premise of the arbitrary relation between signifier and signified to its logical conclusion—the loss of the signified. Yet this loss presumes a prior presence of an undifferentiated absence: an absence of meaning, language and subjectivity. In language, the disjunction between presence and absence is re-presented rather than represented in dualities: male, female; light, dark; right, wrong...The distinction between re-presentation and representation is a distinction between the

---

1. Imagine language and subjectivity, or more accurately, the thetic movement into language and subjectivity, hung above the abyss of absence and meaningless-ness as a piece of brittle rice paper held tight like the skin of a drum, cloudily trans-parent, and fragile, so that a flick of a finger might shatter its veneer and reveal the abyss which it masks imperfectly. See also Derrida's wordplay, 'Tympan' (Derrida 1982: ix–xxix), his reference to the hymen (1981: 43), and Kristeva's picture of the 'skin on the surface of the milk' (1982: 2–3): all variations on the thin skin motif depicting the fine line between language and its absence.

2. The technical term for the representation of the semiotic in the symbolic order is *mimesis* (Kristeva 1984: 57–61).

metaphorical, metonymical, mimetic quality of language as discussed by Kristeva, and the notion that language does actually represent that which it purports to represent (objects, events, people—'real' entities).

How does the identification of dualities occur? To some extent the identification of dualities is intuitive. That is, there is no formal process for discovering them other than:

1. the assumption that they are present; and
2. the discernment of the particular dualities embodied in a particular discourse by reading or listening.

This response seems facile, and yet the presence of such dualities is generally assumed, to the point where statements asserting their presence pass without footnote or reference in many texts. Jay, for example, identifies both logical and social binaries in the formal theoretical inheritance of western philosophy from the Greeks, and the popular informal distinctions of society at large (Jay 1981). These identifications do not require justification. Although Jay does spend some time in exploring the exact nature of these binary relationships, the existence of the binary distinctions is accepted. It could be argued that the identification of dualities is an imposition on a discourse: a constraint dictated not by language itself, but by the metalanguage of theory.[3] Even if this imposition is the case, the broad acceptance of the proposition that the language and subjectivity of western culture is dominated by dualities would appear to have made it demonstrable, or at least validated it as a proposition. In any case, it is my contention that the accentuation of dualities, even partially discernible in the text, creates the environment whereby the text itself may be subverted through a programme of poetic reading.

In arguing my case, I use the biblical pericope of the story of the Canaanite woman (Mt. 15: 21–28) as the focal text for analysis using the method of poetic reading. The subsequent reading from this method is the key illustration for the overall argument of this chapter.

In paraphrase, the pericope depicts Jesus travelling to a foreign territory and being confronted by one of its residents who demands the healing of her daughter. Jesus apparently ignores her request. Jesus' disciples appear in the story. They are distressed by the woman's demands. Jesus indicates that the woman does not belong to the people to whom he was sent, i.e. the people of Israel. The woman

---

3. Lévi–Strauss' desire that his mythology of dual organizations might 'become a reality in the mind of the reader' (1979: 6) may have been achieved.

pleads again and Jesus reiterates his previous meaning in stronger imagery. The imagery is highly derogatory of the woman, obliquely referring to her as a 'dog'. Still the woman persists. Taking into her discourse the derogatory image Jesus has used, she suggests that even dogs receive leftovers. In effect, the woman has engaged in debate over the identity of the people whom Jesus may benefit. Jesus' response to her entering into debate is to praise her faith and to grant her demand. The story concludes with the instantaneous healing of the woman's daughter.

As a story from the Gospel of Matthew, the pericope is generally regarded as belonging to the deliberations throughout that Gospel over the relationship between the emerging Christian movement and the Jewish religion, and, together with that, the rights (or otherwise) of non-Jewish people to access the work and teachings of Jesus. (For example, see Patte 1987: 215–16; Hill 1972: 66–72; Fenton 1963: 17–27). It is a text, however, which has often been overlooked in church practice (e.g. by omission from lectionaries). When used, it has generally been interpreted in a way which honours the central character of the gospel narrative, Jesus, to the point where no affront to the woman character in the story is countenanced. Even in this interpretation's mildest form, the healing of the woman's daughter is attributed to the woman's demonstration of faith and wisdom, and not to a change in the mind of Jesus. In its more misogynistic variations, the responses of Jesus are seen to be a deliberate test of the woman's faith with no recognition of the possible cruelty which this interpretation may imply. For example, Augsburger suggests that the woman's request is fulfilled when she comes to worship Jesus (Augsburger 1982: 195); Dicker, that the woman's request is granted because she demonstrates herself as 'a person of great faith' (1983: 62); Hill, that it is her humility (1972: 254); Patte, that it is her recognition of Jesus' true vocation (1987: 221–23); and Gundry, that it is a demonstration to the disciples (and hearers/readers of the text) of the faith of the Gentiles (1982: 311–17). Elaine Wainwright (1995: 140, n. 27, 28) refers to Davies and Allison (1991) as providing a 'recent example of this interpretation', and points to further examples provided in Fiorenza (1992: 161). Fiorenza particularly outlines the modern preoccupation with attempting to 'explain away' the apparent 'offensiveness' of Jesus' initial rebuff to the woman (1992: 161–62).

My reading of the story of the Canaanite woman is indebted to the textual work of Wainwright, who seeks to identify an inclusive tradition within the redaction of the Matthean text despite its patriarchal repressive tendencies. In her doctoral thesis (1991), Wainwright argues that there is significant evidence to suggest the existence of at least some 'house-churches' in the Matthean community that operated with a model of organization which rejected prevailing societal patriarchal household arrangements. The article (Wainwright 1995) that is the primary focus for my work continues this exploration by offering a reading of the story of the Canaanite woman which closes with an imaginative reconstruction of just such a house-church retelling the incident (Wainwright 1995: 152–53). My reading of Wainwright's account of the pericope identifies nine significant dualities which Wainwright understands as operating in the textual and socio-cultural context of the Matthean story of the Canaanite woman. It should be noted that Wainwright's reading of the story of the Canaanite woman also relies on considerations of her own reading context in feminist critical and biblical scholarship and as 'an Australian woman of Anglo-Irish origin who is affiliated with one of the mainstream Christian traditions', i.e. Roman Catholicism (1995: 134–35).

In part, this identification of dualities is also an identification (or reading) of dualities in Wainwright's reading; and through her reading, in my own reading of the text; and through my own reading, in the text itself. Such is the complexity of the hermeneutical focus from a poststructuralist perspective where the text is never the unique and authoritative holder of its own meaning. Wainwright herself does not specifically formulate my identified dualities *as* dualities or in the list format that I employ below. Nevertheless, inherent in her characterization of the story of the Canaanite woman are the implicit recognition of dualistic divisions and the prospect of subversion related to these. For Wainwright, the story of the Canaanite woman is a focal discourse in the Matthean narrative where 'the androcentric perspective and patriarchal structures encoded in the text' are decentred by 'the ethnic and gender otherness surrounding the female in the symbolic universe that the narrative creates' (1995: 137).

As I have formulated them, then, the identified dualities in the Matthean story of the Canaanite woman are:

Male	Female
Lord/Master	Supplicant
Lord (*kyrios*)	Wisdom (*sophia*)
Jew (ethnicity)	Canaanite (ethnicity)
Jew (religion)	Gentile (religion)
Immigrant (occupier)	Indigenous Person
Public Realm	Private Realm
Androcentrically Alone	Gynocentrically Related
Centre	Periphery

These nine form three sets of three related items which are, in turn, parallel to each other. This list of nine dualities is not an exhaustive list. Undoubtedly, other dualities are also present within the pericope. In the context of this argument, however, I have chosen to limit the list of identified dualities to those outlined above and discussed below.

Jesus, as male, is confronted by the woman, who is female: the first duality. According to Wainwright, this is the first woman's voice raised and heard in the text (Wainwright 1995: 139). An earlier female voice, that of the woman with haemorrhage is neither raised nor heard (Mt. 9: 20). Other female characters, few in number, remain voiceless (1995: 137). The non-response of Jesus to the raised voice is 'uncharacteristic' of his response to similar requests such as that of the blind men (Mt. 9: 27–28). This non-response emphasizes the woman's otherness, as does the intervention of the disciples 'who in the androcentric world of the text are characterized as male'. A threat is posed by the voiced appearance of a woman in 'a gender-structured world' (Wainwright 1995: 139). For Wainwright, this gendered interjection is one of the essential confrontations in the 'ethnic and gender otherness' of the unnamed Canaanite woman. For me, it is a clear narrative confrontation of a basic sociocultural duality constructed in the wake of linguistic and subjective formative processes.

The woman calls Jesus 'Lord' (*kyrios*). Her words present her as 'a supplicant seeking favor' (Wainwright 1995: 144–45, 148). Jesus maintains honour throughout (1995: 149) as the 'Master'. It is his gesture of healing and affirmation that closes the pericope: a gesture from the 'Master' to the 'Supplicant'. This particular duality underlies many contemporary popular interpretations of the story of the Canaanite woman as a test of the woman herself. Some of these were canvassed earlier in this chapter in the initial description of the pericope. They rely on inherent variations on the Lord/Supplicant duality—Master/Slave, Master/Pupil, Lord/Serf—for their interpretative approaches.[4] The link between these dualities and the Male/Female pair reflects the gendering of these relationships.

The image of Jesus as 'Master' or 'Lord' to his disciples and followers is contrasted by Wainwright with the 'Wisdom' or sophianic imagery surrounding the story textually, and contained within the pericope itself (1995: 138–39). I have characterized the third duality, then, as Lord (*kyrios*) contrasted with Wisdom (*sophia*). In part, this is another refinement or variation of the Male/Female duality: *kyrios* is masculine; *sophia* is feminine. Nevertheless, the refinement is significant because it brings the gender duality into the realm of conceptualizing divinity, not just humanity. For Wainwright, the story of the Canaanite woman stands at the centre of a chiastic structure of stories containing bread motifs. These stories begin and end with feeding of the thousands stories (Mt. 14: 13–21; 15: 32–39) and invocations of the disciples' 'little faith' (Mt. 14: 28–33; 16: 5–12). Following the argument of Fiorenza (1992: 13), Wainwright links the chiastic section dominated by bread imagery with the preceding section (Mt. 11: 1–9 to 14: 13a) characterized by Wisdom imagery, so that the motif of 'Jesus–Sophia', the identification of Jesus with Wisdom, is carried through both (Wainwright 1995: 138). Yet within the story itself, the androcentric tradition is maintained through the use of the title *kyrios* (1995: 144–45). The tension in this duality is already apparent, but the use of that tension in a subversive move belongs to the second stage of the method of poetic reading. Here, the noting of the duality is sufficient.

The next three dualities form a set around the theme of ethnicity. The fourth duality refers specifically to ethnic identity: Jesus is a Jew; the woman, a Canaanite. This duality is highlighted by Jesus' statement, 'I was sent only to the lost sheep of the house of Israel' (Mt. 15: 24). For Wainwright, ethnicity is the crucial partner to gender in the characterization of the woman's otherness (1995: 139–40). This ethnic 'otherness' is compounded by religious and historical factors. Thus, the fifth duality focuses on the religious division of Jew and Gentile, highlighted by another of Jesus' statements, 'It is not fair to take the children's food and throw it to the dogs' (Mt. 15: 26). For

4. Since the woman requests something that is for her child (Mt. 15: 22) and for the 'children' (Mt. 15: 26), the Parent/Child duality is another pair which can be identified here but is not discussed in this chapter.

Wainwright, the reference to 'dogs' is a double slur against Gentiles and 'those not learned in the Torah' (including women).[5] The dualities of ethnicity and gender, thereby, become overlaid in the religious realm with 'ritual or cultic dimensions' (1995: 140). Ethnicity also calls to mind historical circumstances. Jesus, as a Jew, is a member of the conquering race of the Canaanite woman's homeland. Jesus is conquering immigrant; the woman, conquered indigenous person. This duality was more clearly present in the earlier draft of Wainwright's paper (1993: 14). In the published version, in a footnote, Wainwright points out the anachronism of the term 'Canaanite' in the text and suggests that political, ethnic and religious nuances can be drawn from this (1995: 143). Her recognition of the Australian contextual considerations of the position of indigenous people informs the political, ethnic and religious nuances which she suggests (1995: 140–41). I want to maintain Wainwright's earlier observation that the ethnic designation of the woman 'aligns her symbolically with the indigenous of the land whom Jesus as representative of male Israelite or Jew had dispossessed' (1993: 14). This reading, in itself, may be anachronistic. Nevertheless, the duality is relevant for a contemporary reading of the text in an Australian context as demonstrated implicitly, if not explicitly, by Wainwright's published paper.

The final set of three dualities is organized around the Public/ Private pair. Jesus as male belongs to the public realm. The woman as female belongs to the private realm. This division is emphasized by the woman being 'out of place' in the story. The pericope begins with Jesus alone, although later the disciples enter also. Androcentric aloneness is a male provenance. The woman is gynocentrically defined by her relationship in the private realm to a family member, her daughter. Nevertheless, an association with a male relative is missing and this gap serves to highlight her out-of-placeness also (Wainwright 1995: 144). The setting of the story emphasizes the Public/Private duality from a different perspective. Geographically, the region of Tyre and Sidon is peripheral to the central Gospel action in Galilee and Jerusalem. The story of the woman is a peripheral story to the central drama of the Gospel, and the character of the woman a peripheral character to Jesus, the central figure of the Gospel narrative (1995: 141–42, 144). This last duality—Centre/Periphery—can serve

5. Note also the Sheep/Dog duality developed in this exchange.

as a guiding pattern for attending to the subversive potential contained within these identified dualities since all of the dualities essentially revolve around the primary opposition of the characters, Jesus and the Canaanite woman.

Displacing the Order

In the context of the second stage of the method of poetic reading, attention to alterity in relation to the prior identification of dualities contained within the focal discourse involves attention to points where the apparently distinct poles of the dichotomies move, overlap, change places or undermine the position of their opposites. It also involves attention to additional terms in the discourse which present themselves, not as other points on a continuum but as prior concepts which participate in both terms in a dichotomy through similar relations without being characterized by either of them. Recall the definition of dichotomy as a juxtaposition of terms identified as 'A' and 'Not-A', and the subsequent identification of alterity as 'a multiplicity, which is simultaneously A, Not-A, both and neither'.

The illustration of the reading of the story of the Canaanite woman continues here in order to demonstrate this type of attention. Each of the nine dualities identified above are considered, beginning with the ninth, i.e. Centre/Periphery, and working in reverse. The key opposition in the pericope remains the juxtaposition of the main characters, Jesus and the Canaanite woman. The other nine identified dualities relate to this central one. In the course of dealing with these nine dualities, the seven strategies for the second stage of the method of poetic reading are identified. The whole stage is characterized in this illustration by a privileging of the lesser term of the central opposition, the Canaanite woman.

Centre/Periphery

The story of the Canaanite woman is set in 'the district of Tyre and Sidon' (Mt. 15: 21). The district is outside of both Judea and Galilee, away from Jerusalem and Nazareth, from Jesus' religious home and his familial one. The story is contrasted with the immediately prior accounts of a dispute with the Pharisees from Jerusalem (Mt. 15: 1–9); miracles performed in the Galilean region (Mt. 14: 13–36); and Jesus' rejection in his home town (Mt. 13: 54–58). These last two accounts are divided by the reporting of the death of John the Baptist, Jesus' precursor, at the hands of the political authority, a Jewish ruler administering a Roman charge. In the focal pericope, the character Jesus is placed outside both the source of his identity in terms of his Jewish heritage and the source of his authority in terms of his religious identity. In this place, Jesus is other and his imperviousness to this change in status is challenged by the character of the woman. Wainwright observes that 'the man of honor, withdraws from the center'. The centre is 'the place where that honor would be less threatened'. On the periphery, 'a place of tension and ambiguity', Jesus is out of place. There, he encounters another who is also 'out of place'. Both Jesus' 'out-of-placeness' and that of the woman, who assumes a dominant role in the pericope itself, is a threat to the honour accorded to the central figure of the Gospel (1995: 144). The categories of centre and periphery, honour and shame, are reversed and re-emphasized in this reading. Jesus, the central figure of the Gospel genre, is moved to the periphery geographically. The Canaanite woman, a minor player, is centralized in this text. The Jesus character is faced with the potential of a shameful response in the face of the woman's persistent request. By rendering the Not-A figure of the Canaanite woman as A, a Derridean reversal of the characters' positions is achieved in the interpretation of the story (and perhaps even in the text itself). Alterity is approached because the prior dualistic identifications are maintained underneath the reversal. This is precisely the tension which renders the reversal significant. The possibility of *jouissance* is promoted through the original identifications *and* their reversal. In the tension created, the ambiguity of the subjectivity of the characters is highlighted. At the point where this tension ceases to exist, through either a return to the original identifications or the advent of the reversal as the new dominant dualism, attention to alterity is thwarted and *jouissance* prevented.

Androcentrically Alone/Gynocentrically Related

Despite the setting of the story of the Canaanite woman in a place of limitations for a Jew, within the story itself and in the context of the Gospel narrative, Jesus' movements and presence are unquestioned. The character Jesus is at first alone in this pericope. The disciples enter later. A lone male figure in a public place requires no explanation. The woman is also alone, but in a more noticeable manner. She is defined by a familial relationship and its associated concern, but not by a male relative. While the isolation of the male figure in this cultural setting is unremarkable, the absence of any definition by association with a male relative of this woman ensures that she is depicted as 'out of place'. Without reference to male relatives, she is 'like a woman who is divorced or widowed': 'sexually aggressive and hence dangerous' (Wainwright 1995: 144). She is alone, and she speaks on behalf of her daughter, another female without apparent male support. Yet, the woman defines her own situation, and also that of the character of Jesus, by demanding of Jesus a suitable response to her situation. Her action challenges the dominant androcentric culture in that it and she are defined by her relationship to her daughter 'tormented by a demon' (Mt. 15: 22) and not to a male relative. It is a gynocentric relationship not an androcentric one. The A, male, as a pre-condition for identifying the Not-A, female, is denied. Indeed, in this story, it is the woman who forces the definition of the Christic figure, by her persistent request. The Not-A prompts the A to define itself in terms of its response to the Not-A. This movement again blurs the distinctions between the dual terms by asserting that the identification of the 'positive' term is predicated on the 'negative'. This is not an identification of the A with the Not-A, but it is a recognition of the dependency of the relationship from an inverted position. Whereas the A is usually presumed to determine the Not-A, in this reading, the opposite dependency is highlighted. The independent identity of the positive term is challenged. Its ambiguity revealed.

Public Realm/Private Realm

The woman's 'out-of-placeness' in the story is particularly highlighted by her transgression into public culture. She 'came out and started shouting' (Mt. 15: 22), moving from the private culture of family (and hence of women) to the public culture of men. As a Canaanite 'from that region', her geographic presence may be acceptable. Her social presence is not. As a Not-A, she has crossed over into the realm of the A but she has not become an A. In some senses, this movement of terms is a kind of slippage, although I want to reserve this particular strategy description for specific words. It is a displacement of terms, but not a reversal as in the manner of the Centre/Periphery reversal.

It does represent a gap in the discourse, an apparently deliberate transgression of the character and her appropriate setting for the purpose of establishing a tension within the story which, in narrative tradition, begs resolution. The gap is created apparently by the narrative and its requirements. This creation assumes the necessity of resolution and, thereby, reveals the gap between character and setting: a space of tension in the story. The highlighting of this displacement, in its own right and not as a narrative device for a later progression, challenges the dualities which allow it to be used thus in the first place. The 'out-of-placeness' of the Not-A in the realm of the A is challenged and highlighted. Again, the tension remains because it is a challenge. Should the tension dissolve by removal of the character to a more appropriate place or the loss of the transgression implied in the narrative, attention to alterity is thwarted again, as it is in the resolution of the narrative itself.

Immigrant (Occupier)/Indigenous Person

The dualities related to ethnicity provide particularly fruitful sources for attending to alterity. The anachronistic use of the term 'Canaanite' can be read as a significant slippage of terms in the text. The significance of this slippage is recognizable in the intertextual associations of the story. Intertextuality is not simply the presence of or indebtedness to other literary sources by the focal discourse, but the 'transposition' that such cross-referencing reveals, i.e. the movement of one or more signifying systems into another. Kristeva's classic example of this is the incorporation of carnival, courtly poetry and scholastic discourse into the advent of the modern phenomenon of the novel. A clear consequence of this transposition is the renewed articulation of a thetic position, a rearticulation of the manner in which meaning is constructed, and therefore, of meaning itself: an alteration of 'enunciative and denotative positionality' in Kristevan terms (Kristeva 1984: 59–60). The movement of the signifying systems produces an observable change in the signifying process: in the construction of meaning. The story of the Canaanite woman, and the three dualities which surround the issue of ethnicity within the pericope, provide a good illustration of how the phenomenon of intertextuality can be identified and used in the interpretive process of the text.

Described as a Canaanite, the woman presents a complex figure of multiple nuances. She is both in her place and out of it. Anachronistically, she should not be present in the story, but through her presence described in such a manner, she brings with her a wealth of other associations. She is a member of the indigenous people historically recorded as being dispossessed by the Hebrews, the ancestors of the Jews. The description calls forth the stories in the Hebrew scriptures of the antagonistic relations between these two groups. The confrontation of Canaanite and Jew is a clear device of the story.[6] The woman's 'out-of-placeness' is emphasized by this ethnic distinction, as is that of Jesus in this foreign territory. The tension created by this device is multi-layered. She is clearly a Not-A, a person without identity in the contemporary geo-political situation of both the setting of the story and its writing. Yet this identity, 'ontologically prior' to that of Jesus as Jew, challenges the neat dismissal or 'infinitization' of this negativity, as does her confrontation with the Jew. With the Canaanite woman identified with the prior occupiers of the land of the Jews, both figures are essentially displaced in 'the region of Tyre and Sidon'. The woman is not simply Not-A because she is also precedent and precursor to A: an A which is itself displaced in the focal pericope. The ambiguity of both characters is highlighted in the observation of the slippage of the term and its intertextual connotations, emphasized in the religious aspects of their ethnic distinction.

Jew/Gentile (Religious Distinction)

The Canaanite woman speaks in careful Jewish theological terminology persistently despite the insinuation in the text that this is beyond her realm. Wainwright writes: 'A first-century reader would recognize the intertextuality operative here'. In the psalmic tradition of the Hebrew scriptures, 'the language of the religious insider'

6. A comparison of the story of the Canaanite woman, as it occurs in Matthew's Gospel, and, in its parallel form, in the Gospel of Mark (7: 24–30) reinforces the significance of this device. While Matthew, the latter Gospel of the two which draws on Markan sources, identifies the woman as Canaanite, Mark describes the woman as Syro-Phoenician (Mk 7: 26). Mark, identified as containing Latinisms and therefore probably written in the context of Roman law and administration (Koester 1982: 166–67), has the woman as a conquered person of the Roman Empire. Matthew, probably located in a Syrian context and involved in dialogue with Judaism (Koester 1982: 172), has her as prior occupier to the Jews.

(Wainwright 1995: 145), the woman pleads for a consideration which is outside the apparent bounds of her religious rights or implied inclinations. This disjunction is emphasized in the story itself by the reference to dogs, indicating not only non-Jewish ethnicity but also referring derogatorily 'to those not learned in the Torah': those ineligible and/or ignorant of the Jewish religious law, among them, women (1995: 140). As a Canaanite, a Gentile and a woman, the unnamed female is expected to be thus ignorant but clearly she is not. This Not-A, the woman, engages in conversation with the A, Jesus, in a manner befitting of another situation: a 'challenge-riposte' between equals. The transposition of styles in the pericope 'creates extraordinary tension for the reader' as the woman claims and 'acquires honor beyond the cultural limitations placed on her by her gender' and her ethnicity (Wainwright 1995: 148–49). This acquisition is another aspect of the privileging of the lesser term in a reading of the story of the Canaanite woman.

Jew/Canaanite (Ethnicity)

Because of the intertextual considerations, the address of the woman is ambiguous. She is not a Jew religiously yet she speaks in Jewish religious language. While she comes as a supplicant to a miracle worker, her submissive request is accompanied by some assertive argument to justify her case. She is not a Jew ethnically, not 'a lost sheep of the house of Israel' (Mt. 15: 24), yet she demands a relationship with the Jewish faith-healer. She is a Not-A claiming the status of A and, therefore, somehow neither A nor Not-A, neither both nor either. The character of the woman breaks the tendency towards dichotomy of the binary opposition by its specific 'otherness': an otherness which is not simply the lesser side of the duality. She can be identified as a figure of alterity: a possible third term introduced into the reading of the text in order to destabilize the rigidity of the dualities that may also be read there. This destabilization is achieved by highlighting the constructed nature of the dualities through the portrayal of the third term as existing beyond such categories and yet because of them.

The slipperiness of this assertion is clear. The character of the woman as a figure of alterity relies first, on the depiction of the character as the lesser term in the primary character opposition within the story. This primary opposition is then destabilized through a revaluing of this lesser term and, consequently, of the dominant term also. It could be argued that, in reading the character of the woman as a figure of alterity, the Jesus character also gains a certain ambiguity which opens the way to a similar interpretation. However, attention to the character of the Canaanite woman as a figure of alterity is probably a little easier to sustain than a similar attention to the Jesus character. Such ease is associated with the character of the woman beginning as the lesser character. To read the alterity in this lesser character, a privileging of that part of the duality is required. In a reading context where preference on the basis of gender and ethnic difference is at least in part recognized as inappropriate, the privileging of the lesser term seems far easier than the consequent revaluing of the dominant term (the Jesus character), at least for those reading within a Christian theological tradition. The dominance of the Jesus character makes it extraordinarily difficult to consider the alterity of this character, since it is not privileging that the dominant term requires, but de-privileging. De-privileging is not the same as denigration, but it does involve the withdrawal of the reading of the dominant term as inherently dominant, without the assertion of the inverted triumphalism which celebrates the de-privileging of the term as a further sign of its dominance. While this process is theoretically possible, it does have implications for a Christian theological context.

Both characters hold the potential to be interpreted as figures of alterity. The character of the woman stands out, however, because, she is the lesser term which is privileged. The Jesus character, as the dominant character dethroned, presents a different set of difficulties in identifying its 'otherness', and perhaps even a more threatening set. Nevertheless, in the process of reading, either or both of them as figures of alterity, neither of them, in fact, lose their original status. That is, in part, the reason that they can obtain a position of alterity: because at one point they each are identified with one side of the duality. This identification in turn is overturned, and ambiguity is highlighted.

Lord (Kyrios)/*Wisdom* (Sophia)

The duality observable in the text in its textual context, although not readily apparent simply from the verses of this pericope, concerns the imaging of Jesus as *kyrios* (masculine) and *sophia* (feminine): Master or Lord, and Wisdom. This duality presents itself in Wainwright's reading of the redaction of the Gospel of Matthew. Earlier in Matthew,

Jesus is cast as *sophia*, i.e. Wisdom.[7] The bread imagery which continues through to and past the pericope of the Canaanite woman underscores this imagery (Wainwright 1995: 138). In contrast, the woman's address to Jesus as 'Lord', the depiction of the Jesus character in the context of disciples who look to him for action, and the closure of the story with a pronouncement from Jesus concerning the woman, all present the Jesus character as 'representative of the kyriocentric structures and discourses that characterize the Matthean narrative'. The privilege assigned to the Jesus character because of his gender and ethnicity is 'divinely sanctioned' in his identification with the messianic 'Son of David' imagery (Wainwright 1995: 140). There is a clear tension here. Jesus, identified with Wisdom earlier, is depicted upholding the gender and ethnicity prejudices of the kyriarchal messianic tradition, until challenged. At the point of challenge, Jesus moves his position. Nevertheless, his authority is reasserted in the closing admonition to the woman. Furthermore, the image of the woman crying out in the streets carries with it sophianic associations from the Hebrew scriptures (Proverbs 8). The answer to the question as to which character should be identified with the Wisdom motif at this chiastically central pericope is unclear. Neither the Jesus character nor the woman character is completely identifiable with it. But then, neither of the characters is devoid of associations to it. Both characters, in a sense, are neither Not-A nor not Not-A: a further variation on the complex formula of the (il)logical description of alterity. There are considerations of intertextuality here, as well as varying interpretations of the story laid alongside each other. The story of the Canaanite woman can be read with either of the characters filling the Wisdom role. In the process of the possibility of such dual (and multiple) interpretations of the text, the ambiguities of the text and its reading(s) are highlighted.

Master/Supplicant

This ambiguity is further highlighted in the Master/Supplicant duality. It is the woman who comes seeking the master, a supplicant with a request. Initially, the request is ignored: an appropriate 'brushing aside of the challenge of an inferior' in the manner of the culture of the 'challenge-riposte' where only equals may engage in dialogue. Yet later in the story, the woman's request is acknowledged,

7. For discussion on the imagery of Jesus-Sophia, see Johnson 1992: 94–100.

her challenge validated and her request granted (Wainwright 1995: 148–49). In being included in such an exchange, the woman is lifted out of her status as Not-A, and treated as an A. In elements of the woman's argument being accepted by the Jesus character, her role as teacher or colleague is validated, while the Jesus character's role is changed to one who learns from another for a brief moment—not simply an A. Indeed, a kind of mutuality is affirmed by an exchange of teaching for healing as the outcome of this dialogue conducted as if between two social equals. This is not really a reversal of terms. It certainly is a re-privileging of the Not-A, together with a corresponding de-privileging of the A, but not so that a mirror hierarchy is produced. Mutuality between terms is the outcome here.

Male/Female

Perhaps the major binary opposition underscoring the whole passage, outside of the opposition of the characters themselves, is the male/female one. Jesus is male. The woman is female. Her very lack of nominal identification indicates the tension inherent in such a public meeting. Truly, she is 'out of place'. But it is this out-of-placeness that ensures her character cuts across the contextual dichotomies within which the story is found. She is the alterity which stands outside of, and yet within, the dichotomous structure. She is also the ambivalence which forces the other central character, Jesus, into a more ambivalent position as well. The re-privileging of the character of the woman in the reading of the story allows a reading of ambivalence to occur where the gender roles become confused.

Re-Presenting the Discourse

Having recounted seven suggested strategies for the second stage of the method of poetic reading through the illustrative reading of the story of the Canaanite woman, I offer a re-presentation of the focal discourse attending to the particular task of attempting to enunciate alterity. The pattern of the discourse thus unfolds:

Jesus (A) moves to a place outside Jewish territory (Not-A). He is approached by a woman (Not-A) defined by her relationship to another female (Not-A). She is also Canaanite (both A and Not-A and neither i.e. alterity). Her approach is public (alterity) in suitable language but her mission is private (Not-A). Jesus ignores her. The disciples defined in relation to Jesus (A) are annoyed by the presence of the woman (Not-A). They complain to Jesus (A) who reaffirms her status as Not-A. The woman reaffirms her need despite the apparent impropriety of her request (alterity). Jesus again reaffirms her status (Not-A). The woman assents to the status but requests a different understanding of the way in which Not-A's are treated (alterity). Jesus affirms the woman's faith.

There are two particular aspects of the character of the woman where alterity clearly emerges. First, it is in discourse that the alterity of the woman is expressed and through which it challenges the accepted dichotomies. The text, drawn from an oral culture, is steeped in oral terms ('shouting'; 'did not answer'; 'urged him, saying' etc.). It is precisely the woman's presence orally that establishes her transgression subjectively. Second, the alterity of her being is expressed through the ambivalence of her ethnicity, i.e. her identification as Canaanite, the displaced indigenous person. As woman (Not-A), she enters into the realm of A by speaking publicly, engaging in theological debate and approaching a male on her own. She has become a displaced other, no longer simply Not-A, but operating as both Not-A and A, and therefore, necessarily, as neither. As Canaanite, similarly, she is displaced. Not merely Not-A, she is in fact displaced prior subject: A become Not-A and therefore neither. Theologically addressing a Jew in his own terms, a lone woman yet prior resident of the region and of the claimed homeland of the addressee, shouting in the public arena but in the careful words of a Jewish religious devotee, the character of the Canaanite woman breaks the power of binary opposition as dichotomy since she is both A and Not-A and neither. In the gaps and silences of this oral text, readers are invited to consider the transgression further.

The account of the character of the woman moves us to the crucial Jesus/Not-Jesus dichotomy and the impact of the story of the Canaanite woman on the characterization of Jesus as Christ. In the theological arena, the proposed poetic reading of the story of the Canaanite woman creates an enormous impact on the Christ/Not-Christ dichotomy. In the story, Jesus is out of place and not simply geographically. As Wainwright points out, he also does not conform to the *basileia* vision previously enunciated (Wainwright 1995: 142). The woman, displaced herself, holds the vision and re-imparts it to Jesus, performing the role of the Christ herself. Jesus is thus both A and Not-A and neither, as is the woman. The imagery of the Christ becomes much more diffuse and less focussed on a particular historical individual or, at least, his characterization and a reading of the text is established which clearly emphasizes ambiguity.

How does this reading of the story of the Canaanite woman differ from Wainwright's? Wainwright is certainly concerned with the possibilities of the woman's ethnic and gender otherness for decentring the patriarchal traditions within the texts and its interpretations. Her particular reading of the text leads her to uphold the woman as a symbol for the prophetic resistance of woman against injustice, as a reminder of the necessity for women to construct their own discourses in the face of the dominance of masculine discourse, and as an impetus to the reconstruction of women's stories marginalized in the Christian tradition (Wainwright 1995: 149–50).

The story of the Canaanite woman is a story of political action, particularly when read through the deconstructive/reconstructive lenses proposed by poetic reading. With Wainwright, I want to claim the revolutionary impetus readable in the story, the encouragement to voice new positions, and the necessity of reconstructing the tradition. I want to focus more specifically, however, on the nature of the otherness detectable in the text, particularly through the figure of the woman, but concomitantly, also through that of the Jesus figure. By constructing this otherness as alterity and relating this alterity to the semiotic of the Kristevan map of language and subjectivity, the method of poetic reading has particular implications for a new theological reconstruction. My reading of the story of the Canaanite woman using a method I have named 'poetic reading' leads me to a reconstruction of the text which posits the ambiguity of the characters within it, not only their otherness, but also their sameness as products of the semiotic economy. In making this claim, I recognize that there are many other elements within the text (notably some of its imagery, e.g. the animal associations) which would prove fruitful sources for further investigation of the presence of the semiotic within the text.

Chapter 7

RE-PRESENTING THE (M)OTHER: A THEOLOGY OF
AN-OTHER COMING

Making a Case

A duality implied by varying interpretations of the story of the Canaanite woman is that of the virgin/whore dichotomy of female representation. Following from the illustrative use of the reading of the Matthean story of the Canaanite woman (Mt. 15: 21–28), this chapter takes the method of poetic reading into the realm of the development of theological position(s) from such a hermeneutic. A key theological implication from the method of poetic reading is a confrontation with the feminine other, the (m)other. The (m)other is a means of designating, without defining or delimiting, the repressed otherness of language and identity, i.e. the semiotic. A confrontation with this feminine other is made possible through attending to the dual characterization of women as virgin and whore in Western Christian tradition. In keeping with the strategies of poetic reading, the subversion of the virgin/whore duality via the privileging of the lesser term, the whore, will provide a means of approaching the (m)other and the alterity of language and identity. Thus, the outline of this chapter follows the three stage method of poetic reading:

1. The identification of the duality of the virgin/whore, both within interpretations of the story of the Canaanite woman, and the Western Christian socio-cultural milieu.
2. The subversion of that duality through attending to the lesser term of the duality, the whore, and privileging it.
3. The attempted re-presentation of alterity in discourse through the device of the (m)other.

In a theological context, a key means of privileging any term is to equate its characteristics with the concept of divinity. Hence, it is through an exploration of the concept of God as whore that the confrontation with the (m)other is proposed, and the outcome of *jouissance* suggested. Through the use of an unpublished paper entitled 'God is a Black Lesbian Whore!' (Henman 1994), an encounter with graffiti on a University toilet cubicle wall, I explore the nature of the confrontation with the image of God as whore. This exploration is followed by an account of the nature of the (m)other concept in the context of Kristeva's analysis of the semiotic motility of the archetypal mother, and Martha Reineke's relocation of the victim of the archetypal primal murder as the (m)other. I return to the story of the Canaanite woman and engage momentarily with Kristeva's encounter (1982: 115–16) with the Markan parallel (7: 24–30) to this biblical text. Drawing from the poetic reading of the Matthean pericope from the previous chapter, the analysis of the (m)other in this chapter, and my exploration of the encounter with God in the image of the whore, I argue that the goal of *jouissance* sought by the method of poetic reading demands a confrontation with the character of the woman as a divine figure, and that this divinity is encountered through the characterization of the woman in the whore image, the unruly feminine uncontrollable by patriarchy. The result of this confrontation with the woman as a divine figure is a splitting of the God imagery contained within the story between the character of Jesus and that of the woman. In this manner, this reading also confronts the ambiguous subjectivity of the divine. The response to this confrontation, provided it is entered into and not avoided, for the Christian subject is *jouissance*.

Virgin and/or Whore

Interpretations of the story of the Canaanite woman tend to fall into two characterizations of the woman. Formerly dominant interpretations suggest that the woman is earning her daughter's health through proving her faith, wisdom, or persistence in the face of a test by Jesus. Feminist interpretations such as that suggested by Wainwright, or the method of poetic reading, tend to read the woman as challenging Jesus and causing a change in his intentions.[1] This split in interpretations mirrors a division in the characterization of

---

1. See also feminist accounts of the parallel story of the Syro-Phoenician woman in Mark 7: 24–30 by Tolbert (1992: 268–69) and Fiorenza (1992: 11–13; 96–100; 103; 160–63).

women in the Western Christian tradition through the dichotomous images of the virgin and the whore: the feminine supporter of patriarchy, and the feminine challenger to patriarchy.

Philosopher Nel Noddings, in her book, *Women and Evil* (1989), describes the dualistic stereotypes of women in the Western Hellenistic Judeo-Christian tradition as 'the angel in the house' (1989: 59–89) and 'the devil's gateway' (1989: 35–58). The latter term is drawn from the writings of second-century Christian theologian Tertullian. For Noddings, women 'appear as angels or as innately moral and beautiful as long as their sphere of activity remains severely limited' (1989: 88). This assertion is encompassed in the distinction made by feminist liberation theologian and ethicist Beverley Wildung Harrison (1985) between what is deemed appropriate and inappropriate femininity as a corollary of a series of underlying 'false dualisms' which lie at the core of patriarchal ideological control. Notions of what is deemed to be appropriate femininity (sweetness, goodness, non-assertiveness, gentility, weakness, receptivity, sexual propriety) are contrasted with what is deemed to be inappropriate femininity (aggressiveness, hostility, assertiveness, independence, self-reliance, strength, sexual availability). Neither femininity is considered appropriate to the masculine public realm although inappropriate femininity is seen as a threat to it, while appropriate femininity is understood as supporting it. Appropriate femininity may share in the reflected glory of the masculine 'rational and spiritual' world while inappropriate femininity is relegated to the '"lower", "animal" modalities of existence that have to be tamed or in some way overcome and transcended'. Appropriate femininity is associated with a sanitized and de-physicalized notion of sexuality as parental obligation. Inappropriate femininity is associated with carnality, physicality, sensuality and bodiliness (Harrison 1985: 135–39).

A further means of characterizing this duality is through the caricature of the biblical figures of Mary, the mother of Jesus, and Eve. For Noddings, the duality of appropriate and inappropriate femininity is perpetuated in the notion of the 'immaculately conceived virgin' and the myth of the 'demon-Eve' (Noddings 1989: 55). Similarly, Rosemary Radford Ruether, in *Sexism and God-talk* (1983), distinguishes the image of Mary as 'obedient female' and reverser of the destructiveness of Eve (Ruether 1983: 150), the archetype of woman 'as the primordial cause of evil' (Ruether 1983: 165–66). In her self-identified movement outside of Christianity, *Beyond God the Father* (1985), originally published in 1975, Mary Daly also explores the Mary-Eve dichotomy in relation to Christian understandings of fall and redemption.

A final mention of alternative terminology for the dualistic characterization of appropriate and inappropriate femininity is relevant to my Australian context. In 1975, Anne Summers' groundbreaking book *Damned Whores and God's Police: The Colonization of Women in Australia*, argued that the 'traditional Judaeo-Christian notion' that women were 'exclusively either good or evil' ('virgin Mary' or 'Mary Magdalene') was imported to Australia with the first permanent European settlement. In the Australian context, this duality was further reinforced by the nature of the European settlement. Summers asserts that 'almost *all* women were categorized as whores' during the first sixty years of the European occupation of Australia: convict women, whatever their crime; Aboriginal women, doubly burdened by racial dualities; and female immigrants with neither of the apparent burdens of criminal conviction or racial difference. Later the imagery of 'God's police' became important as women were again burdened by the myth of the feminine with the new task of curbing the excesses of the male members of the colony and turning a 'continental gaol' into a 'respectable society' (Summers 1975: 267, 276–77, 291–92).

The dualistic image of damned whores and God's police has been effectively incorporated into feminist political analysis in Australia. For example, in an exploration that probably owes its genesis to comments made by Summers about the categorization of women's mental health (Summers 1975: 98–103), Jill Julius Matthews ponders images of 'good' and 'mad' women in twentieth century Australia (1984). Matthews traces a ferocious double-bind for women in Australia where the living of the ideal of femininity, however that is characterized in different times and communities, is impossible; the failure to do so is labelled; and the deliberate disregard of the ideal is cause for 'legitimate' punishment in the hope that other deviators will be warned 'of the dangers of non-conformity'. Matthews' argument relies on case studies from the records of admissions to a psychiatric hospital in South Australia between 1945 and 1971 (Matthews 1984: 7, 199, 201, 202–203). The virgin/whore dichotomy is firmly established as extant in an Australian context through such analyses.

I have retained the generic terms of the virgin and the whore rather than any of the other alternatives for several reasons. First, avoiding the Mary-Eve characterization allows for specific re-readings of those characters outside of their dualistic interpretations. Second, the terms 'virgin' and 'whore' signal specific sexual connotations associated with the stereotypes. Such connotations can be minimized in notions of appropriate and inappropriate femininity but cannot be in the context of an approach based in psychoanalytic theory. The sexual connotations of these terms are also powerfully connected to concepts of bodiliness, that which is repressed, and the specific characterization of women in sexual and bodily terms. Noddings, who argues that the dichotomous stereotypes of women have played a powerful role in 'the violent struggle to control women's sexuality' (Noddings 1989: 57), associates her 'devil's gateway' image with three related characterizations: 'the denigration of the body and its functions, the notion that demonic forces work through the feminine unconscious, and the pernicious scapegoating of women in myths of the Fall' (Noddings 1989: 36). The terms 'virgin' and 'whore' maintain such connections through their specific sexual references. They have the added convenience of being single words: shorthand references to concepts which encompass highly complex and interactive ideas and phenomena. Finally, the virgin/whore terminology is significantly reminiscent of Summer's characterization of the duality of God's police and damned whores, a useful trace for an Australian context.

The significance of the virgin/whore duality lies not simply in the observation of its existence but also in its political significance at several levels. The virgin/whore dichotomy is an accomplice in limiting the autonomy of individual women; characterizing the role of women *en masse* in a society, thereby confining their spheres of influence to certain realms, notably domestic family arrangements; perpetuating corresponding dichotomies such as body/mind and nature/culture, thereby contributing to the denigration and destruction of entities representing the lesser terms of those dualities; and maintaining the ideological domination of patriarchy in general. The breaking of the power of such a paradigm is regarded by people such as Noddings, Wildung Harrison, Radford Ruether and Daly as a political and ethical imperative. A confrontation with the image of God as whore may be one useful strategy for such an ethico-political movement in a theological context and a key theological implication arising from the proposed method of poetic reading.

The Whore

My definition of the whore begins with an image of woman as challenger to the patriarchal, constructed order. Her sexuality is uncontrolled by that order: either by individual association with a male protector (husband, father, brother etc.) or by moral precept. The image is invested with a tremendous sense of power—the power to seduce sexually and, by analogy, away from the constructed 'moral' order. This investment with power produces a response of fear, and the desire for separation from the possibility of corruption suggested by the image. Because of the power investment, the image also brings with it an almost irresistible attraction. This perceived seductive power demands the repression of the whore. The image of the whore is used to justify the repression of women as the collective potential site for this corrupting power. In this definition of the whore, the image is distinguished entirely from the particularities of women's lives. The whore, as an image, cannot be equated with any individual or any specific aspect of certain women's lives, e.g. prostitutes or prostitution. Rather, women's lives are characterized in their particularities by the vagaries of the image of the larger-than-life, wanton, unrepressed, seductive, dangerous whore: the other of the patriarchal order.

God as a Whore

In a brave and personally spiritually rigorous paper, Paul Henman considers a piece of graffiti that initially confronted him in one of the men's toilets at the University of Queensland. As with much interesting graffiti in University toilets, the locus of attention was not so much a statement as an exchange between two writers. The exchange, however, began with a 'claim': 'God is a black lesbian whore!'. In this version of the statement, the word 'feminist' was omitted, although I have heard of variations which have included this adjective also.

Henman's paper is confronting just as the toilet cubicle graffiti was confronting to him: 'Is it a deep theological statement, or is it the work of a God-hating, racist, homophobic misogynist spreading rumours in the hope of dethroning God from "his" throne?' (Henman 1994: 1). The paper reflects the language of the graffiti which becomes more confronting in its use of sexual slang when a response is added. In some ways, the confrontational nature of both the graffiti and Henman's reflection upon it suggests precisely the significance of the argument of this chapter. A confrontation with the feminine other is the repulsive, attractive imperative of a rigorous application of the method of poetic reading. The language of the graffiti, Henman's paper and my use of the term 'whore' for God is confrontational. Such confrontation is precisely illustrative of the suggested theological imperative of the process of poetic reading. Poetic reading demands the facing and confronting of a disturbing otherness outside of any constructed order with which we find ourselves comfortably, unconsciously familiar. Henman's paper provides a means of exploring the nature of this confrontation.

Henman examines a number of the images evoked by the graffiti: the singular terms 'black', 'lesbian' and 'whore', as well as some of the interrelationships between them, for example, 'lesbian whore'. While Henman asserts that, from his own 'personal theological journey', he is able to affirm that God could be imaged as black and lesbian (1994: 1), it is the whore image that proves to be the most provocative for his own considerations. After considering the images of black and lesbian women as images of the God who '*is* poor and oppressed' (1994: 2), Henman considers the image of God as whore: first, as 'prostitute', again an image of poverty and oppression (1994: 3–4), and then as sexualized feminine object, something which can be 'fucked' (1994: 8). The latter is where the confrontation really begins.

In some ways, Henman's paper is not confrontational enough. In particular, Henman's occasional tendency to resort implicitly to the image of the 'poor, respectable prostitute' is, in its own way, an attempt to move a picture of inappropriate femininity into that of appropriate femininity: the good girl forced into something she would not choose for reasons of necessity and/or altruism. This image is not the confrontational image that I associate with the term 'whore'. The depiction of prostitution in such a manner is not the key to the image of the whore as the inappropriate, repressed feminine other.

In *Reading, Writing and Rewriting the Prostitute Body* (1994), Shannon Bell acknowledges the contradictory images of 'the [female] prostitute body': disease, sufferer, worker, deviant, symbol of urban decay, criminal, abnormality and unrepressed sexuality. Recognizing the contradictions between the traces of acceptable and unacceptable femininity found within this catalogue, Bell claims an 'overarching cultural representation' of 'the prostitute as the other within the categorical other': 'the profane woman', archetypal inappropriate femininity. In arriving at this characterization, she appeals to a reading of Freud's 'marking of the prostitute body as ambiguous'. This ambiguity is characterized by Bell as the imaging of the prostitute body as both the maternal body and a 'lower type of sexual object' and, alternatively, 'the polymorphously uninhibited sexual woman and woman lacking sexual integrity' (Bell 1994: 70–72). It is this ambiguous image which I wish to draw upon in aligning the concept of the whore, with the concept of the (m)other from the work of Julia Kristeva.

Like Bell, and perhaps more emphatically than Bell, I wish to make a distinction between the varying imagery of prostitution and the particular archetype of the profane woman, in my terms, the whore. In part, Bell's suggestion about the connections between the multiple images of the prostitute body and the 'overarching cultural representation' of 'the profane woman' can be read, again in my terms, as an indication that prostitutes have the capacity to re-present alterity to some extent because of their multiple characterizations. Indeed, Bell does argue that prostitute performance art 'balances the presentation of the prostitute body as an abused body and as an empowered body, refusing any bifurcation', in my terms again, subjecting ambiguity. For, according to Bell, in the balancing act of prostitute performance art, the dichotomous characterization of women as madonna/whore (her description of the dual characterization of women) is deconstructed, leaving space for a 'new philosophical theory of prostitution' (Bell 1994: 188).

Bell sees prostitute performance art as bringing into discourse the ambiguity of the feminine other. Her reading of the possibilities of prostitute performance art is closely related to several of the suggested strategies in the second stage of my articulated method of poetic reading. By highlighting spaces, gaps, slippages, contradictions and diversity in the construction of the prostitute body, prostitute performance art re-presents alterity on a multi-media, multi-dimensional canvas. In contrast, though not contradiction, it is my contention that the privileging of the lesser term of the dual characterization of women by aligning it with the image of divinity produces a similar possibility for the re-presentation of alterity in a theological context.

In my context, as in Bell's, the archetype of the whore is more than any individual notion of the prostitute by being a particular characterization of the 'overarching cultural representation' of the profane woman. Henman begins to make his confrontation with this archetype when he commences his consideration of God as the sexually active, assertive and available whore: 'Below the penned theological statement, "GOD IS A BLACK LESBIAN WHORE!" in the same red ink was an epistemological claim: "(I know, I screwed HIM)" ' (Henman 1994: 6).

Acknowledging the multiplicity of connotations expressed in the word 'screwed' being used to refer to the act of 'carnal knowledge' and the gender ambiguity applied to God by the graffiti exchange (1994: 7), Henman explores three possibilities of meaning indicated by the graffiti conversation. His first consideration concerns the possibility that the primary author of the graffiti (the writer in red) has encountered God in an act of knowing and discovered the female aspects of divinity (1994: 7–8). The second consideration recognizes the hatred inferred against females by such statements and the God-hate thereby readable in such expressions: 'Like the "bum-raped" male prisoner is degraded, no longer considered a man but a quasi-female, so too is God degraded from being a male to become female' (Henman 1994: 8). The third consideration involves a combination of the first two with a twist: 'In the death-fuck of the male he-God (denoted by "HIM") we recognize the reality of God as female (and black, lesbian and "whore"). In the ironic hatred fuck of the he-God, God dies and is resurrected as the she-God' (Henman 1994: 9).

Henman plays with the gendering of God, producing the self-destruction (i.e. death) of the 'patriarchal he-God'. This self-destruction reveals the 'brokenness of humanity' and the prospect of the 'she-God' as 'the possibility of life and its celebration'. The patriarchal he-God is identified by Henman with the writer(s) of the graffiti as 'racist, homophobic and misogynist'. In this third consideration, the 'fucking' by a patriarchal he-God and the patriarchal he-God as 'fucked'[2] evoked by the image of the whore for Henman draws attention to the possibility of a she-God who transcends such an exploitative situation (Henman 1994: 9–10). Again, Henman draws perilously close to the image of the poor prostitute.

---

2.   The term 'fucked' is an Australian colloquialism for something akin to 'at the end of its useful life'.

Nevertheless, his recognition of the importance of the image of sexual activity to the use of the term 'whore' is crucial. His early recognition of the denigration of women inherent in the exchange is important to my own continuing considerations. I would not, however, be so quick to focus on the gender of the 'fucker' as is Henman.

The movement too quickly from the possible image of the female deity to the male, patriarchal one takes away the immediacy of the confrontation with the powerful image of God as 'whore'. In part, this movement is precipitated by the second piece of graffiti penned as a response to the first. The masculine gender of God is maintained and emphasized, albeit ironically, in the statement, 'I screwed <u>HIM</u>'. While Henman briefly dwells on the homophobic considerations suggested by this statement, the statement itself almost immediately moves him to focus on a male God who 'fucks' himself. This movement leaves the feminine deity image in the possession of powerlessness and oppression, whereas the male God is clearly powerful and aggressive, even violent and abusive—'the fucking God is also a fighting God, a God of war'—despite existing on both sides of the homosexual rape image (Henman 1994: 11). Momentarily God stands on both sides of the act of carnal knowledge as the patriarchal God 'fucks' himself to death. For Henman, this death is where the real space for the construction of the feminine deity occurs.

There are two losses in this movement by Henman, for a gain which may not be in the interests of the subversion of the dual characterization of women. First, in focusing too quickly on the patriarchal, 'fucking' God, the female image of God as whore, is in fact lost to another more familiar, less threatening image of feminine deity—the gentle, creative, earth mother.[3] Second, in changing the gender of the one who is 'fucked' to masculine, the recognition of the denigration of women earlier made by Henman is counteracted by an assertion that the victim of death is male, albeit one who is discovered to be female in the act of his death. Henman himself implicitly recognizes the latter element when, at the end of his paper, he provides one last observation which can be read as a recognition of the eruption of the semiotic into the symbolic expression of the graffiti. The graffiti writer has written in red ink. Henman ponders

---

3. Many feminine images of God suggested by contemporary Christian feminist scholars have also tended towards the image of the good, gentle, earth mother, i.e. a variation on the image of appropriate femininity. See, for example, Mollenkott (1984), McFague (1987), and Johnson (1992).

whether this choice of ink references the *'life-sustaining* blood of the oppressed, black, lesbian, "whore"', the *'life-renewing* blood of the cross', the *'life-creating* blood shed in menstruation' and the 'blood of our black, lesbian, "whore" Christ' (Henman 1994: 14–15).

This recognition comes somewhat belatedly especially since Henman has already relied on Andrea Dworkin's retelling of Leo Tolstoy's story 'The Kreutzer Sonata' for the creative impetus to the interpretation of the God who 'fucks' himself (Henman 1994: 9). 'The Kreutzer Sonata' recounts the slow killing of a wife by her husband. Ironically, the killer discovers the personhood of the victim through her death. Ironically, too, for Henman, the victim in his interpretation of the graffiti is male, and the male victim's death brings about the resurrection of a female deity, whereas the recounted story tells of the death of a woman, and the resurrection, through recognition of her personhood, of a woman. The confrontation with the feminine other, then, is one which must take into account the status of that other as victim, but in very specific terms. The feminine other as victim is not the image of the appropriate feminine forced into behaviour which she abhors through necessity. The feminine other as victim is the image of the one murdered continuously for who she is, challenger to the patriarchal order, and who she will not be, conformer to that same order: defiant and uncontrollable to the end.

Henman's encounter with the toilet cubicle graffiti, almost in a stream of consciousness style, moves through several possible layers of interpretation to rest finally with this possibility of God as whore and therefore murder victim. His sustained encounter with the image of God as whore exposes:

1. The desire to destroy the whore through repression, i.e. death.
2. The desire to rehabilitate the whore into an image of appropriate femininity, i.e. earth mother.
3. The failure to recognize when the victim is female rather than male.

Of Henman's three interpretations of the graffiti exchange then the first, an act of knowing, provides the most useful basis for the encounter with the image of God as whore; the second, a recognition of the hatred of the feminine, assists in identifying the dynamic of threat and fear associated with the encounter; and the third, the death-fuck of the he-God offers an insight into the violent, threatening nature of the encounter, and the tendency to misidentify the victim.

In his willingness to follow through the death-fuck of the he-God imagery, Henman has created the space for an authentic encounter with God as whore to occur. In the suggestion made at the end of his paper, Henman begins to approach the crux of this encounter: a confrontation with God as whore as an encounter with the repressed. In Christianity, the key symbol of repression is the death of the God-human Christ who becomes the required sacrificial victim not through circumstance and misfortune but salvific necessity. If it is the death-fuck of the he-God that Henman witnesses in his encounter with the graffiti, the immediate victim is not the patriarchal 'fucker', but the one who is available and 'fucked' without any apparent consequence or remorse. In highlighting God as 'fucked' alongside the recognition of the denigration of women, Henman raises the interesting possibility that, in Christ, we crucify the whore. It then follows that through the Christic imagery, there is the possibility of re-encountering or resurrecting her. The murdered feminine other image leads me to a recounting of the (m)other imagery of Kristeva, particularly as interpreted by Martha Reineke. The resurrection possibilities of the Christic imagery lead me back to the story of an encounter between Jesus and a Canaanite woman.

The Whore as Murdered (M)Other

The figure of the mother in the work of Kristeva holds an ambivalent position. She is the subject who holds within herself the potential for multiple subjectivity. She does not conform to the neat expectations of the singular and unitary identity of an individual. The process of pregnancy calls into question the nature of boundaries between herself and her child, her potential other. From the child's perspective, the mother is both source of life, and entity from which it must become separated in order to establish its own identity. The mother's ambivalent position and the necessity of the child's separation from the mother contribute to the process of the mother's 'abjectification' as the child enters into the symbolic realm, the place of language and identity. In this process, the mother becomes the child's other, the entity over against which the child defines itself, and to which the child is continually drawn. The drawing power of this (m)other is the drawing power of desire, the yearning for reunification with some primeval, preconscious state or entity. Desire is generally unconscious, unacknowledged, displaced and fetishized. It cannot be satisfied, for reunification with the (m)other threatens identity. The image of the (m)other is thus invested with an horrific power both of repulsion and attraction. It is this 'power' of the 'abject' feminine which Julia Kristeva explores in her book *Powers* (1982). It is the position of ambivalence in which individuals find themselves in relation to this (m)other that holds both the key to the dilemma and the possibility of moving beyond the impasse of strict dualisms. The displacement of desire is an important clue to the necessity of confronting the image of God as (m)other or, in my terms, whore.

In *Revolution* (1984), Kristeva explores her imagined double helix of human life: a double helix pertaining to psychic and linguistic development. The two strands of the double helix—the semiotic and the symbolic—represent the heterogeneous potential for meaning and the attempted homogeneous construction of meaning. These two components of language and meaning construction are assigned genders: the semiotic is feminine, the symbolic is masculine. Gender and sex are both regarded as constructs, and not necessarily distinguishable as separate constructs. There is no suggested ontological or biological correlation within the terms 'masculine' and 'feminine' in this context. Their use, however, polarizes sexual and/or gender identity. The semiotic/symbolic split and the accompanying constructs of polarized gender and/or sex is understood as underlying the profound tendency for people in Western European patriarchal cultures to organize their world in terms of binary oppositions or dualities. Nevertheless, it is important to note again that neither the semiotic nor the symbolic are regarded by Kristeva as existing without the presence of the other. Both are discovered to be present in the tenuous and ambivalent status of the 'speaking subject' or the *'sujet en procès'*, the subject-in-process, the continuous search for individual and corporate identity.

The symbolic component of the 'signifying process', i.e. the process of language and identity formation, represents that which is readily observable in language: the order, arrangement and selection of signs, syntax, grammatical constructions and their corresponding social constraints. This component is equated with the 'paternal function', the construction and maintenance of an order into which human beings are invited and indeed compelled to enter as they begin to gain their identities even as very young children. This paternal function is the 'Law' or 'Name-Of-The-Father' with which Lacan suggests individuals must eventually identify in order to attain stable psychic identities. Kristeva identifies this law as the logic and power of the number '1' (1980: 69–91). It represents law, definition, 'linguistic, psychic, and social "prohibition"' and God. This is the site, for Kristeva, of theology and dogma. It is the site of certainty and the positing of 'truth' but in that respect it is also the site of illusion and subterfuge. It is a necessary component of language and of identity but it is not the only component. Failure to recognize the complexity of language and identity formation is a denial of the countering aspect of the signifying process: the semiotic, an equally important component of that process. Failure to recognize the complexity of language and identity formation also results in an overvaluing of the symbolic. This overvaluing has pathological consequences as does its undervaluing.

In *Revolution* (1984), Kristeva's image of the semiotic is clearly contrasted with her understanding of the symbolic. The semiotic exists prior to language and identity formation as well as within the continuing process of both. It is heterogeneous, unformed, undefined, non-unified, akin to rhythm and movement rather than to word and definition. It carries the whole potential of possible meanings without signifying any. The Lacanian correlation is the Real: the complex indescribable and unknowable actuality of human identity and interaction. The semiotic is imaged by Kristeva as the Greek *chora*, a womblike vessel or receptacle which surrounds the emerging subject. In order to gain identity, a separation from the semiotic must occur. This process of separation occurs through the 'mirror stage' and the 'thetic process'. The mirror stage refers to the identification of a child's own reflection in a mirrored surface and in the perspective of its primary caregivers. The thetic process refers to the positing of statements, the emergent use of language and particularly of the pronoun 'I', and the corresponding emergence of individual identity. The process of linguistic and subjective separation is symmetrical to the process of separation of a child from its primary caregiver, usually its mother at such an early stage of life. The semiotic is thus identified with the mother as the symbolic is with the father. The gender/sex construction referred to above occurs thus. The mother from which 'I' must separate has been established as the mother which threatens to devour and to prevent the development of my own identity. The father has been established as the principle with which I must identify, although the way in which I must identify with that principle will be determined by my assigned sex. The identification process involves a repression of that which has been constructed as the true 'feminine' nature, the devouring mother, the whore.

Within Kristeva's conceptual framework, the possibility of moving beyond such a dichotomy does exist. It exists in the power of poetic language to call upon multiple meanings and significations in the one process: the power and logic of the number '2' (1980: 69–91). The semiotic is assigned the number '0'. The problem of moving beyond the power and logic of '1', the symbolic, to that of '2' is confronted. The ambivalent logic of '2' encompasses both '1' and '0' but '0' is impossible to define and very difficult to detect. The semiotic is only available in the spaces, slips and silences in and around language: in the 'traces'. The would-be poet must confront and embrace the transgressions of language and identity which originate from the semiotic. This confrontation is a fearful and horrific task because it threatens the boundaries of language and identity which I have established both for myself and my understanding of my world. In the process of repressing this feminine other, I have abjectified the feminine principle, women in general and a myriad of other boundary crossers which I identify with both women and the feminine, e.g. the pain and 'mess' of birth and reproduction; people and things which allow themselves to be penetrated, i.e. to have their boundaries crossed; people and things which do not present a clear and unambiguous identity e.g. a pregnant woman, a dead person; bodily fluids and emissions which are secreted/excreted. It is the process of abjectification which establishes an immense fear of the other who is identified as mother: the (m)other and her perceived destructive/ procreative power. It is also this process of abjectification which must be confronted in order that the ambivalent position of language and identity might be appropriately addressed.

For Reineke, the identification of the object of fear as feminine is the key to Kristeva's psychoanalytic project. The fear of the other is the impetus for the maintenance of the symbolic order. In Reineke's analysis, Kristeva reveals the real victim of the Freudian primal murder to be the mother, not the father. The process of abjectification and defilement of the feminine has established an alternate, acceptable victim for the constructed order: the father is acceptable victim for it is outrage to commit murder against the symbolic, whereas the repression of the semiotic is an everyday occurrence. The practices of 'defilement' account 'for the myriad substitutions that have functioned to conceal the gender of the victim over whose body society has arisen' (1992: 77). This monumental substitution and its effects are astounding. The site of the grave of the (m)other who dies for the sake of language and identity is marked with the name of an other who is a patriarchal impostor, false claimer of the glory of the sacrifice. This camouflaged identity has enormous significance for a theological context.

Reineke, again relying on Kristeva, suggests that paganism 'wards off the mother through elaborate rituals that separate the pure from the impure'; Judaism 'cuts off the mother' in the ritual act of circumcision; and 'Christianity binges on and purges the mother' in the Eucharistic rite (Reineke 1992: 78–79). Clearly, in Christianity, the sacrificial victim has been male. Confronted with the knowledge of the symbolic substitution of the victim's identity, Reineke interprets Kristeva's conclusion to *Powers* as ambivalence about the use of this knowledge: does the 'whirl of abjection' portend 'carnival or apocalypse'? 'Do we swallow words of death, or do we vomit up mother death? Do words kill us or are they our freedom?' (Reineke 1992: 80). It would be tempting to answer either/or, but I think that Kristeva also offers the promise (both hopeful and despair-filled) of ambivalence. The implications for theology of Kristeva's revelation are not simply that the feminine and, therefore, women bear the burden of the substitution. Kristeva's revelation also presents the possibility of new rites, interpretations and theologies which, seeking to take into account the knowledge of the murdered mother, attempt to address the burden of women: in Reineke's words, to 'diffuse the terror' (1992: 82). Reineke looks to Kristeva's *Tales of Love* (1987b) for the possibility of this hope. Kelly Oliver in a conference paper, 'The Paradox of Love', looks towards a possibility outside of Kristevan theory: a social mother and an embodied father (1996). For me, the hope is already contained in *Powers* itself. Its imperative, in a theological context, may well be the development of a concept of a social mother, through the imagining of God as (m)other, not in the meek earth mother model, but in the image of the whore.

Kristeva speaks of 'confronting the maternal' (1982: 54) in a chapter in *Powers* entitled 'Something to be scared of'. It contains the rationale for the 'representative of the paternal function' taking 'the place of the good maternal object' when that is found 'wanting' (Reineke 1982: 45), leaving the way clear for abjectification of the feminine which no longer satisfies. For Kristeva, 'devotees of the abject', the 'borderlanders' of identity, are fascinated by 'the desirable and terrifying, nourishing and murderous, fascinating and abject inside of the maternal body'. This 'misfire of identification with the mother' suggests perversion. Yet its categorization is not so easily determined. It is not simply an avoidance of 'castration', i.e. of the necessary separation for identity, that the borderlander attempts, but more like a game played out between precipices. The fascination with the abject, i.e. its 'erotization', is not death but 'a threshold before death, a halt or a respite'. This threshold is clearly the result of an attempt at 'incorporating the devouring mother'. The identification with the mother as well as the father, for the symbolic is apparent since identity has not completely collapsed, is precisely the way in which the borderlander retains a position 'in the Other'. This is an ambivalent position, but it is not death, but 'a self-giving birth ever miscarried' for 'the advent of one's own identity demands a law that mutilates, whereas *jouissance* demands an abjection from which identity becomes absent' (1982: 54–55). The confrontation with the (m)other heralds the advent of a 'second thetic' which is neither static identity, nor its complete loss: a jouissance in the ambiguity of identity.

The second thetic relates to Kristeva's notion of the 'second truth' of mimetic activity (1984: 60) and her concept of the 'second-degree thetic'. Essentially, it refers to the re-emergence of the semiotic within the signification of language (1984: 50). The positionality of this second thetic assumes the success of the mirror stage and the acceptance of castration and separation from the mother. This acceptance, however, is not the endorsement of a 'sacred and unalterable' signification (1984: 51), a dogmatic repression (1984: 61). Rather, the 'reactivation' of the Oedipus complex in puberty sets up the thetic, not as a wall, but as 'a transversable boundary' (1984: 51). Hence, 'Poetic mimesis maintains and transgresses thetic unicity by making it undergo a kind of anamnesis, by introducing into the thetic position the stream of semiotic drives and making it signify' (1984: 60). The semiotic process receives *some* exposure, and the subject posited in the thetic is prevented from attaining the statue of 'transcendental ego' (1984: 58). The instability of the symbolic order is revealed, as well as its indebtedness to the semiotic forces. In this process, signification is multiplied, but not destroyed. If the advent of the thetic is an imposition of the Law-of-the-Father, then the arrival of the second thetic is a re-contextualization of the status of that law, both its valid effect in signification and communication, and its unforeseen consequences in the repression of otherness. In effect, it is the recognition of a second type of 'law'. In this recognition, and in the account of the second thetic, rigid identification and signification become as pathological as the failure to develop identity of any kind. Thus, the second thetic, as sociolinguistic and subjective position, bears the mark of *jouissance*, a joying in the truth of self-division—a recognition of the subjective ambiguity of any speaking subject.

In the face of this recognition and the enjoyment of *jouissance*, a theological position is demanded that resists and/or subverts the temptations and intentions of dogma. Since the second thetic is in effect a confrontation with the otherness of language and identity, then it follows that a theological position that adequately encompasses the positionality of the second thetic must also be involved and come to terms with such a confrontation. While no signifier can represent the semiotic, I am arguing that, given the current gender/sex stereotypes, the image of the (m)other, as oppositional figure to the 'Father' who projects the 'Law', and as acceptable metaphor for the semiotic precondition of language is a useful image for producing a theological confrontation that would engender a second thetic response. I have aligned the (m)other with the lesser term of the dual characterization of women, the whore. I am, thus, suggesting that a confrontation with the image of God as whore is one possible means of producing the poetic language demanded by the second thetic, and the re-presentation of alterity anticipated by the method of poetic reading.

The Canaanite Woman as (M)Other

For Kristeva, the Markan story of the Syro-Phoenician parallel to that of the Matthean Canaanite woman is an opening up to the 'mother' and to symbolic relations in Christ (1982: 115). There is no doubt that this assessment is based on the traditional interpretation of the woman as penitent supplicant. Correspondingly, the Christ who feeds her, providing 'food' for the woman to sustain her daughter, is identified with her as the 'good mother' (1982: 119). The redemptive mechanism of Christianity is characterized as the sanctification of the divided subject, who has internalized abjection as sin, by the incorporation of the heterogeneity of the sublimated body of Christ, producing not 'a being of abjection but a lapsing subject', at once sanctified and cognisant of 'incompletion' (1982: 117–20). This process is also a reconciling act with the 'maternal principle', but not a revalorization or rehabilitation of it (1982: 116–17). The Christian subject thus wavers between awareness of the abject otherness of self and the sublimated symbol of Christ: between the abject mother, and the good one. The subject is pluralized, torn between guilt based on a sense of internal self-defilement, and momentary reconciliation with the redeemer— the one true heterogeneous body (1982: 119–20). This reconciliation, dependent as it is on self-abjection, is, for Kristeva, *jouissance* (1982: 124–25). The story of the encounter between Jesus and the Syro-Phoenician/Canaanite woman is an account of such reconciliation.

There are *major* difficulties with this account of *jouissance*, and the corresponding characterization of the divided subject: difficulties of which Kristeva herself is aware. Certainly, the internalization of defilement and the movement to a concept of sin does bring an ambiguous subject into discourse. The ambiguity of this subjectivity, however, is not one which is accepted except in the very specific, and probably masochistic, cases of the mystics who enjoy the abjection of asceticism (1982: 127). More commonly, the recognition of defilement within humanity has rendered condemnation, inquisition, censorship and punishment (1982: 131). Furthermore, this account of *jouissance* and subjectivity retains the dual characterization of women, and the sublimation of the other in symbolic relations. The Christ is the symbol of the heterogeneous other, but in the process of symbolization, the 'real' transgressive nature of the other is sublimated. The 'real' nature of the (m)other is repressed: 'To eat and drink the flesh and blood of Christ' is a transgression of 'the Levitical prohibitions' and a satiation 'at the fount of a good mother who would thus expel the devils from her daughter' at the same time as being 'reconciled with the substance dear to paganism' (1982: 119).

The reconciliation is never named for what it is. It is always sublimated in masculine imagery and spiritual language. The (m)other is disembodied through her reproduction as the eternal masculine. I particularly want to underscore the inadequacies of such a subjecting of ambiguity, both from a feminist perspective, and a systematic theological one. It is not appropriate for contemporary theology to be playing with language in the symbolic order, several levels beyond the deep psychic attitudes which are implicit in the play. The lack of recognition of the nature of the play is precisely the source of the repressive dogma that demonstrates an inability to 'master' the 'second thetic'. This inability is, in a sense, a failure to develop beyond a certain psychological stage. When Christianity repels 'pagan' imagery without recognizing its existence within its own systems, it risks taking itself too seriously, i.e. it risks a rigidity of identification which is the object of the apocalyptic laughter of those who enjoy subjective ambiguity and have learnt to play with the precious images of theology.

Kristeva looks to speech, a development from the act of confession, to bring the next movement in the process of bringing the ambiguous subject to birth: 'only on the fringes of mysticism...can the most subtle transgression of law...the enunciation of sin in the presence of the One, reverberate not as a denunciation but as the glorious counterweight to the inquisitorial fate of confession' (Kristeva 1982: 131). This moment of enunciation (without condemnation) is the point of joy in the ambiguity of identity. Recognizing the difficulties of this moment as identified earlier, i.e. the masochistic results of self-abjection, it is essential that the power of the moment is also identified. The penitent in naming self as sinful in Christian theology is confronted with the resounding acceptance of that self by the One, the symbolic Father and Law-Giver. The sinful self is named as 'justified'. Undoubtedly, this experience is *jouissant*. From a feminist perspective, however, it is extremely dangerous for women.[4]

It is my contention that an alternate strategy for moving towards the acceptance of an ambiguous subject is the placing of confessional speech in the mouth of the One who proclaims its hidden otherness by declaring its relationship to the (m)other. In a sense, this is the double production of an embodied father, since the site of the One has generally been determined in patriarchal terms, and a social mother, since the bringing of the (m)other's bodily associations into the Godhead demands a re-evaluation of the believer's relationship with both the deity and the (m)other. An extraordinary gnostic poem recorded by Elaine Pagels suggests the possibility of such a divine confession where 'first' is 'last', 'whore' is 'holy', 'wife' is 'virgin', 'bride' is 'bridegroom', foolishness is wisdom, 'life [Eve]' is 'death' (Pagels 1988: 67). The echoes of Christian texts are heard within this declared heretical discourse. Such a confessional proposition is, unlike its prior counterpart, a revalorization of the maternal principle, as well as an invitation to reconciliation with that principle. This

4. The significant problem with this pattern for women was specifically high-lighted by Valerie Saiving in 1960 (1979). Feminist scholars have built on Saiving's observation in the intervening period, e.g. Plaskow (1980).

revalorization stands in contrast to Kristeva's account of Christianity as a reconciliation without revalorization. It is necessary, then, to ground this proposition in biblical terms.

Of the two central characters in the pericope, the Canaanite woman is the primary other. She is the interloper to the Gospel story. Persistently, she names her situation, if not herself, causing the Jesus figure to incorporate something into his speech which was not at first present: acceptance of the woman, her daughter, and, by implication, the validity of ministry to the Gentiles. Through this incorporation, the Jesus character is enabled to contribute something to the woman and her daughter. In effect, a mutual exchange has taken place: an opening of the two characters to each other. Now, if it is accepted that the story of the Canaanite woman is an opening to Christic relations, then it must also be accepted that the mutuality of this exchange blurs the distinctions between the Jesus character and the woman, as both act in the role of the good mother, Christ, feeding her companion. But this assessment can only be rendered if the persistence of the woman is read, not as submission, but as demand, i.e. if the woman is characterized, not as the appropriate feminine, but as the intrusive, persistent, threatening inappropriate feminine, in my terms, the whore. Once rendered, the association of the woman with Christic feeding ensures that Christ is both identified with the good mother and the abject mother, and the boundaries of valorization and vilification are transgressed. How can a Christian subject vilify the Christ? How also can it valorize the whore? Thrown into sensual confusion, the product is *jouissance*, a joying in the truth of self-division engendered by a recognition of the ambiguous subjectivity of the Godhead. It is not sufficient to acknowledge the dynamic of Christic relations in the symbolic. It is also important that the dynamic be exposed. By re-presenting the (m)other as part of the Godhead, i.e. by explicitly acknowledging the underlying dynamic of reconciliation, the Christian subject is forced into dealing with its own ambiguity, not via self-abjection, but by acceptance of the other. If the Christic journey moves towards a bringing into speech of the ambiguity of subjectivity, then identifying God as whore remains *a* strategy for precipitating this.

Conclusion

RESURRECTING EROTIC TRANSGRESSION: 'WITHOUT END, FOR NO REASON'

The Remainder

The method of poetic reading is a hermeneutical tool for reading biblical texts, a conceptual tool for exploring theological topics, and a practical tool for understanding and promoting the development of particular types of communities. This method uses a Kristevan psychoanalytic and linguistic framework as its underlying philosophical base, and Derridean deconstructive processes as the templates for the strategies developed within that framework. In the development of the method, the emphasis has been on the linguistic implications of these theoretical positions. The non-linguistic and in particular the bodily implications of this theoretical base have not been explored to any significant extent; nor indeed have the issues of power inherent in such a philosophical base. Such considerations are topics for future projects. The current project has been set in the context of a personal desire to develop a feminist theological methodology that deals with diversity, ambiguity, and integrity in relation to the multiplicity of identity. I have argued that such a methodology necessarily requires the bringing of ambiguity into subjectivity more overtly through its explicit introduction into relevant discourses such as biblical interpretations, theological expositions and community interactions. Four questions then remain:

1. Has this project been successful within the bounds of its limitations?
2. What has this project been unable to do within those bounds?
3. What further project(s) does this project point towards?
4. What responses/results is this project likely to evoke?

Successes and Limitations?

Since language is phallologocentric, there is a sense in which it must be taken to its extremes in order that possibilities outside and within its limitations are recognized. If poststructuralism also serves to deconstruct poststructuralist projects, then this internal critique is particularly welcome in a feminist environment. Critique, reclamation and reconstruction has always been the threefold process of feminist methodologies (see Christ & Plaskow 1979: 3–7). This threefold process has retained a circular motif where every new possibility remains open to constant critique; every old tradition, be it feminist or patriarchal, is treated with a degree of suspicion and an eye for reclamation; and no position has yet been hailed as *the* final word on any matter.

I still value the epithet 'poststructuralism' in its account of its theoretical roots and as a pointer to the significant deconstructive movement. That movement is crucial to this project. If anything can be regarded as foundational to this project, it is the twofold movement which I have variously called deconstruction/reconstruction and death/resurrection. Within that movement, the significance of the *process* and the importance of the *moment* between the two elements of the movement are stressed. In that moment, loss of meaning is confronted fully, and the unfulfilled possibility of reconstructing genuinely alternative meanings emerges briefly. That brief space is the moment of *jouissance*.

The notion of ambiguity requires that any account of such a twofold movement, and indeed of dualities of any kind, must be aware that the polarities feed into one another: we are not busy being born *or* busy dying, we are busy being born *and* busy dying. The aim of this project has been the subjecting of ambiguity: the development of a feminist theological methodology that might bring ambiguity more overtly into discourse in theological arenas, thereby dealing more effectively with the ambivalence of human life hermeneutically, theologically and practically. I believe that I have been able to demonstrate some of the methodological possibilities for subjecting ambiguity in theological arenas in the three examples I have explored: a reading of the story of the Canaanite woman; a theological exploration of the notion of God as whore; and the practical application of the methodology to a community situation, the 3rd

National Gathering on Women in The Uniting Church in Australia. In that demonstration, I have sought to allow the deconstructive movement and the reconstructive one, endeavoured to indicate that such explorations, as constructions, are valid only insofar as they may be deconstructed also, and attempted to mark points where such explorations may fail in their attempts to subject ambiguity because the deconstructive movement is avoided in the privileging of reconstruction.

This project does not fulfil its own intentions if it does not internally critique itself. What is already written is already open to deconstruction. The images which may still seem so provocative to a first time reader are now becoming mundane and transgressively ineffectual in the minds of those who have read them many times before. The project itself demands that its own dissonances be recognized and explored. An initial first-stage poetic reading of what I believe myself to be engaged in here suggests that the binary opposition between the need to explore dissonance and the desire to create synthesis is an important ambiguity of which to be aware, although it is not always juggled or balanced in a way that achieves anything remotely confronting *jouissance*.

Further Projects?

For the moment I have named this project 'erotic transgressive resurrection'. The name itself signals more its motives and concerns than its methods. It also signals significant aspects that relate to poststructuralist theory that this project has been unable to explore to a great extent: power, bodiliness, the erotic and the relationship between these. Because this project has deliberately focussed on language, the extensive implications of the semiotic as far more than that which bubbles into language, and the symbolic as far more than the ordering of language and identity, remains open to further exploration.

There are other issues that arise from theological concerns of this project. Both the passage used initially to explicate the method of poetic reading (Mt. 15: 21–28; the Canaanite woman), and the graffiti image of God as the whore and the reflection on this by Henman, raise major questions about the direction that such a method might take a fully developed Christological exploration.

This project, with its focus on ambiguity, originally arose out of a concern for the question of Christian theodicy from a feminist perspective in a pastoral ministry context. Since that time, Kathleen Sands (1994) has produced a work dealing with this issue using poststructuralist theory and the concept of tragedy. Nevertheless, the justice of God remains an issue in the context of subjecting ambiguity, as does the understanding of the nature of humanity. These areas remain significant theological issues in an environment where diversity, ambiguity and multiplicity are valued. They are also areas of major interest for an unfolding theological project.

A further aspect for exploration that immediately emerges from this thesis is the facilitation of the loss of singular identities in community which remained unaddressed in the programme strategy for the 3rd National Gathering on Women in The Uniting Church in Australia. Because that strategy focussed on the shattering of a singular identity for a community by prompting the articulation of multiple identities, it did not address the necessity of individuals with strong singular identities facing their own multiplicity. Such a confrontation is much easier for those who have not yet been given the opportunity to articulate strong, singular identities in a communal context. What does it mean to shatter identity in community? This question is a key question for feminist theology in a phallologocentric sociolinguistic environment and a patriarchal sociopolitical system.

This project is unfinished because it is committed to poststructuralist principles which cannot deem any linguistic communication to be complete. It has been a heuristic adventure: an exploration that has certain validity and certain limitations. There are no more obvious limitations than that spawned by poststructuralism itself in the eternal rhythm of its deconstructive/ reconstructive processes: 'Their only sustenance lies in the beauty of a gesture that, here, on the page, compels language to come nearest to the human enigma, to the place where it kills, thinks, and experiences jouissance all at the same time' (Kristeva 1982: 206).

Likely Responses?

In a theological context, this book is provocative in both its methodology and the images/examples it has confronted in explicating that methodology. I do not think that it could have been otherwise although I am sure that it could have been even more confrontational than it is already. Provocation must envisage reaction. I do not think that this project will be an easy work for many Christian theologians to approach. Yet I would like to re-affirm its place in the Christian theological spectrum.

The key motifs of this work are strongly influenced by my own Christian background: the death/resurrection imagery as the centrepiece for the deconstructive/ reconstructive process; the ambiguity of the identity of Christ (fully human, fully divine) as the paradigm for the ambiguity of all identity; the identification of God with the most vilified in the discussion of God as whore. These are all orthodox Christian motifs which cannot immediately be discounted even though their interpretation in poststructuralist categories will inevitably be disputed.

This project is also provocative in a feminist environment. The development of subjectivities for women by women has been an important component of the women's movement generally. When theoretical bases that seem to challenge these hard-won developments are introduced, the prospect is understandably frightening. I hope that I have demonstrated some of the possibilities that such a theoretical base offers a movement which is already involved in the processes of deconstruction and reconstruction in order that it remains relevant to its time.

A Final Word

The following factors are continuing marks of the methodology proposed here:

- A continuing exploration of dissonance without reconciliation or synthesis.
- A continuing political programme of transgression.
- A revolutionary focus which remains movably identified with the unwanted, repressed otherness of language and subjectivity wherever that may be.
- A lack of definitiveness in its product.
- A constant openness to transformation.

It is dissonance in discourse that will always expose the 'otherness' of language and identity, and transgression that will always ensure that that otherness cannot be ignored in successive attempts to repress it. But because the otherness is already part of language, the danger of any new account of its existence solidifying in language must always be countered by a willingness to find otherness expressed in the repressed whatever that is or may become. This necessity ensures that any project, such as this, that attempts to confront alterity is by definition unable to be definitive, and must always be open to transformation.

BIBLIOGRAPHY

The biblical translation quoted throughout is the *New Revised Standard Version*.

Alcoff, Linda
    1988   'Cultural Feminism Versus Poststructuralism: The Identity Crisis in Feminist Theory', *Signs* 13 (3), 405–36.

Allen, Jeffner & Iris Marion Young (eds.)
    1989   *The Thinking Muse: Feminism and Modern French Philosophy* (Bloomington: Indiana University).

Augsburger, Myron S.
    1982   *Matthew*. Communicator's Commentary (Waco: Word).

Bell, Shannon
    1994   *Reading, Writing, and Rewriting the Prostitute Body* (Bloomington: Indiana University Press).

Bettenson, Henry (ed.)
    1963   *Documents of the Christian Church* (London: Oxford University Press, 2nd edn).

Braidotti, Rosi
    1994   *Nomadic Subjects: Embodiment and Sexual Difference in Contemporary Feminist Theory* (New York: Columbia University Press).
    1991   *Patterns of Dissonance: A Study of Women in Contemporary Philosophy* (Trans. Elizabeth Guild; Cambridge: Polity).

Brock, Rita Nakashima
    1988   *Journeys By Heart: A Christology of Erotic Power* (New York: Crossroad).

Cameron, Deborah
    1985   *Feminism and Linguistic Theory* (London: Macmillan).

Céline, Louis-Ferdinand
    1968 (1957)   *Castle to Castle* (Trans. R. Manheim; New York: Delacourte).

Chopp, Rebecca S.
    1989   *The Power to Speak: Feminism, Language, God* (New York: Crossroad).

Chopp, Rebecca S. & Sheila Greeve Davaney (eds.)
    1997   *Horizons in Feminist Theology: Identity, Tradition, and Norms* (Minneapolis: Fortress Press).

Christ, Carol P. & Judith Plaskow (eds.)
    1979   *Womanspirit Rising: A Feminist Reader in Religion* (San Francisco: Harper & Row).

Clément, Catherine

    1983 (1981)   *The Lives and Legends of Jacques Lacan* (Trans. Arthur Goldhammer; New York: Columbia University Press).

Collins, Adela Yarbro

    1984   *Crisis and Catharsis: The Power of the Apocalypse* (Philadelphia: Westminster Press).

    1979   *The Apocalypse*. New Testament Message Vol. 22 (Dublin: Veritas).

Cooey, Paula M.

    1994   *Religious Imagination and the Body: A Feminist Analysis* (New York: Oxford University Press).

Daly, Mary

    1985 (1975)   *Beyond God the Father: Toward a Philosophy of Women's Liberation—With an Original Reintroduction by the Author* (Boston: Beacon Press).

Davies, William D. & Dale C. Allison

    1991   *The Gospel According to Saint Matthew Volume II Chapters VIII–XVIII* (Edinburgh: T. & T. Clark).

Derrida, Jacques

    1982 (1972)   *Margins of Philosophy* (Trans. Alan Bass; Chicago: University of Chicago Press).

    1981 (1972)   *Positions* (Trans. Alan Bass; Chicago: University of Chicago Press).

    1978 (1967)   *Writing and Difference* (Trans. Alan Bass; London: Routledge & Kegan Paul).

Dicker, Gordon S.

    1983   'The Community of Disciples—The Church (Matthew 14–18)' in Hugh McGinlay (ed.), *The Year of Matthew* (Melbourne: Desbooks & JBCE): 59–69.

Dutney, Andrew

    1993   *Food, Sex and Death: A Personal Account of Christianity* (Melbourne: Uniting Church).

Fenton, J.C.

    1963   *The Gospel of St Matthew* (Harmondsworth: Penguin).

Fiorenza, Elisabeth Schüssler

    1992   *But She Said: Feminist Practices of Biblical Interpretation* (Boston: Beacon).

    1991   *Revelation: Vision of a Just World*, Proclamation Commentary (Minneapolis: Fortress Press).

    1985   *The Book of Revelation: Justice and Judgment* (Philadelphia: Fortress Press).

    1983   *In Memory of Her: A Feminist Theological Reconstruction of Christian Origins* (London: SCM).

Freud, Sigmund

    1955   'Beyond the Pleasure Principle' in *The Standard Edition of the Complete Psychological Works of Sigmund Freud Volume XVIII (1920–1922): 'Beyond the Pleasure Principle', 'Group Psychology' and Other Works*. Translated under General Editorship of J. Strachey in Collaboration with Anna Freud (London: Hogarth/Institute of Psycho-Analysis): 1–64.

Fulkerson, Mary McClintock
    1994   *Changing the Subject: Women's Discourses and Feminist Theology* (Minneapolis: Fortress Press).

Gallop, Jane
    1982   *The Daughter's Seduction: Feminism and Psychoanalysis* (Ithaca: Cornell University Press).

Gilligan, Carol
    1982   *In a Different Voice: Psychological Theory and Women's Development* (Cambridge: Harvard University Press).

Griffin, David Ray
    1989   *God and Religion in the Postmodern World: Essays in Postmodern Theology* (Albany: State University of New York Press).

Grosz, Elizabeth
    1990   *Jacques Lacan: A Feminist Introduction* (London: Routledge).
    1989   *Sexual Subversions: Three French Feminists* (Sydney: Allen & Unwin).

Guberman, Ross Mitchell (ed.)
    1996   *Julia Kristeva Interviews.* European Perspective Series (New York: Columbia University Press).

Gundry, Robert H.
    1982   *Matthew: A Commentary on his Literary and Theological Art* (Grand Rapids: Eerdmans).

Harrison, Beverly Wildung
    1985   'Misogyny and Homophobia: The Unexplored Connections' in Carol S. Robb (ed.), *Making Connections: Essays in Feminist Social Ethics* (Boston: Beacon Press): 135–51.

Hegel, G.W.F.
    1931 (1910)   *The Phenomenology of Mind* (Trans. J.B. Baillie; London: Allen & Unwin, 2nd edn).

Henman, Paul
    1994   'God is a Black Lesbian Whore!' Unpublished.

Hill, David
    1972   *The Gospel of Matthew.* New Century Bible Commentary (Grand Rapids: Eerdmans).

Jay, Nancy
    1981   'Gender and Dichotomy', *Feminist Studies* 7 (1), 38–56.

Johnson, Elizabeth A.
    1992   *She Who Is: The Mystery of God in Feminist Theological Discourse* (New York: Crossroad).

Keller, Catherine
    1994   'The Breast, the Apocalypse, and the Colonial Journey', *Journal for Feminist Studies in Religion* 10 (1), 53–72.

Kim, C.W. Maggie, Susan M. St. Ville & Susan M. Simonaitis (eds.)
    1993   *Transfigurations: Theology and the French Feminists* (Minneapolis: Fortress Press).

Koester, Helmut
  1982   *History and Literature of Early Christianity: Introduction to the New Tes-*
            tament Volume 2 (Philadelphia: Fortress Press).
Kristeva, Julia
  1995 (1993) *New Maladies of the Soul* (Trans. Ross Guberman; New York: Columbia
            University Press).
  1993 (1990) *Nations Without Nationalism* (Trans. Leon S. Roudiez; New York: Co-
            lumbia University Press).
  1991   *Strangers to Ourselves* (Trans. Leon S. Roudiez; New York: Columbia
            University Press).
  1989 (1981) *Language: The Unknown—An Initiation into Linguistics* (Trans. Anne
            M. Menke; London: Harvester Wheatsheaf).
  1987a (1985) *In the Beginning was Love: Psychoanalysis and Faith* (Trans. Arthur
            Goldhammer; New York: Columbia University Press).
  1987b (1983) *Tales of Love* (Trans. Leon S. Roudiez; New York: Columbia University
            Press).
  1984 (1974) *Revolution in Poetic Language* (Trans. Margaret Waller; Introduction
            by Leon S. Roudiez; New York: Columbia University Press).
  1982 (1980) *Powers of Horror: An Essay on Abjection* (Trans. Leon S. Roudiez; New
            York: Columbia University Press).
  1980   *Desire in Language: A Semiotic Approach to Literature and Art* (Trans.
            Thomas Gora, Alice Jardine & Leon S. Roudiez (ed.), Oxford:
            Blackwell).
Kurzweil, Edith
  1980   *The Age of Structuralism: Lévi-Strauss to Foucault* (New York: Columbia
            University Press).
Lacan, Jacques
  1978   *The Four Fundamental Concepts of Psycho-analysis* (ed. Jacques-Alain
            Miller, trans. Alan Sheridan; New York: Norton).
  1977 (1966) *Écrits: A Selection* (Trans. Alan Sheridan; London: Tavistock).
Lechte, John
  1990   *Julia Kristeva* (London: Routledge).
Lévi-Strauss, Claude
  1979 (1964) *The Raw and the Cooked: Introduction to a Science of Mythology I* (Trans.
            John & Doreen Weightman; New York: Octagon).
  1977 (1973) *Structural Anthropology Volume II* (Trans. Monique Layton; London:
            Allen Lane).
  1968 (1958) *Structural Anthropology* (Trans. Claire Jacobson & Brooke Grundfest
            Schoepf; London: Allen Lane).
MacDonald, Diane L. Prosser
  1995   *Transgressive Corporeality: The Body, Poststructuralism, and the
            Theological Imagination* (Albany: State University of New York Press).
Matthews, Jill Julius
  1984   *Good and Mad Women: The Historical Construction of Femininity in Twen-
            tieth-Century Australia* (Sydney: George Allen & Unwin).

McFague, Sallie
    1987   *Models of God: Theology for an Ecological, Nuclear Age* (Philadelphia: Fortress Press).

Miles, Margaret R.
    1989   *Carnal Knowing: Female Nakedness and Religious Meaning in the Christian West* (Tunbridge Wells: Burns & Oates).

Mitchell, Juliet & Jacqueline Rose (eds.)
    1982   *Feminine Sexuality: Jacques Lacan and the École Freudienne* (Trans. Jacqueline Rose; London: Macmillan).

Mollenkott, Virginia Ramey
    1984   *The Divine Feminine: The Biblical Imagery of God as Female* (New York: Crossroad).

Noddings, Nel
    1989   *Women and Evil* (Berkeley: University of California Press).

Nye, Andrea
    1987   'Woman Clothed with the Sun: Julia Kristeva and the Escape from/ to Language', *Signs* 12 (4), 664–86.

Oliver, Kelly
    1996   'The Paradox of Love', Women in Philosophy Conference, 13 July, Brisbane. Unpublished.

Ostrovosky, Ruth
    1971   *Voyeur Voyant: A Portrait of Louis-Ferdinand Céline* (New York: Random House).

Pagels, Elaine
    1988   *Adam, Eve, and the Serpent* (Harmondsworth: Penguin).

Patte, Daniel
    1987   *The Gospel According to Matthew: A Structural Commentary on Matthew's Faith* (Philadelphia: Fortress Press).

Pattel-Gray, Anne
    1995   'Not Yet Tiddas: An Aboriginal Womanist Critique of Australian Church Feminism' in Maryanne Confoy, Dorothy A. Lee & Joan Nowotny (eds.) *Freedom and Entrapment: Women Thinking Theology* (North Blackburn: Dove): 165–92.

Pippin, Tina
    1992   *Death and Desire: The Rhetoric of Gender in the Apocalypse of John* (Louisville: Westminster/John Knox Press).

Plaskow, Judith
    1980   *Sex, Sin and Grace: Women's Experience and the Theologies of Reinhold Niebuhr and Paul Tillich* (Lanham: University Press of America).

Porter, Elisabeth J.
    1991   *Women and Moral Identity* (Sydney: Allen & Unwin).

Psych & Po
    1996   'Woman is Never What We Say' in Ross Mitchell Guberman (ed.), *Julia Kristeva Interviews* (New York: Columbia University Press): 97–102.

Raschke, Carl
   1992   'Fire and Roses, or the Problem of Postmodern Religious Thinking'
             in Phillipa Berry & Andrew Wernick (eds.), *Shadow of Spirit:
             Postmodernism and Religion* (London: Routledge): 93–108.
Reineke, Martha
   1992   'The Mother in Mimesis: Kristeva and Girard on Violence and the
             Sacred' in David R. Crownfield (ed.), *Body/text in Julia Kristeva:
             Religion, Women, and Psychoanalysis* (Albany: State University of New
             York Press): 67–85.
Rose, Jacqueline
   1982   'Introduction—II' in Juliet Mitchell & Jacqueline Rose (eds.), *Feminine
             sexuality: Jacques Lacan and the École Freudienne* (Trans. Jacqueline Rose;
             London: Macmillan): 27–57.
Ruether, Rosemary Radford
   1985   *Women-Church: Theology and Practice of Feminist Liturgical Communities*
             (San Francisco: Harper & Row).
   1983   *Sexism and God-talk: Toward a Feminist Theology* (London: SCM).
Russell, Letty
   1987   *Household of Freedom: Authority in Feminist Theology*. The 1986 Annie
             Kinkead Warfield Lectures (Philadelphia: Westminster).
Ryan, Anne
   1997   'Women in the Uniting Church' *Trinity Occasional Papers* XVI(1), 44–
             49.
Sands, Kathleen M.
   1994   *Escape from Paradise: Evil and Tragedy in Feminist Theology* (Minneapolis:
             Fortress Press).
Saussure, Ferdinand de.
   1966 (1959)   *Course in General Linguistics* (Charles Bally, Albert Sechehaye, Albert
             Reidlinge (eds.); trans. Wade Baskin, New York: McGraw-Hill, 3rd
             edn).
Seung, T.K.
   1982   *Structuralism and Hermeneutics* (New York: Columbia University
             Press).
Stace, W.T.
   1955 (1924)   *The Philosophy of Hegel: A Systematic Exposition*. New York: Dover.
Summers, Anne
   1975   *Damned Whores and God's Police: The Colonization of Women in Australia*
             (Harmondsworth: Penguin).
Talbert, Charles H.
   1994   *The Apocalypse: A Reading of the Revelation to John* (Louisville: West-
             minster John Knox).
Taylor, Mark C.
   1997   'Theology of Life: Case Studies Based on the 10 Affirmations' *Echoes:
             Justice, Peace and Creation News*, November, 21–28.
   1990   *Tears*. Intersections: Philosophy & Critical Theory (Albany: State
             University of New York Press Press).

1987   *Altarity* (Chicago: University of Chicago Press).

1984   *Erring: A Postmodern A/Theology* (Chicago: University of Chicago Press).

1982   *Deconstructing Theology*, American Academy of Religion Studies in Religion 28 (New York: Crossroad).

The Uniting Church in Australia Assembly Liturgy Commission

1988   *Uniting in Worship Leader's Book* (Melbourne: Uniting Church Press).

Tilley, Terrence W. (ed.)

1995   *Postmodern Theologies: The Challenge of Religious Diversity* (Maryknoll: Orbis).

Tolbert, Mary Ann

1992   'Mark' in Carol A. Newsom & Sharon H. Ringe (eds.), *The Women's Bible Commentary* (London: SPCK): 263–74.

Trudgill, Peter

1983 (1974)   *Sociolinguistics: An Introduction to Language and Society* (Harmondsworth: Penguin, rev. edn).

Wainwright, Elaine

1995   'A Voice from the Margin: Reading Matthew 15:21–28' in Fernando F. Segovia & Mary Ann Tolbert (eds.), *Readings from This Place Volume 2: Social Location and Biblical Interpretation in Global Perspective* (Minneapolis: Fortress Press): 132–53.

1993   'A Voice from the Margin: Reading Matt. 15:21–28 in an Australian Feminist Key' Work in Progress. Unpublished.

1991   *Towards a Feminist Critical Reading of the Gospel According to Matthew*. BZNW 60 (Berlin: de Gruyter).

Weber, Hans-Ruedi

1988   *The Way of the Lamb: Christ in the Apocalypse—Lenten Meditations*. Risk Book 36 (Geneva: WCC).

1981   'Salvation to God' in *Experiments with Bible Study* (Geneva: WCC): 260–66.

Welch, Sharon D.

1990   *A Feminist Ethic of Risk* (Minneapolis: Fortress Press).

Whorf, Benjamin

1956   'The Relation of Habitual Thought and Behavior to Language' in John B. Carroll (ed.), *Language, Thought, and Reality: Selected Writings of Benjamin Lee Whorf* (Cambridge: MIT Press): 134–59.

Winquist, Charles E.

1995   *Desiring Theology* (Chicago: University of Chicago Press).

Wyschogrod, Edith

1990   *Saints and Postmodernism: Revisioning Moral Philosophy* (Chicago: University of Chicago Press).

Index of Biblical References

INDEX OF AUTHORS

Printed in the United Kingdom
by Lightning Source UK Ltd.
119472UK00001B/145-177

9 781845 531041